Cannabis on Campus

D1262991

Cannabis on Campus is a comprehensive resource on the implications of marijuana legalization for college campuses. It is essential reading for college administrators and other professionals responsible for overseeing drug policy and addressing marijuana use in higher education. The authors use their considerable experience in college alcohol and other drug (AOD) counseling to provide a sweeping look at the cannabis culture found in our universities. Chapters alternate between historical context, research and analysis, and student interviews, providing an evidence-based and nuanced understanding of the role of marijuana use in today's college campuses as well as insights and recommendations for a post-legalization future.

Jonathan C. Beazley, LADC, LMFT, is a licensed substance abuse counselor and marriage and family therapist with 38 years of experience. He has done numerous presentations, lectures, webinars, and podcasts on various aspects of substance abuse treatment and prevention, many of which have focused on college students and young adults. He is presently the AOD interventionist at the University of Connecticut and has a private practice in Chaplin, Connecticut.

Stephanie Field, PsyD, is a licensed clinical psychologist in private practice in Glastonbury, Connecticut, and sits on the board of directors for the Connecticut Psychological Association. She has served as the AOD specialist at the University of Hartford and is the principal author of *Treating Traumatic Stress in Adults: The Practitioner's Expressive Writing Workbook.* Her specialties include traumatic stress, substance use disorders, and expressive writing therapy.

Cannabis on Campus

Changing the Dialogue in the Wake of Legalization

Jonathan C. Beazley
and Stephanie Field

Routledge
Taylor & Francis Group

NEW YORK AND LONDON

First published 2018
by Routledge
711 Third Avenue, New York, NY 10017

and by Routledge
2 Park Square, Milton Park, Abingdon, Oxon, OX14 4RN

Routledge is an imprint of the Taylor & Francis Group, an informa business

Library of Congress Cataloging-in-Publication Data
Names: Beazley, Jonathan C., author. | Field, Stephanie Leigh, author.
Title: Cannabis on campus : changing the dialogue in the wake of legalization / Jonathan Beazley and Stephanie Field.
Description: New York, NY : Routledge, 2018.
Identifiers: LCCN 2017041537 (print) | LCCN 2017048493 (ebook) | ISBN 9781315160177 (eBook) | ISBN 9781138039117 (hardback) | ISBN 9781138039124 (pbk.)
Subjects: LCSH: College students—Drug use—United States. | Marijuana—United States. | Marijuana abuse—United States.
Classification: LCC HV5824.Y68 (ebook) | LCC HV5824.Y68 B4326 2018 (print) | DDC 362.29/50973—dc23
LC record available at https://lccn.loc.gov/2017041537

ISBN: 978-1-138-03911-7 (hbk)
ISBN: 978-1-138-03912-4 (pbk)
ISBN: 978-1-315-16017-7 (ebk)

Typeset in Sabon
by Apex CoVantage, LLC

Contents

Expanded Contents

Preface

A few years ago I found myself being in charge of a game called "Stump the Expert" at a university-sponsored student information fair. These events are routinely held on college campuses at the beginning of each academic year as part of student orientation and are characterized by rows of booths sponsored by clubs and organizations, all with the goal of introducing students to the vast array of activities available. Others promote social, political, and health issues. Very often these groups will employ games as a way of luring students to their booths. I was asked to run such a game by the Wellness and Prevention Department, focusing on substance abuse awareness. As the university's alcohol and drug interventionist, my attraction was named "Stump the Expert" and involved a "Wheel of Alcohol and Drug Questions" where curious students spun the wheel and read aloud the question selected. I encouraged each contestant to try to answer the question before I offered mine, lending at least some suspense and competition to the activity. One question on the wheel was, "Smoking marijuana is less dangerous than tobacco, true or false?" The official answer was "false": an average marijuana joint contains up to five times as much carcinogenic chemicals as a regular tobacco cigarette; smoking four joints was the equivalent of almost a pack of cigarettes.[1] Not only did I know this to be factual, but I had been supplied a cheat sheet with answers as well (why it was thought their so-called expert needed a cheat sheet still eludes me). But I found myself nagged by one small problem, then and now: if this is true, then where are all the bodies?

After decades and millions of dollars in research grant money, we still have not been able to show a robust relationship between cannabis smoking and later terminal respiratory illnesses—bronchitis, yes, but not cancer or Chronic Obstructive Pulmonary Disease (COPD).[2] Meanwhile, the World Health Organization (WHO) estimates that tobacco is strongly associated with the deaths of one in ten adults over age 30 throughout the world[3]—not one in ten smokers; one in ten adult human beings, period. The WHO further predicts that if current trends continue, tobacco, by the end of this century, will be directly associated with close to one billion fatalities. To put that number into perspective, and with a little research and arithmetic, we could sum the estimated total deaths caused by AIDS, World Wars I and II, the Spanish influenza pandemic of 1918, the Black Death of the fourteenth century, the Plague of Justinian, and even throw in the biblical flood and still not reach that number. Perhaps adding smallpox and malaria to that list would tilt the scale back, but the point remains inarguably that the relative dangers between the two substances would not be remotely close. And tobacco is a legal substance for those over age 18.

Despite this knowledge, I became aware of a reticence to inform students of this factual distinction. Somehow it did not seem right. In truth, it felt heretical. So, I did what seemed to be the only course available to me at that time: I waffled. While admitting that tobacco was statistically a much more dangerous substance, I quickly cautioned that it did not mean smoking marijuana was safe, adding that research was hampered by confounding variables—the jury was still out. I emphasized the potential consequences of breathing hot gasses and debris of any kind regardless of what research demonstrated and then educated about marijuana's short-term effect on memory and cognition. What I was really doing was not so much educating but trying *not* to convey the message that marijuana was—in any way, shape, or form—acceptable to use.

It was only later and after much reflection that I could pinpoint some of the origins of my discomfort. Among them was an early experience that I had almost forgotten and that involved my first exposure to drug prevention education when I was around 10 or 11 years old. Rather than at school, it happened at a church father-and-son dinner in the late 1960s. After a serviceable meal, probably consisting of some sort of chicken stew slathered over a couple of biscuits, we were given a drug-abuse presentation by one of the area policeman. Whether this was a local effort or part of a larger initiative, I cannot remember, for this was over 20 years before the onset of the D.A.R.E. program. The officer started by pulling out a fold-up display case with fake or inert samples of various illicit substances to inform the youth of what to avoid and the fathers of what to dread. This was followed by a film of maybe a half hour in length.

Memory this remote is always clouded, fragmented, but what remains with some clarity are images from a scene in the film about marijuana use at a party. The protagonist is a young male hanging out with other teenagers and young adults. The party is in a large living room, or maybe a finished basement, with psychedelic flashing lights and a soundtrack of canned mod music, all of which now seems a feeble attempt to make the message sound hipper to the younger members of the audience. The narrator's voice is staccato-like and inflectionless. With an economy of words, he educates the viewers about marijuana, alternately using its street aliases such as pot, grass, tea, and Mary Jane. He tersely lists the initial effects of smoking this substance, speaking the words "pleasurable" and "euphoric" in such a flat, colorless way that it belies their denotation. The young man "tokes" on the joint being passed. The scene quickly begins to shift; the lights become brighter, glaring, flashing, as the background music melds into the sound of the participants' growing laughter. He takes another hit. The narrator's voice, suddenly grave, cautions the viewers that marijuana use will inevitably lead to another experience: "A bummer. A bad trip." At some point, the scene begins to change, devolving into something nightmarish, a depiction of hell from a Hieronymus Bosch painting. The laughter turns maniacal, the lights a blinding, rapid strobe; the music increasingly cacophonous. Where the surroundings had been previously mirthful, the hapless protagonist suddenly finds himself encircled by faces now distorted, grotesque, malevolent, while all he can do is close his eyes, cover his ears, and curl whimpering into a fetal position.

How accurate is my memory? I do not know, as I could not find anything resembling the film for comparison. Memory is not a faithful recording; the brain's reconstruction of events is never perfectly replicated and is subject to gradual loss over time. What is probably more significant was the lasting emotional impression it had on me. Of all the events in my life those decades ago, these scraps of memory were among those that remained. How influenced was I by this and other early prevention messages? Upon what sort of fear-imbued foundation had I built my own beliefs about cannabis and other illicit substances, and how was this influencing my work in treatment and prevention to this day?

We are now in the midst of a nation-wide tectonic shift in how we approach marijuana. As of this writing, eight states and the District of Columbia have legalized the recreational use of cannabis. Twenty-eight states have passed medical marijuana laws, over half of the United States. Throughout the country, there is an increasingly accepted belief that these states are but the first trickle in an impending torrent of statutory changes, all centered on this controversial plant, this weed. Where it is now legal, new cannabis consumer cultures are taking root and becoming part of the normal social and commercial landscapes. These states hope to earn millions in taxes and potentially win back substantial funds from those previously drained by marijuana's cost of law enforcement, judicial processes, and incarceration. The immensity of this transformation cannot be overstated: legalization would represent the reversal of a policy on cannabis that has guided this country since the 1930s, dismembering a major appendage from the trillion-dollar apparatus that is the War on Drugs.

For those who counsel college students, or any young adult, the conversation about marijuana has always been sticky. Discussions on the dangers of more heavyweight illicit drugs such as heroin, crack cocaine, or methamphetamine are much easier for professionals like myself. Even talking about alcohol is more straightforward from a health standpoint. The dangers are known and generally accepted. In contrast, cannabis is and always has been different. We may feel as though our feet are not firmly planted, our convictions more malleable. We may wrestle with a perception of hypocrisy—while an overwhelming majority of us can claim to have never tried heroin, far fewer of us can do so with marijuana. Persuading students who fully embrace the marijuana culture can sometimes seem like trying to achieve a religious conversion. We may feel like unwelcome missionaries: preaching a god they find absurd and even repugnant. Our literature, our research, our facts fall on deaf ears. These students may view us as misinformed at best or at worst as tools of a long-standing, immoral government hegemony.

It is our hope this book will start a discourse on ways to breach the divide. It is important that we continue to try, for many of the students we work with are convinced that cannabis is not only completely benign and non-addictive but unquestioningly good for them in any amount or frequency. They cling to this conviction even in the face of plummeting grades, failed relationships, empty bank accounts, increased anxiety, unstable mood, and lost jobs. To be heard more clearly, we must first *really* listen to them. We must examine our own filters. We must take an honest look at how we have been acculturated through our experiences with marijuana and at how it has shaped our beliefs, just as our students' beliefs have been shaped by their own experiences. We need to start this discussion now because as Bob Dylan, that Pied Piper of marijuana use in the early 1960s, sang: "The times they are a-changin'." And they are changing fast.

Jonathan Beazley
July 2017

Notes

1 BMJ Specialty Journals. (2007, August 2). Impact on lungs of one cannabis joint equal to up to five cigarettes. *Science Daily*. Retrieved July 17, 2017 from www.sciencedaily.com/releases/2007/07/070731085550.htm.
2 Tashkin, D. P. (2013). Effects of marijuana smoking on the lung. *Annals of American Thoracic Society*, 10(3), 239–247. doi:10.1513/AnnalsATS.201212–127FR
3 World Health Organization. (2012). WHO *global report: Mortality attributable to tobacco*. Retrieved from www.who.int/tobacco/publications/surveillance/fact_sheet_mortality_report.pdf?ua=1

Introduction

Over half a century since the start of the Information Age, we have begun to experience profoundly and personally the dark side of that era's vision of exponentially increased communication, knowledge, and productivity. As the universe of information continues to expand, we may find it harder and harder to sort out what is factual from what is specious. Complex theories are expounded on the internet, in books, or in other media—many constructed on a foundation of data that have been misinterpreted, taken out of context, or completely fabricated. The collective effect of all this reached a peak during the presidential election in 2016. Democratic and Republican voters, often sitting at the same family dinner table, argued to constant stalemate over the issues influencing their political positions. Both sides were armed with evidence derived from sources that did not intersect at any point, seemingly originating from entirely separate dimensions. In 2017, the words "alternative facts" entered the national vocabulary. In what may be the seventh decade of the Information Age, we also found ourselves in a Misinformation Age.

Students may be struck the first time they experiment with cannabis by the discord between what older adults have taught them and how good the drug makes them feel. Their friends spread even more doubt. To find some truth in this confusion, they look to what is being touted in the media. In our research, the sheer amount of conflicting information was eye opening and daunting—a dilemma that we will further explore. We hope to provide a guide through that informational morass to clarify the extent and effects of this ongoing debate.

In constructing this book, we sought opinions from researchers and higher education prevention and treatment professionals. Since this continues to be a controversial topic, some of these individuals are identified while others remain anonymous so that an honest yet unpopular opinion will not mar their careers. Chapters are also interspersed with interviews and shorter comments provided by students to capture the wide and diverse spectrum of relationships and experiences with marijuana.

Given the sensitive nature of the topic and to promote honest disclosure, students will remain anonymous with disguised identities. We are both thankful for and humbled by all their courage and candor.

Following the first of the student interviews, *Cannabis on Campus* will begin with a description of cannabis and a history of its evolution from an essential crop at the dawn of civilization to a controversial and illicit drug in most countries. We must revisit the history preceding our current situation to fully understand our present set of beliefs about cannabis, as well as how we came to this point. It has also been our experience that many working in the field of substance abuse prevention and treatment know surprisingly little about the fascinating and controversial stories behind this substance. It is not our intention for this volume to serve as an exhaustive text on the history of cannabis, since other writers have already offered more comprehensive and valuable accounts. We beg the readers to forgive the whirlwind tour; it is difficult to boil down 10,000 years of our past with marijuana into a single chapter while still providing something of substance. Instead, we employ a series of brief biographical sketches depicting key figures that have played major roles in influencing the course of how we view marijuana, thereby putting a human face on the history. Their stories are woven into the book to contextualize current issues surrounding cannabis prevention and treatment and how we can proceed moving forward. There are noticeably more "heroes" in the pro-marijuana historical pantheon, while several of those characters that orchestrated and enforced prohibition come off as misguided, or worse. We have tried to present a balanced depiction of the latter group. This overall bias suggests something about the available record. It could be that the pro-marijuana movement self-identifies as the underdog in this struggle, and underdogs in any major movement tend to cultivate Robin Hoods. Or it reflects a basic part of us that connects with those who defy authority—that is how this country began, after all. As Wilt Chamberlain—not enormously popular despite his immense basketball prowess—once conceded: "Nobody pulls for Goliath."

We also recognize that the issues surrounding marijuana will change swiftly. Therefore, elements of this book will become historic markers within a very short time. This is inevitable and unavoidable with a subject this dynamic and fluid. The text required numerous updates before being finished. But any snapshot capturing a moment in time is important to the entirety of the evolving record.

Chapter 5 will be an interview with a pro-legalization student activist, and Chapters 3, 8, and 11 will be interviews with other student consumers from across the nation, each with a very personal story to share about cannabis. There was no intention in these interviews to ultimately arrive at some predetermined point guided by an ulterior agenda. Any moral to their stories will be the interpretation of the reader. We simply wanted to give these students the opportunity to share their histories, their relationships, their thoughts, their fears, and their hopes about this substance that has played such a central role in their lives.

Chapter 4 is a panoramic view of cannabis within the college milieu: how students obtain, experience, use, and share it as well as the role it plays in the domains of Greek life, student conduct, law enforcement, housing, and collegiate sports. In surveying this landscape, we hope to show how imbued the overall fabric of collegiate culture is with cannabis use—how pervasive it is compared to years ago when it was a little-known drug used only by those on the fringe of university life.

Chapter 6 serves as a prelude to Chapter 7 and explores the multitudes of different information about cannabis that students are regularly exposed to and how these influences inform their beliefs. The sources of this material have their own agendas and biases; examining these sources should be part of any overall determination students need to make. The trick is in weighing those biases accurately. Readers already influenced by one side or the other can easily dismiss sound data as propaganda or embrace the latter as fact.

In Chapter 7, we will examine some major issues in the point and counterpoint existing between those who believe that marijuana should remain illegal, if decriminalized, and those that want it made legal to adults, regulated like alcohol. We do not intend this to be a polemic, nor at the conclusion will we declare a winner in the argument about whether marijuana is something beneficial or harmful to humankind. That would contribute little more than adding another contestant to the debate. Rather, we hope to provoke (re)thinking about cannabis during this period of great uncertainty.

Chapters 9 and 10 cover the past and present state of cannabis prevention, intervention, and treatment in higher education. As in previous chapters, we will describe how understanding the evolution of both fields as they pertain to marijuana led to our present status. Unlike other domains within the arena of health and wellness promotion, the fields of college substance abuse prevention and counseling have been influenced and entwined with its criminal status—fiscally, administratively, and theoretically—hampering efforts at meaningful discourse.

In Chapter 12, we will attempt to peer into the future, painting a picture of what this country might look like and how legalization could alter the present landscape of college campuses. We already have such glimpses in universities in states such as Colorado and Washington that have a several-year head start, and representatives from those institutions are already beginning to forecast what is coming for the rest of the nation's schools.

In the final chapter, we will attempt to consolidate the information amassed in the writing of this book and offer some recommendations for improving communications between college officials and student consumers of marijuana. This chapter will be viewed through the lens of the psychotherapists (that we are), and our suggestions will reflect that bias. We are neither professional researchers nor prevention specialists—though we have a great deal of exposure to both and have delved deeper into these areas to prepare this book. What component we do offer is innumerable hours of intimate, often intense, conversations with individuals who use marijuana and other substances, much of which occurs in the college environment. We find that students, if given the chance, free of judgment, *want to talk about this*. Accordingly, as psychotherapists, we further recognize in our work that when our clients are unwilling or unable to change, hammering away at them with the same interventions and expecting different results usually ends in impasse. Therefore, *we*, as college professionals from all facets of higher education, need to self-examine and make a shift ourselves. Change our script.

When we started, we had only our basic theses and a vague idea of where our journey would lead us. The final objective crystallized only when we were well on our way. The creativity in the process was organic, exploratory. As Frank Gehry, world famous architect, stated, "I've always felt if you know what you are going to do in advance, then you won't do it. Your creativity starts with whether you are curious or not."[1] So, for our readers, we invite you to join us in the process.

Note

1 MasterClass. (2017, March 10). *Frank Gehry teaches design and architecture.* [Video film]. Retrieved from www.youtube.com/watch?v=8LwK5-yN_NE

Acknowledgements

Firstly, I would like to thank all of the higher education professionals who took time out of their hectic schedules to provide essential insights into this book. I know how difficult it can be just to carve out time and answer emails. Secondly, I am also in debt to those students willing share their experiences openly and, at times, fearlessly. They brought to the text an intimate component that speaks in ways no amount of research or skilled writing can match.

Thirdly, I owe starting this journey to my co-author and colleague Stephanie, who over lunch one day, three years ago, suddenly challenged me with the following: "So, you want to write a book with me?" Taken by surprise, my immediate response was, "I don't know if I have the discipline to write a book." To this she responded swiftly, "Well, then, I guess *that's* off the table." Having been in sales long ago as a young man, I now recognize this gambit as "the old take-away." When I backtracked with, "Well, let me think about it," the hook was set. Well played, Stephanie.

Finally, I owe so much to my loving wife, Kim, for her patience and understanding as this effort consumed much of the time available to us outside our normally busy lives. Your days as a book widow are over Hon. Thank you.

—Jonathan Beazley

Thank you, Jonathan, for challenging my proposal. Your persistence through hectic periods of transition has been impressive and openness to learning with me very much appreciated. I am also grateful for the leagues of patience and support shown by loved ones. Dan, you too are a book widower no more!

—Stephanie Field

Chapter 1

Tom

"I actually started smoking weed kind of late, my senior year of high school." Tom has a slight build and is politely soft-spoken, with dark hair and gauges in both ears. He shares an apartment in an old late-Victorian house just outside of Boston, typical of the places students inhabit in that college-rich city. The décor is classic college male, and so starkly functional. Chairs and the sofa are for sitting, listening, and watching; tables are for writing and eating. Beds remain unmade. Old plaster walls, in need of fresh paint, are intermittently covered with posters that might also hide damage from past renters. There is a singular variant: covering much of a small kitchen table is an impressive display of specialty teas. It is dark inside, the sun's rays blocked by flags of various countries covering the windows, affording some privacy from passersby on the street just feet away. Levity comes into the living room in the form of a purring, flopping cat named Zoe, who is preternaturally friendly to complete strangers.

"My father owned a wood-carving business. He did the carving you see on some of the historical buildings in the city. He had intended on being a state policeman, so he was very against marijuana. Anyway, he couldn't be a cop because he accidently cut his hand really badly while working on a carving one day. He used to fly into rages—we both have borderline personality disorder, I think—and he would accuse me of being stoned, even when I wasn't. I hadn't started yet." It becomes clearer as the interview progresses that the relationship with his father is complex, with intense emotions including sadness. "My father is an alcoholic. He's not going to be with us much longer." Tom states this as fact, undeniable and unavoidable. He does not linger on this subject.

We move on to the beginnings of his relationship with weed. When asked about the first time he ever smoked marijuana, Tom is clear about his experience. "It was right before college, on a drive during that summer. I felt the loss of anxiety that I had held in my chest. I think it helped with my depression. So, I started smoking regularly. I became more social. It helped with sleep. If I haven't smoked, I won't fall asleep." This led to the question of whether he had tried any prescription medications for his insomnia, anxiety, and depression. He asserts that he had tried Benadryl and melatonin for sleep and was prescribed citalopram for his anxiety and depression. "I didn't like the effects. It was worse than the borderline personality stuff." As for other therapy: "I had seen a number of therapists as a kid and I was tried on a bunch of things that just messed me up." He adds that he also suffers from severe acid reflux, and cannabis helps him cope with that condition.

Tom now smokes daily. "I smoke a concentrated form of marijuana. I now tend to do dabs because I developed a slight case of asthma from smoking the plant so much." On the topic of dabs, he becomes the teacher: "Dabs are highly concentrated with THC, 80%–95% versus the 19%–20% even really good weed has. I have an array of devices to use it; it depends on the form I am using. There are the oils, or it can be waxy. I also use a lot of what is called 'shatter,' because it looks like drops of amber and breaks into shards." Tom confides that he gets this cannabis product from a person whom he watched process it. He describes this person packing high-quality marijuana plant into a pre-frozen large glass tube, with one end covered in cheesecloth. Butane is then pumped through the tube, separating active from inert ingredients. "Only the cannabinoids pass through the cheesecloth onto a collection dish, except for maybe 5%–10% of the plant material or butane." When oils or waxes are unavailable, Tom must buy whatever cannabis is available for sale through connections. The varieties and quality vary, but it is generally not a problem, because he has several friends who smoke regularly.

"When I got to college my smoking became an amplified version of what it was in high school." No longer having to co-exist with his volatile father, Tom paints a picture of unbridled substance exploration. "College was an incredible sense of freedom. I had this roommate who was very much into the pot culture—you could say she was a hippie. Weed was a social lubricant and I had smoked enough to be able to handle myself in social situations. Non-smokers became curious. I remember there were these girls who asked to smoke with us because they wanted to study the effects." Tom's voice becomes more solemn: "Then, further into college, things got darker." He describes moving into a place with one roommate who was a serious drug dealer. "We even had a gun in the house and if someone came into the house, we might have [needed] to shoot him." Tom admits to being exposed to a variety of drugs. "For a while I did a lot of MDMA, cocaine, and Adderall." Throughout this period, he was trying to write his thesis, despite blacking-out one time while high on cocaine and trashing the apartment. His roommates moved out. "I was using so much Adderall that I eventually got sick from uppers. I ended up being hospitalized after taking 200mg of Adderall. Alcohol took over at this point."

Tom becomes painfully open about his losses as his life spiraled downward. "I failed out of college and got real depressed. I became dependent on alcohol. I was drinking 151 rum, 1.75 liter bottle and killing half of it in a day." Somehow during this period, he developed a serious relationship with a girl and intended to get married. "But alcohol and depression took too much. She left. I take full responsibility for destroying my relationship. I wasn't able to really get my shit together." After a pause, he becomes more upbeat: "I haven't drunk in several months, and before that a whole year. But, I am extraordinarily dependent on oil. I can't say that it is necessarily good, but it has replaced alcohol, amphetamines, cocaine, and prescription drugs." He notes discovering that the combination of dabs and caffeine seem to mimic the effect of Adderall on his brain; this is significant, as he has returned to writing. "It took me years to be able to write without amphetamines." Asked about the differences between what he uses now and speed, he answers, "Adderall made relationships with family and others difficult, dabs don't."

What does he like most about cannabis? Tom is unequivocal: "It is comforting to know that in a flash I can change how I am feeling. I've been very suicidal in the past, but it has kept me away from that." He has considered stopping or severely limiting his use. "I have [reduced use] several times, usually for financial reasons. But friends have helped by pitching in." He is asked for any negatives about his relationship with marijuana. "More of the social. It's tough, always having it around; I have a lot of friends who are also fans. People will come over and expect to get high. I might not have enough." He goes on to tell about a time when a friend, in preparing to do dabs with him, tried to break off a piece of some of the "shatter"—which did exactly that, sending expensive shards all over the room. Travelling is also nerve-racking: "How do I do this on the road?" It is clear that dabs create a lot of complications in his life. It is just as clear that he is not yet prepared to stop.

Tom ends on an upbeat note. "Lately, there have been a lot of positive things happening." He has been working as of late. He is writing. He declares that he intends to finish his degree. "Having goals has been much more of a saving grace."

Chapter 2

Cannabis, the Plant, and Its History With Humankind

Arabians, Indians, Sabaeans,
Sing not, in hymns and Io Paeans,
Your incense, myrrh, or ebony.
Come here, a nobler plant to see,
And carry home, at any rate,
Some seed, that you may propagate.
If in your soil it takes, to heaven
A thousand thousand thanks be given;
And say with France, it goodly goes,
Where the Pantagruelion grows.
                    —Francois Rabelais[1]

Cannabis, if anything, is versatile. The utility of the plant and its ability to adapt to a variety of environments has historically been a major part of its impact on humankind. Cannabis, for much of its 10,000-year history with humans has been cultivated mainly for the usefulness of its stalk. Hemp is the name used most commonly to differentiate this variety from the psychoactive herb we now refer to as marijuana. The plant was given its scientific name, *cannabis sativa*, by Carl Linnaeus, the father of taxonomy, in the mid-eighteenth century. The latter name means "cultivated."[2] *Sativa* is characterized by slender leaves and can reach heights of over 20 feet, and it may have been these great, fibrous stalks that first attracted humans. Thirty years later, the French naturalist John-Baptiste Lamarck proposed that the plant found in Europe was different from the one found in warmer climates such as India and that they were actually two separate varieties. He reclassified them accordingly, giving the name *cannabis indica* to the variety from those sunnier climates, after the country where it was so prevalent. *Indica* is much shorter and bushier with broader leaves than the more trim and vertical *sativa*. A century and a half later, a third possible variety named *cannabis ruderalis*, was found in Russia. Scrawny compared to the others, *Ruderalis* lacks the psychoactive properties of its siblings.[3] More recently, there has been a growing majority of cannabis experts who agree that all three are but variants of *sativa*.[4]

Cannabis is dioecious: there are male and female plants. And in rare instances it can be hermaphroditic.[5] It is wind-pollinated in the wild. Under proper conditions, *cannabis sativa* grows at a prolific rate—up to 5 inches a day. When grown commercially for its psychoactive properties, male plants are typically destroyed before fertilization happens as this leads to increased resin production in the remaining female plants. Most of the resin produced by cannabis is on its flowers but also found to a lesser extent on its leaves. By contrast, the stalk and seeds have little to no resin. Cannabis was probably first cultivated for the fibers of its stalk, which are remarkably strong and resistant to rot.[6] These fibers were processed from the stalks through a process known as retting. Earlier in history, this arduous method involved soaking the stalks in water until they began to soften, then thrashing them against a hard surface until the fibers finally separated. Archaeological evidence suggests that humans were using hemp as far back 7000 BC for rope and cloth. The importance of hemp earlier in our past cannot be overstated, as it was an essential ingredient in clothing, rope, paper, and building material.[7] Later in history, hemp cultivation was vital during the rise of shipping and naval power. The fiber it provided was remarkably resistant to the ravages of seawater and was necessary in the production of all the ropes used in riggings for sails. Governments strongly encouraged its cultivation because hemp production was so important in pre-revolution American colonies. In some areas, such as seventeenth-century Virginia, farmers were mandated to grow it under English law.[8] It is a very elite botanical club that includes only members grown in response to legal edicts.

The necessity of cannabis's cultivation to early humans, including its value as a food source, may have contributed to the rise of agriculture and thus civilization. Overshadowed by its other properties, the use of cannabis seeds as a source of food has often been underappreciated. The prevailing belief is that ingesting cannabis for nutrition long predates its psychoactive use.[9] Hemp seeds have been eaten for millennia and are still a regular staple in the diets of rural India and sub-Saharan Africa. More recently, seeds, powders, and other non-psychoactive edible hemp products have become increasingly available in the health food sections of supermarkets. High in protein and rich in nutrients, hemp seeds contain omega-3 and omega-6 fatty acids as well as other important vitamins such as E and A. It has been written that Buddha once survived for a year solely on hemp seeds; it should be added that the story depicts him somehow managing this on only a few seeds a day.[10] Along with hemp seeds, hemp oil derived from non-psychoactive plants can be used as food. In the past, hemp oil was also an important source of fuel for lamps.

Humankind eventually discovered additional, remarkable characteristics about some of the plants found in warmer climates: they possessed medicinal properties and the power to intoxicate. Cannabis can be found in Chinese writing as early as 2700 BC and was included in the first Chinese pharmacopeia *Shennong Bencoajing* during the first century BC. *Cannabis sativa* was probably brought to South America in the fifteenth and sixteenth centuries,[11] where it evolved into the mind-altering plant known today. The species *cannabis indica* had been known for its psychoactive properties by Europeans (and later Americans) for much longer—so much so that up until the twentieth century, marijuana associated with intoxication was associated with India and often referred to as "Indian Hemp," even though much of the psychoactive plant being used may have been sativa. Sufficient photoperiod, or length of available sunlight, unavailable in the northern climates of Europe, is essential for cannabis to produce psychoactive resin on its flowers. Presently, some of the available marijuana are hybrids, *sativa* bred with *indica*, cultivated for specific properties based on the marketing goals of the growers and sellers.

Cannabis, the plant, contains over 400 compounds.[12] Among these are over 60 (and counting) identified chemicals unique to the plant itself, known as cannabinoids. The most prominent are delta-9 tetrahydrocannabinol (THC) and cannabidiol (CBD). THC is the chemical in marijuana that creates the sense of being high. It acts on the brain, distorting sense of time and space and heightens perceptual experiences. This cannabinoid also gives the user "the munchies"—an increase in the brain's reward signals to food, leading to greater consumption. The other main cannabinoid, CBD, does not make a person high but has other properties including mild sedation. As we learn more about cannabis, CBD emerges as increasingly important for its potential medical benefits. Other chemicals found in a wide range of plant life, known as terpenes or terpenoids, are believed to be important in the various actions of cannabis, but their role is far less understood.[13]

Cannabis as a psychoactive substance is used in several ways with each pathway dictating the intensity and longevity of the effects. Early in history, cannabis was primarily ingested, often mixed with a fatty liquid as it was done in ancient India.[14] The psychoactive chemicals in cannabis cannot easily be dissolved in water or injected; as a result, *hashish* prepared from resin of the flowers of fertilized female plants was often blended with milk. Hashish is processed and pressed into cakes where it can be ingested or smoked. It typically has more than twice the level of THC than the rest of the plant containing psychoactive properties. Hashish can be further refined by extracting the cannabinoids, creating an oil with an almost 85% THC level. In the Middle East, before smoking became more prominent, hashish was often blended with nuts and spices into a paste served on pieces of flatbread.[15] There is a trade-off between smoking and ingesting marijuana in any form. When smoked or vaporized, the active cannabinoids reach the lungs and so the arterial blood swiftly, producing a pleasant, manageable, and quicker high that is relatively short-lived—a few hours at most. Much of the THC, upward of 50–90%, is lost to the heat of burning with smoking. When ingested, the results can be dramatically different. Eaten or drunk, THC is absorbed into the blood stream through the intestines where it is initially metabolized in the liver. It is first stored in the fatty tissue surrounding the liver for close to 30 minutes before being released back into the blood stream where it eventually reaches the brain, creating a potentially intense effect that can last for hours. Cannabis with high levels of THC is made into cookies, brownies, candies, or butter-like spreads. In states where recreational use is legal, a variety of beverages containing—primarily THC—are marketed looking very much like regular bottles of soda. When made with high-potency hashish oils, a tray of brownies, for instance, can contain the equivalent THC of a tremendous amount of marijuana plant.

Aside from different modes of use, changes in marijuana THC percentage over time also impact the longevity and intensity of drug effects. Even when smoked, the THC content of the average joint is far greater than it was just over 20 years ago. According to the University of Mississippi's Potency Monitoring program, the average THC content in confiscated marijuana hovered around 4% in 1995. In 2012, it had risen to 12%, and they had tested hashish samples as high as 36%.[16]

It was in India where cannabis began to be produced and graded according to its effects, medicinal and otherwise. It was revered. According to the twelfth-century BC Hindu texts known as the *Vedas*, cannabis was a gift brought by the god Shiva from the Himalayas for all humanity's enjoyment.[17] The benefits of cannabis seemed unlimited—it was thought to bring enlightenment, sexual awareness, serenity, and energy, depending on the context and who was using the drug. Grading cannabis was based on the quality and potency, how it was prepared, and from what part of the plant it was taken. The top grade, named *charas*, was high-quality hashish—or the resin collected by hand from selected plants grown at higher altitudes and further processed into cakes. The most potent resin, referred to as *kief*, is harvested from the trichomes of the flowers by grinding them over a screen and collecting the sifted product. The next in quality was *ganga* and was made from the dried flowers of the female cannabis plant. The lowest grade preparation was *bhang*, a less expensive form of marijuana commonly available.[18]

The recreational use of cannabis followed knowledge of its medicinal value, and a culture of hashish developed with the rise of Islam in the seventh century. Cannabis ingestion became part of the fabric of life during the Caliphate that emerged following the death of the prophet

Mohammed. The drug was mentioned in poems and stories—it was even central in two of the tales told in *One Thousand and One Arabian Nights*. By the Middle Ages, the culture of cannabis had already reached legendary proportions contributing to western awareness of the plant's intoxicating qualities. All myths have at their base some kernel of fact, but its power emanates from the stories spun thereafter. And so it is with hashish, as one of its most infamous legends brought to Europe was possibly fabrication, sprung from the tales dictated by a man in prison, later known by some as *Il Millione*: Marco of a Million Lies.

Marco Polo, the famous thirteenth-century Venetian, includes this story in the memoir of his journey from Venice to China under Kublai Khan. Many historians believe this journey was pure invention comprised of stories he had heard from actual trips to the Middle East, but new research suggests otherwise.[19] In this story, Marco Polo tells of *The Old Man in the Mountain*.[20] He was probably referring to Hassan Ibn-Sabbah, an eleventh-century leader, and later dissident, believed to have created an Islamic cult in northern Persia. Very little is actually known about Ibn-Sabbah, yet his name has become historically linked with cannabis.

According to Polo, it was in Ibn-Sabbah's fortress of Alumet that young men were enlisted and conditioned there to do anything their leader commanded. To achieve this, recruits were plied with an elixir allegedly made with hashish (and probably opium) that would swiftly induce sleep. When they awoke, they would find themselves in a beautiful garden within the fortress, where they would be fed delicious foods and sexually serviced by lovely maidens: a glimpse of paradise. Once they fell back asleep, they were whisked away, left with this dream and a promise that if they remained loyal servants to their master (even unto death), they would again visit the wondrous garden in heaven. They became fanatical warriors—trained, stealthy killers known as the *hashishin* because of their use of the drug, and throughout history this name was thought (probably erroneously) to be the etymological root of the later word *assassin*.[21] In fact, there is little to connect the assassins employed by Ibn-Sabbah to hashish with the sole exception of Marco Polo's tale retold a century later.

Still, this is not merely cannabis-related trivia: the lurid character of Polo's story lent a certain romance, an exotic and slightly dangerous reputation to hashish as it was revealed in oral tradition and written word to westerners over the next 800 years. Its use for intoxication became the practice of those persons willing to step outside the bounds of social convention: writers, artists, musicians, and poets such as François Rabelais, Eugène Delacroix, Charles Baudelaire, William Burroughs, Jack Kerouac, and Louis Armstrong. It remains true today as cannabis still retains a supra-cultural, if not anti-establishment, status.

Indian hemp, when pure and administered carefully, is one of the most valuable medicines we possess.
—Sir Russell Reynolds, Queen Victoria's physician[22]

William O'Shaughnessy was an Irishman and true polymath who pursued medical and other knowledge with incomparable passion. His was a fertile and relentlessly active mind. O'Shaughnessy's research contributed to the advent of treating cholera patients during an outbreak in 1831 with intravenous electrolyte therapy.[23] It was during his travel to India in the late 1830s where he came upon something else that captured his fascination. In the city of Calcutta—now known as Kolkata—he was introduced to how *cannabis indica* was being used in traditional Indian medicine and had been for millennia. He wrote that the shorter *indica* plant had sticky resin on its flowers that was lacking in the variety of *sativa* he knew from England and Europe. He studied how the local populace grew and harvested this plant. He observed how they processed the resin and prepared it for use in a variety of ways; including blending it with sugar, flour, and butter, making it into a paste that could be spread onto flat bread. What he found most fascinating was seeing how people with pain, spastic disorders, rheumatism, tetanus, and cholera were almost invariably helped by this preparation. He successfully demonstrated how the extractions from the plant could quell seizures in children. Even if these illnesses eventually killed them, it greatly reduced their suffering. O'Shaughnessy later brought his findings back to England, introducing the West to the potential medical value of cannabis.[24]

The word spread throughout the medical communities, and O'Shaughnessy's work ushered in the era of cannabis-based medicines. Tinctures of cannabis—extracts made with alcohol solutions to derive the active, yet undiscovered, ingredients—became part of the United States Pharmacopeia in 1850. Up until 1942, companies such as Eli Lilly and Parke-Davis marketed cannabis extracts. O'Shaughnessy was eventually inducted into the Royal Society and, in 1856, knighted by Queen Victoria for his work establishing a telegraph system in India. It is for his work with *cannabis indica*, however, that he is most remembered.

I believe in some cases one cigarette might develop a homicidal mania, probably to kill his brother. It depends on the physical characteristics of the individual. Every individual reacts differently to the drug. It stimulates some and others it depresses. It is impossible to say just what the action of the drug will be on a given individual, of the amount. Probably some people could smoke five before it would take that effect, but all the experts agree that the continued use leads to insanity. There are many cases of insanity.
—Harry Anslinger in a statement to a congressional subcommittee (July 12, 1937)[25]

When reading about the central figure at some important historical crossroads, seminal moment, or *cause célèbre*, it is not uncommon for that person to be introduced with descriptions such as "a more unlikely character could not be imagined" or "seemed ill-suited for the role." This is patently untrue for Harry Anslinger, the first head of the Federal Bureau of Narcotics: the man looked every inch a cop—and he was during alcohol prohibition under the Volstead Act. Photographs of Anslinger at the height of his power show that he possessed a large head and thick neck, giving him the appearance of a bulldog. And a bulldog he was, with Congress and anyone else, for that matter, who stood between him and his goals. Without the unbridled ambition and indefatigable drive of Harry Anslinger, the modern prohibition against cannabis would not exist. He cut his teeth during the early 1920s as an investigator on the Pennsylvania Railroad and worked as an assistant commissioner for the Bureau of Prohibition in the latter part of that decade. He built a reputation as being implacable and incorruptible during his service on the bureau, where many other government officials during Prohibition were otherwise. It may have been for this reason he was appointed as the first director of a brand-new department—the Federal Bureau of Narcotics (FBN), although the fact that his wife was the niece of Andrew Mellon, the Secretary of the Treasury and among the richest men in the world, should not be overlooked.

Unfortunately, this remarkable leap up the ladder of success within the government system came with a serious problem: there was not much for this new department to do. After the repeal of Prohibition, regulation of the now-legal alcohol fell under the purview of the Treasury Department. There were no illicit inebriants out there for Anslinger to fight other than opiates, which affected a very small percentage of the population at the time. He also inherited his fledgling agency at the height of the Great Depression, and, therefore, the future looked bleak for his department unless he could demonstrate that it deserved fiscal support at a time when the federal coffers were very low. Anslinger needed a worthy and terrible villain, his own Professor Moriarty or Evil Empire, to combat and demonstrate to the world that his battle was worthy and righteous.

Ironically, cannabis did not initially interest him. He complained that it was a weed, that it grew "like dandelions," so prolifically that trying to interdict it would be impractical and doomed to failure.[26] Early on, he thought it would be best controlled on a local and state level. It was then that he became aware of legislation that was occurring in some of the southern and western states, especially those that bordered Mexico. These states had passed laws designed to prohibit the distribution of *marijuana*, a name used with increasing frequency to connect it with the Mexican immigrants introducing it into the United States.[27] Racial fear existed in those states that this little understood drug would be used by local black and Hispanic men, disinhibiting them and resulting in crime, violence, and sexual behavior with the white female population.

Anslinger did not invent the racial fear cannabis could inspire, but he apparently saw in it a means to conjure the demons he needed to justify his crusade. Very few Americans had even heard of the words "marijuana," "cannabis," "reefer," or "muggles." It was an absolute unknown. But, the fear of Negroes and Mexicans, miscegenation, and corruption of the nation's white youth—these could all be exploited for his campaign. Anslinger used press clippings describing violent crimes, murders, madness, and wanton sex relentlessly, often mined from articles in the "yellow journalism" newspapers owned by the media magnate William Randolph Hearst.[28] He seemingly had no need for facts to support his portrayal of cannabis and the horrors it would bring to the user and society.

In fact, he defied scientific research at times, even going toe-to-toe with the head of the American Medical Association (AMA), Dr. William Woodward. Woodward led the opposition against the Marihuana Tax Act, a bill being pushed hard by Anslinger. Woodward and the AMA were concerned that many physicians did not grasp how the law would affect their ability to prescribe medicinal cannabis for analgesia and other ailments. They did not make the connection between this feared drug marijuana and the cannabis preparations to which they were accustomed. Dr. Woodward and the AMA also presented studies demonstrating that there was no scientific evidence supporting the purported evils of cannabis claimed by the Federal Bureau of Narcotics. In the end, Anslinger and his forces won the day. Legislation for the Marihuana Tax Act passed in 1937, due greatly to his ceaseless canvassing, fear mongering, and general combativeness. Harry Anslinger knew that Congress and the public were most vulnerable not in the head but in the viscera, and he would always swing for the gut.

The Marihuana Tax Act, Anslinger's signature piece of legislation, was the seminal law in the federal government's campaign prohibiting cannabis, though it did not actually make marijuana illegal. What it did was mandate a tax of $100 per ounce every time marijuana changed hands. This is in 1937 dollars, when the median cost of a home was $4,100.[29] The Marihuana Tax Act made selling of any cannabis (including hemp)— for recreation, medicine, industry, or any other purpose—all but illegal through the tax law.

In 1944, he took on the popular and powerful mayor of New York, Fiorello LaGuardia, who had organized a commission comprised of renowned members of both the medical and the scientific communities to determine the true dangers cannabis posed and to publish their findings. What this commission found after a five-year review refuted many of the claims Anslinger and the Federal Bureau of Narcotics had been making about marijuana. As expected, Anslinger went on the attack with a fusillade of rhetoric, condemnation, and arm-twisting. He even managed to get the American Medical Association, the very organization with which he had crossed swords seven years before, to join him in what was eventually a successful discrediting of the report.

Anslinger was instrumental again in the passing of the Boggs Act (1951), which set mandatory sentencing for narcotic possession. First offenses were punishable by two years in prison; the second offense five to ten years; the third up to 20 years.[30] No longer needing to exploit racial fear, Anslinger instead tapped into the nationwide fear of communist infiltration. He preached that drug use was an overall campaign by our enemy—Communism—to destroy our national will. This was at the height of McCarthyism, so once again Anslinger was canny in matching his message with the zeitgeist of America in the early 1950s.

Finding an unbiased portrayal of Harry Anslinger is not easy. He is vilified by most of the contemporary authors, many whom represent the anti-marijuana prohibition contingent. Isolating the original source of his more egregious alleged racial comments can be difficult; writers and bloggers appear to be referencing each other. The true depth of Anslinger's racist beliefs is not fully known, but, in the news flashes collected for his "gore file," the suspects in those marijuana-crazed crimes were often blacks or Latinos.

He was certainly using this information in a calculated way. Anslinger was savvy in preying upon racial fear and did not appear to be internally conflicted by such tactics. Yet it must be remembered that this was America in the 1930s: Jim Crow laws still ruled the south, and the lynching of blacks was still chillingly common. As a nation, we were—at least overtly and certainly legally—more racist.

Although he has been dead for over 40 years, Harry Anslinger remains a lightning rod for the pro-marijuana groups, his life and work cited as testimony to the immoral roots of cannabis prohibition. His tireless promotion of the FBN laid down the foundation for the War on Drugs. The FBN was eventually reorganized into the Bureau of Narcotics and Dangerous Drugs (BNDD) in 1968 and finally transformed into the Drug Enforcement Administration (DEA) under the Nixon administration.

> *I believe that the cannabinoids represented a medicinal treasure trove which waits to be discovered.*
>
> —Raphael Mechoulam[31]

Raphael Mechoulam, a man who could be considered the father of modern cannabis science, in the early 1960s embarked on a quest to investigate the constituents and action of the cannabis plant. Mechoulam was admittedly clueless to the difficulties he would encounter obtaining an illegal drug for his research. Armed with such naiveté, he blithely went into the police department in Rehovot, Israel, where he was junior faculty at the Weizmann Institute, and requested 5kg of good-quality Lebanese hashish that had been seized. He later recounted that he apparently "seemed reliable" to the police, and he obtained much of his specimens from them thereafter.[32] His scientific studies into the properties of cannabis are historical highlights in the evolution of our understanding of this plant. After re-isolating cannabidiol (CBD), the second-most prominent cannabinoid (a term Mechoulam claims to have coined) in marijuana, he and Yahiel Gaoni synthesized what they named delta[33] tetrahydrocannabinol—later renamed delta[34] tetrahydrocannabinol (THC).[35] Up to this point, almost all research on marijuana had ground down to the point of non-existence. No pharmaceutical company wanted to risk investing money in a substance that had been so thoroughly scourged internationally by the still-Anslinger-led American anti-narcotic forces.

Mechoulam, a Bulgarian Jew whose family left its homeland in 1949 and immigrated to Israel, had his first taste of research in the army. Later, at the Rockefeller Institute in New York, he conducted post-doctoral research on steroids, giving him a taste for studying chemistry on the perimeter of normal inquiry. This sparked interest inevitably led him to the unexplored territory of cannabis compounds. Over the next several decades, Mechoulam was at the forefront of much of the research describing the chemical make-up, effects, and potential therapeutic value of cannabis. His work with Alyn Howlett and others led to the discovery of the *endocannabinoid system*.[36] They had already accepted that the brain had receptor sites to which THC could bind, but they further hypothesized that these receptors were there for an important chemical produced *within* the body. A first receptor, dubbed "C1," was found throughout the brain.[37] In 1992, that binding endogenous chemical was finally discovered, isolated, and named "anandamide"—after a Sanskrit word meaning "bliss" (N.B. anandamide is not only produced by the body but also present in chocolate).[38] Later, a second receptor type, "C2," was discovered in the immune system.[39]

Since then, other receptors and endocannabinoids have been isolated, and their roles in the body are beginning to be understood and articulated. As of this writing, Mechoulam still teaches at the Hebrew University in Jerusalem at age 86. He has published over 350 articles, many of which pioneered our understanding of cannabis.

Most users, young and old, demonstrate an average or above-average degree of social functioning, academic achievement, and job performance.

—Shafer Commission report 1972 (commissioned by Richard Nixon)[40]

There can be little controversy over what President Richard Nixon thought about marijuana. He expresses himself on the matter quite clearly in the White House tapes, which came to public knowledge during the Watergate Hearings. It was Nixon who bequeathed us the term "The War on Drugs," a title he gave his 1971 campaign against "public enemy number one," just prior to making his Special Message to Congress on Drug Abuse Prevention and Control.[41] Given the American attraction to bellicose language, the name stuck. In those now-infamous tapes, Nixon's authoritarian leadership style and anti-Semitic paranoia are undeniable as he rants to his chief of staff, H. R. Haldeman, about the National Commission on Marihuana and Drug Abuse and the pro-legalization movement that opposed him:[42]

May 26, 1971, Time: 10:03 am—11:35 am—Oval Office
Conversation: 505–4—Meeting with Nixon and HR 'Bob' Haldeman

Nixon:	"Now, this is one thing I want. I want a goddamn strong statement on marijuana. Can I get that out of this sonofabitching, uh, Domestic Council?"
Haldeman:	"Sure."
Nixon:	"I mean one on marijuana that just tears the ass out of them. I see another thing in the news summary this morning about it. You know it's a funny thing, every one of the bastards that are out for legalizing marijuana is Jewish. What the Christ is the matter with the Jews, Bob, what is the matter with them? I suppose it's because most of them are psychiatrists, you know, there's so many, all the greatest psychiatrists are Jewish. By God we are going to hit the marijuana thing, and I want to hit it right square in the puss, I want to find a way of putting more on that. More [unintelligible] work with somebody else with this."
Haldeman:	"Mm hmm, yep."
Nixon:	"I want to hit it, against legalizing and all that sort of thing."

Even more important and as enduring as the title he bestowed upon America's anti-drug abuse effort was the Controlled Substances Act of 1970 (CSA) that he signed into law.[43] This legislation expanded the federal government's authority to regulate the manufacturing, importation, selling, and distribution over a large swath of substances. Further, it categorized drugs into one of five schedules in rank order of the potential harm it posed, coupled with any medical utility.

Marijuana was listed in Schedule I, which includes heroin, LSD, MDMA, among others. Schedule I drugs are all deemed as having a high potential for abuse and no proven medical value, and lack evidence of acceptable safety. None of the substances in Schedule I can be prescribed or possessed for any reason without violating federal law. Under the CSA, new drugs may be added or the schedule of a drug changed internally by the Drug Enforcement Administration through a scientific evaluation and recommendation process done by the Department of Health and Human Services, employing the Food and Drug Administration and the newly created National Institute on Drug Abuse. Marijuana was grouped along with substances like heroin, whereas more hazardous drugs such as cocaine and methamphetamine were placed in Schedule II. Even more inexplicable was that Nixon pushed for this classification despite the findings of his own hand-picked committee: the National Commission on Marihuana and Drug Abuse. Headed by Raymond Shafer, this committee was charged with examining the evidence of marijuana's purported health and social hazards going back to the early part of the twentieth century. It ultimately found that marijuana use did not lead to[44] illness, and harder-drug addiction, though it did not directly recommend ending its illegal status. Nixon was presented with the committee's findings in 1973. He chose to ignore them. But other researchers in the scientific and medical field did not; some also found fault with the commission's findings. One, published under the auspices of the New York Academy of Medicine, concluded with:

> The medical profession should not accept the recommendations of the marihuana commission without further analysis of the forgotten facts of the record. To do otherwise is to forego the age-old admonition of our mentor Hippocrates: 'Above all, do no harm.'[45]

The regulatory exile of cannabis due to the CSA has been a source of much controversy. In a bureaucratic, catch-22 way, it closed the door on any federal funding for research into the medical potential of marijuana because marijuana was deemed to have no proven medical value. In doing so, the CSA sowed the seeds for an organized, political, and social backlash against marijuana's prohibition that is even now still gaining a fierce momentum.

We have since learned more about Nixon's Machiavellian use of his anti-drug legislation to further his political goals. His former aide John Ehrlichman revealed how Nixon's policies were designed to target groups he considered political obstacles—the youth culture of the 1960s and African Americans:

> The Nixon campaign in 1968, and the Nixon White House after that, had two enemies: the antiwar left and Black people . . . you understand what I'm saying? We couldn't declare it illegal to be against the

war or black, but by getting the public to associate the hippies with marijuana and the Blacks with heroin. And then criminalizing them both like crazy, we could disrupt those communities. We could arrest their leaders, raid their homes, break up their meetings and vilify them night after night on the evening news. . . . Did we know we were lying about the drugs? Of course we did.[46]

Offering a balanced view of someone like Richard Nixon is not easy to do. For many of the baby boomer generation, reviling him is considered not only normal but a moral duty. Yet, Nixon was a very complex figure, and, because of his policy-making, some initiatives continue to play a vital and helpful role this day. The Controlled Substances Act, despite its present controversy, had some profoundly positive effects. It eliminated the draconian mandatory sentences for marijuana possession that had been in existence for 20 years since the passing of the Boggs Act. Moreover, from a substance abuse treatment standpoint, Nixon was the first head of state to approve federal funds for the care of those struggling with chemical abuse and dependency problems.

It was also under his administration that the first confidentiality regulations were passed as part of the Drug Abuse Prevention, Treatment, and Rehabilitation Act of 1972.[47] This law more globally set down the framework for federal drug abuse policy-making, much of which still governs prevention and treatment efforts today. A National Drug Abuse Training Center was established to develop, conduct, and support a full range of training programs relating to drug abuse prevention functions. In 1974, the National Institute on Drug Abuse was created within the National Institute of Mental Health to administer drug abuse programs. A new grant program was authorized to assist states in coping with drug abuse, and four advisory bodies were established to provide recommendations on means of curbing drug abuse. These were the Drug Abuse Strategy Council, the National Advisory Council on Drug Abuse, a Federal Drug Council, and the National Advisory Council on Drug Abuse Prevention.[48]

> *Seriously ill Americans are caught in the crossfire as drug warriors on both sides of the cultural divide try to turn the sick into cannon fodder.*
>
> —Robert Randall[49]

Robert Randall was embarking on a life as a professor in the early 1970s when he gradually became aware that he was having problems seeing well. He noticed "halos" around things like the streetlights outside his home.[50] When he went to have it checked by his doctor, he received a terrifying diagnosis: he had glaucoma—a condition caused by increasing pressure from intraocular fluid slowly and irreversibly damaging the optic nerve. He would be blind by age 30.

After several failed treatment trials and eye surgery, Randall was left absolutely bereft of options and hope, facing a future of increasing darkness. It was one evening thereafter he noticed something peculiar when smoking some marijuana given by a friend: the ocular halos no longer appeared around the lights. He started smoking marijuana more frequently and continued to experience decreased glaucoma symptoms. To ensure he always had marijuana available and to save on expenses, he began to grow a few plants in his yard.

Around this same time, a study by ophthalmologist Robert Hepler of UCLA (1971) suggested that marijuana use decreased eye pressure.[51] Hepler's research had been funded by the National Institute on Drug Abuse to find out if marijuana use could be indicated through eye tests given by policeman. These tests were like the field eye exams used in DUI to ascertain nystagmus (involuntary eye movement) associated with alcohol intoxication or marked pupil dilation resulting from amphetamine use.[52] While his research did not lead to the hoped-for outcomes, Hepler was so captivated by evidence of reductions in intraocular pressure that he subsequently treated some glaucoma patients with cannabis.[53]

In 1975, Robert Randall came home one day to find it ransacked, a search warrant on the table. He was soon arrested for marijuana possession. He later wrote in his memoir, "I could not know at the time, but being arrested was about the best thing that could have happened to me. Being arrested saved my sight."[54] Rather than just plead guilty to a misdemeanor charge, he did something extraordinary; he decided to fight. He claimed in his defense that the marijuana he was smoking was an act of "medical necessity" and that he needed it to forestall blindness after all other conventional treatment had proved ineffective.

To mount such a defense—the first of its kind—Randall sought assistance from a fledgling group in Washington, D.C., known as NORML, the National Organization for the Reform of Marijuana Laws. That group referred him to Dr. Hepler, who was continuing his research on the potential therapeutic effects of marijuana. After rigorous testing and evaluation, Dr. Hepler determined that Randall's marijuana use was indeed impeding the progression of his glaucoma.[55] Armed with Hepler's findings and an affidavit from a doctor that Randall would go blind without regular use of marijuana, Randall went to trial . . . and won.

However, Randall's battle did not end with his exoneration. He still had the problem of where he could obtain his hard-fought-for substance. His next move was even more audacious—he petitioned the federal government to provide him with a steady supply of cannabis so that he no longer needed to break the law by procuring it through the black market. At the time, and still true today, the only marijuana cultivated by the federal government came from a facility near the University of Mississippi.[56] After a long, wrangling process, Randall was eventually able to obtain his requested marijuana, and 300 cigarettes were shipped to him monthly, although he complained about the quality.[57] Riding the crest of this victory, he and his partner, Alice O'Leary, became advocates for all people using marijuana for the treatment of a medical condition. Randall and O'Leary went on to found the Alliance for Cannabis Therapeutics and later the Marijuana AIDS Research Service. Randall was no fan of those who wanted to combine the legalization of recreational marijuana with that of its therapeutic capacity, believing that the association weakened the validity of the medical movement. Robert Randall continued his fight for these causes until his death in 2001 of AIDS, continuing to smoke his government-issued pot. By then his efforts had contributed to the passing of California Proposition 215: the Compassionate Care Act that ushered in a new era of marijuana as medicine and that led to other states passing similar laws. He never lost his sight.[58]

> *Leading medical researchers are coming to the conclusion that marijuana, pot, grass, whatever you want to call it, is probably the most dangerous drug in the United States.*
>
> —Ronald Reagan (1980)[59]

While Richard Nixon coined the term "War on Drugs," it took Ronald Reagan to really wage it. In his second year in the White House, Reagan announced his intentions in his radio address on October 2, 1982, when he finished with the following declaration:

> We're making no excuses for drugs—hard, soft, or otherwise. Drugs are bad, and we're going after them. As I've said before, we've taken down the surrender flag and run up the battle flag. And we're going to win the war on drugs.[60]

In the late seventies, the momentum of Nixon's War on Drugs had slowed, and there was discussion within the Carter administration about possibly legalizing marijuana. Nevertheless, under Reagan there was a sharp reversal in government policy. Those federal agencies directly involved in interdiction saw increased expenditures and expanded powers, while treatment for drug abuse—a major component in Nixon's Controlled Substance Act—experienced cuts in funding from Washington. The amount of funding for eradication and policing increased from an annual average of $437 million during Carter's presidency to $1.4 billion during Reagan's first term alone.[61] Roughly $24 million was cut from the budget for programs of education, prevention, and rehabilitation.

Besides being essentially more politically conservative than Nixon, and certainly Jimmy Carter, Ronald Reagan's first term coincided with a dramatic increase in cocaine distribution in the United States. Violence was associated with this increase as drug cartels from places like Colombia vied for control of the American market; parts of Miami in the early 1980s at times seemed to be an actual war zone. Yet the Reagan administration's policies did not differentiate between using drugs like cocaine, heroin, and cannabis: all were treated as equally criminal behavior.

To strike at the drug cartels economically, he sponsored the Comprehensive Forfeiture Act (1984), which gave authorities the right to seize assets and properties of convicted drug dealers (limiting their financial resources) and then use the funds obtained through the auctioning of these possessions to offset the costs of their efforts.[62] It authorized a court to take appropriate action preserving the availability of property during the pre-indictment period effective for up to 90 days. While much was confiscated from criminal drug lords, many less-dangerous drug-using Americans became collateral damage. Citizens had assets and property initially seized without being charged or convicted of the crime to which the property was purportedly connected.[63] In addition to supply interdiction, the demand for drugs was also targeted. The Anti-Drug Abuse Act of 1986 increased mandatory prison sentences for drug possession, and, though the primary target of this "zero-tolerance" initiative was cocaine, marijuana too fell under blade of this law. Possession of 100 plants would carry the same sentence as having 100 grams of heroin.[64]

Ronald Reagan's expansion of the War on Drugs appears to have been motivated by little other than his entrenched ideology, his concern for his country's welfare, especially its young people. In contrast to Nixon whose policies may have been driven by more unscrupulous political motives, Reagan, a life-long conservative, seemed to truly believe in the just nature of what he was doing. His belief in the virtue of his campaign is clear from the patriotic fervor in his speeches. "In this crusade," he pronounced in a televised address, "let us not forget who we are. Drug abuse is a repudiation of everything America is. The destructiveness and human wreckage mock our heritage."[65]

In addition to the expansion of law enforcement powers, the legacy of the Reagan years brought continuous growth in the field of substance abuse prevention. And in the world of higher education, it started with the passing of the Drug-Free Schools and Communities Act, Title II of his Drug-Free America Act of 1986. This law made funds available to State Departments of Education to implement alcohol and drug programming in the public schools. This was one of six titles in the initiative, all of which granted increased powers and funding to combat drug use. In a departure from his earlier interdiction-heavy policies, it also funneled money into substance abuse treatment. Three years later, amendments to the Drug-Free Schools Act were passed, including the Drug-Free Schools and Campuses Regulations stating that any higher education institution that received federal funding or any other form of financial aid from the government was required to implement programming "to prevent the unlawful possession, use, or distribution of illicit drugs and alcohol by students and employees," on its campus or in any sanctioned activity.[66] Further, colleges were mandated to do biennial reviews detailing their anti-alcohol/anti-drug-use efforts and submit them to the Department of Education. These regulations represented a set of minimum standards, and institutions may also have had other regulations, state and otherwise, to which they had to adhere. The Drug-Free Schools and Communities Act has ended up serving as the major branch of the War on Drugs from which college prevention has bloomed.

The Reagan years were marked by a sharp turn away from more progressive attitudes about drugs and their use in our society. This was certainly due to the stature of Regan himself—an icon for political conservatives. But this escalation in criminalizing substance use also arose as the government's reaction to the perceived threat of cocaine, crack, and the lawlessness associated with its distribution. Reagan's stance against drugs was no different than how he had stood in the Cold War against the Soviet Union: resolute, unyielding. However, in the case of the War on Drugs, there was no Mikhail Gorbachev on the other side reaching his hand across the divide. In the slipstream of Reagan's dogma, everything connected was pulled along, including college substance abuse prevention policies.

The inability to stop is the essence of what addiction is.
—Nora Volkow[67]

Nora Volkow was possibly destined to live an extraordinary life being the great-granddaughter of Leon Trotsky—architect of the Red Army during the establishment of the Soviet Union. Her parents fostered in their children an appreciation for the arts and sciences. Volkow earned her college degree in Mexico and came to the United States for post-graduate work after becoming fascinated with the new technology of positron emission topography (PET). PET scans are those that show where blood is flowing in the brain, indicating what centers are being activated during certain circumstances. Special dyes with radioactive tracers—tagged to chemicals naturally found in the body—are injected into the blood stream and, under PET scanning, light up as they are broken down in the areas being most activated. Unlike other types of imaging such as CT and MRI scans, PET scans are unable to determine the size or shape of a specific structure in the brain but can demonstrate how that structure is working. Volkow opted to do a psychiatry residency at New York

University where they were pioneering PET neuroimaging in their study of schizophrenia with the Long Island laboratory, Brookhaven. After completing this residency in 1984, Volkow went on to further work with PET scans at the University of Texas. Unfortunately, there were no patients with schizophrenia to study.[68] Instead, what they did have were plenty of people abusing cocaine. When given PET scans, Volkow and her colleagues saw "deranged" areas of blood flow in the brain that they likened to strokes.[69]

This research suddenly became more salient and vigorous when, in 1986, basketball pro Len Bias died after smoking a relatively new, powerful form of cocaine called "crack" and "rock." Following this tragedy, Dr. Volkow's work with neuroimaging became a priority of the National Institute on Drug Abuse (NIDA). She returned to Brookhaven and embarked on a crusade to map not just the geography of the brain but the very processes of the brain when it is eating, smoking, experiencing mania, and getting high. We could now watch the black box at work. They also made important discoveries in the action of dopamine in the brain, finding that persons who abused drugs appeared to have less dopamine receptors (known as D2 receptors) than the general non-using population.[70] Her seminal work in this field eventually led to her appointment as the director of NIDA in 2003. She has continued to champion the field of the neuroscience of addictions—whether it be addiction to alcohol, drugs, or, her favorite, chocolate.

She is not without her detractors, which include Stanton Peele, researcher in the field of addiction and a prominent author of such books as *Love and Addiction* and *The Diseasing of America*.[71] He argues that Volkow's emphasis on addiction being a chronic, incurable brain disease marked by repeated relapses limits the treatment options available to only those that fall within a narrow and unproven paradigm. He supports this contention by pointing to studies suggesting that most persons battling addiction who recover get better on their own.[72]

Criticism aside, it is indisputable that Nora Volkow's work has allowed us to learn more about the workings of the brain in the last 30 years than in the preceding 300. We can now peer into this previously unknown world—a realm that had only revealed itself post-mortem or via severe neurological injury. The veil is now lifted to explore how cannabis acts on and alters its environment.

The first few years in this industry, I had nightmares every night of my kids watching me dragged out of the house in handcuffs. But after we saw Charlotte and all these patients' successes, it just became very real that you are living a life worth living and you are doing the right thing.

—Joel Stanley[73]

The words "evangelical Christians" and "marijuana growers" are not typically associated and are almost never read in the same sentence. But in 2009, Josh Stanley, with the help of his brothers Jared, Jordan, Jon, and Joel, decided to start growing marijuana at their farm near Colorado Springs. At first, they were trying to help a family member struggling with the effects of chemotherapy. The Stanley brothers were brought up in a conservative, Christian family, yet they considered marijuana to be "God's plant" and saw no ideological conflict in their enterprise. They began to grow a strain of marijuana very low in THC while high in cannabidiol (CBD), a cannabinoid believed to have therapeutic properties, including anti-seizure effects.[74] By cultivating high-CBD strains with industrial hemp, the Stanley brothers could grow plants with THC levels below 0.5 percent. The strain was christened "Hippie's Disappointment" due to the distinct lack of any high that could be experienced from it, and the Stanley brothers hoped to market it to cancer patients in Colorado since the state had legalized medical marijuana.

Then, in 2011, they were contacted by the parents of Charlotte Figi, a 5-year-old girl with Dravet Syndrome, also known as myoclonic epilepsy of infancy or SMEI—a rare disorder marked by frequent, uncontrollable seizures. Charlotte would have as many as 300 seizures a week, many of them prolonged, and she had lost the ability to walk and talk and had even stopped eating. Standard medications were no longer effective, and her parents were running out of medical options. They had read online about some cases of intractable epilepsy being successfully managed in California with high-CBD/low-THC marijuana and managed to have a friend extract the oil from a small amount remaining at a dispensary in Denver. The results were dramatic; Charlotte was seizure-free for a week. But they were going to run out soon. That is when they found the Stanley brothers, who had since developed a CBD oil extract but could not yet find a market for it. This connection proved providential for both Charlotte's family and the Stanley brothers. Word of Charlotte's remarkable improvement spread, and, when the story was featured in a CNN television documentary, the market for the oil, now named "Charlotte's Web," blew up.[75]

The story of "Charlotte's Web" has not had a simple fairy tale ending, however. The demand for the oil quickly overwhelmed the Stanley brothers' ability to produce it. Desperate parents and other adults were put on a waiting list for the drug that was inescapably dependent on the growing cycle of the marijuana from the Stanley's farm. Also, like any other medication—pharmaceutical or herbal—it did not help everyone. Studies on CBD and its potential as an anti-seizure agent since 2009 have been promising but far from being a slam-dunk.[76] There was some question of the consistency of the CBD content: medical marijuana in any form does not have FDA oversight, and quality control is still in relative infancy.[77] Parents seeking the oil had to travel to Colorado just to have a chance to buy some of the extract, knowing full well they would have to go home only to return once the supply was finished as the oil could not be shipped across state lines without violating federal law.

The Stanley brothers, now operating under the foundation named the "Realm of Caring," made major shifts in production methods to accommodate the demand for Charlotte's Web. They refined their oils to ensure that the THC levels are no greater than 0.3%; this threshold is essential, as it allows the brothers to legally market the oil as an industrial hemp product. In 2015, they planned production of their hemp product from land they had bought in Uruguay, with the goal of providing oil to up to 9,000 customers who live in other states.[78] Why Uruguay? Because in the convoluted and perplexing world of America's legal system, hemp—cannabis with THC levels less than 0.3%—can be *imported* and sold in a variety of products such as clothing, shampoos, health supplements, and foods. However, it still cannot be produced in this country and shipped throughout the states. Thus far, the federal authorities have looked the other way in states where marijuana has been legalized, but not around interstate commerce. The Federal Farm Bill was passed in 2014, allowing states to grow industrial hemp, but only for research purposes; and, in 2015, the Industrial Hemp Farming Act was introduced on the floors of both the House of Representatives and the Senate, receiving bipartisan support.[79] The final step would be for the DEA to separate hemp from marijuana as a Schedule I substance.

Cannabidiol's potential medicinal properties aside, the Stanley brothers and "Charlotte's Web" attracted media attention that has projected medical marijuana beyond those states where it is legal into the national consciousness, adding more fuel to the debate of the plant's future status in our society. The desperate plight of parents with children suffering from these kinds of treatment-resistant diseases supercharged the drive for other states to pass laws in kind.

The leap from cannabis as medicine to cannabis as recreational drug is considerable in many societal and legal ways. The first two states to allow recreational use of marijuana, Washington and Colorado, had medical marijuana laws in place since 1998 and 2000 respectively, perhaps providing an essential step toward the result in 2012. Nevertheless, the legalizing of recreational marijuana in Colorado represented one of the more remarkable examples of a public messaging campaign ever seen in this country. Regardless of one's stance on legalization, the ingenuity, tenacity, and ultimate effectiveness of the "Marijuana Is Safer" crusade is inarguable.[80] Two of the main architects of this movement, Steve Fox and Mason Tvert, proved to be skillful organizers, persuasive communicators, savvy politicians, and, when necessary, effective *provocateurs*. At the foundation of their message lay a clever strategy: rather than argue solely for the legalization of cannabis, they instead embarked on a public education campaign that compared the relative safety of marijuana to that of the legal intoxicant alcohol. Their unique approach was also the result of a 30-year legal backlash against cannabis prohibition that was started during the anti-war movement of the sixties and more formally operationalized in 1970 by a young attorney named Keith Stroup, the founder of the National Organization for the Reform of Marijuana Laws (NORML). The mission of this new organization was to lobby the government to amend the Controlled Substances Act and have marijuana removed from Schedule I status, effectively decriminalizing it so that it could be studied and one day prescribed by physicians. Through the 1970s, Stroup and NORML were successful in getting 11 states to adopt decriminalization laws. Even President Jimmy Carter was seriously considering following suit on a federal level. But this movement came to an abrupt halt and a subsequent about-face with the inauguration of Ronald Reagan.

In 2004, Steve Fox was working as a federal lobbyist for the Marijuana Policy Project (MPP), an organization that had split off from NORML in the 1990s due to some in-fighting between several of the main players. In studying polls that compared opinions of Americans that were supportive of, against, or undecided about legalizing marijuana, he discovered that respondents were split equally about the relative safety of cannabis to alcohol. One third of respondents believed marijuana was less harmful than alcohol, another third thought it was more harmful than alcohol, and the final third thought it was equally as harmful as alcohol. The 75% of respondents who believed marijuana was less harmful than alcohol also supported its legalization. Fox believed that if he could sway the opinions of those who thought marijuana was more harmful than or as bad as alcohol, there would be a groundswell of public opinion to bolster an effort toward legalization.[81] The MPP had already established a track record of successful lobbying in several states, and they agreed to fund his project. Mason Tvert, a pro-marijuana activist in Colorado, initiated this campaign and implemented it at the University of Colorado and Colorado State University partly due to two recent tragic deaths of students directly attributable to binge drinking on those campuses.[82] In 2005, they launched SAFER (Safer Alternative to Enjoyable Recreation) at the campuses in Boulder and Fort Collins. Their initial objective was to spark a referendum among the students to vote on the following proposition: given that marijuana is less harmful than alcohol, penalties for the use or possession of marijuana on campus should be no greater than penalties for the use and possession of alcohol. Despite opposition from an array of sources, the media coverage that ensued paid dividends since it elevated the debate into the public arena.[83]

MPP's next move was to expand the campaign to the city of Denver. They avoided the trap of having to defend marijuana by itself by maintaining a consistent message—that marijuana was proven to be SAFER than alcohol and that alcohol causes a host of societal ills. Those who opposed legalized cannabis would have to justify why alcohol was permissible in the face of these indisputable statistics without sounding like hypocrites. After successfully getting their "Make Denver SAFER" initiative on the ballot for the next municipal election, MPP continued to apply pressure to their opposition. In fact, they seemed to welcome the expected responses since it only seemed to further their argument. Tvert, especially, seemed to relish vexing authorities and opponents. He even challenged the mayor of Denver to a contest where the mayor would drink beer (he owned a microbrewery and pub) and Tvert would smoke marijuana with the winner being the one who remained standing.[84] On November 1, 2005, the citizens of Denver voted to eliminate all penalties for the possession of cannabis by persons over age 21. Even though marijuana remained illegal by both state and federal laws, this represented the first salvo fired in the direction of eliminating recreational cannabis prohibition.

In 2006, a statewide SAFER campaign to legalize marijuana possession up to 1 ounce for an adult, Proposition 44, was defeated. Fox, Tvert, the MPP, and NORML were not discouraged though as the results demonstrated that a large percentage of Coloradans were supportive of legalization. From that point until 2012, they redoubled their efforts since they believed they had already successfully sparked Coloradans to reconsider their views on cannabis.

One reason for their optimism was that Colorado had been a medical marijuana state since 2000, with guidelines that were quite liberal when compared to other states with similar laws. "Caregivers" as defined by the law could grow marijuana on their property, and there was no provision within the statute limiting the number of patients a caregiver could aid. However, this was reduced to five patients in 2010 following several attempted interventions by the DEA and the Health Department.[85] A proliferation of medical marijuana shops then opened, run by persons growing marijuana for those individuals. Marijuana consumption continued to seep into the mainstream and over the rest of the decade created a sense of normalcy around marijuana in the community.

Finally, marijuana was legalized in 2012, after garnering over 53% of the vote. On the same day, the citizens of Washington State voted to pass Initiative 52, also making cannabis legal, though the respective laws differ. For example, Colorado residents could grow their own marijuana up to six plants per person or 12 per household, while Washington's law did not permit home cultivation, regulating production and distribution like alcohol. The initial domino had been tipped. Marijuana was subsequently legalized in Oregon and Alaska (where it already had been so decriminalized that it had been virtually legal, but now regulated). The District of Columbia, which had decriminalized possession in 2014, legalized it for up to 2 ounces by persons over 21. There are, as of this writing, no regulatory ordinances by which it can be sold.[86]

The picture continues to be fluid and changing. The Obama administration removed one of the hurdles that deterred researching marijuana from any angle other than showing its potential harm.[87] However, marijuana has not been re-classified from a Schedule I substance.[88] In 2016, the states of Massachusetts, Nevada, California, and Maine passed laws legalizing marijuana for recreational use by adults, while Florida, North Dakota, Arkansas, and Montana joined the ranks of 28 total states with medical marijuana. It is safe to assume that others are waiting and watching to see how these states fare post-legalization. One of the things they will be looking at carefully is the potential tax revenue that comes with regulation of cannabis. In 2014, Colorado's marijuana tax revenue was 69 million dollars, although this was far less than the projected 118 million. Colorado was hoping that many citizens receiving medical marijuana would purchase their cannabis from recreational businesses, but the 35% tax on recreational cannabis may have deterred consumers.[89] In contrast, Washington State is projecting even better revenue from its marijuana taxes, a hefty $694 million by the middle of 2019.[90] Border states where marijuana is illegal may still face many of the same problems legalization might bring and not be able to realize any of the tax income as their residents make purchasing runs across the border. How legalization will continue to influence the overall picture remains to be seen, but it will not come into full resolution swiftly.

Notes

1 Rabelais, F. (1904). *Five books of the lives, heroic deeds and sayings of Gargantua and his son Pantagruel* (T. Urquhart & P.A. Motteux, Trans.). London: A. H. Bullen. (Original work published 1532).
2 Guy, G., Whittle, B. A., & Robson, P. (2004). *Medicinal uses of cannabis and cannabinoids*. London, UK: Pharmaceutical Press. doi:10.1016/S0768-9179(08)70455-3
3 Booth, M. (2003). *Cannabis: A history*. New York, NY: St. Martin's Press.
4 Watts, G. (2006). Cannabis confusions. *British Medical Journal, 332*(7534), 175–176. doi:10.1136/bmj.332.7534.175.
5 Drug Enforcement Administration. *Cannabis, coca, & poppy: Nature's addictive plants*. Retrieved from www.deamuseum.org/ccp/cannabis/history.html
6 Small, E. (2017). Classification of cannabis sativa L. in relation to agricultural, biotechnological, medical and recreational utilization. In S. Chandra, H. Lata, & M. A. ElSohly (Eds.), *Cannabis sativa L.—botany and biotechnology* [abstract]. Springer, Cham. https://doi.org/10.1007/978-3-319-54564-6_1

7 Ibid.
8 Deitch, R. (2003). *Hemp—American history revisited* (p. 16). New York, NY: Algora Publishing.
9 Robinson, R. (1996). *The great book of hemp: The complete guide to the environmental, commercial and medicinal uses of the world's most extraordinary plant.* Rochester, VT: Park Street Press.
10 Abel, E. L. (1980). *Marihuana: The first twelve thousand years.* Retrieved from http://druglibrary.org/schaffer/hemp/history/first12000/abel.htm
11 Zuardi, A. W. (2006). History of cannabis as a medicine: A review (p. 155). *Revista Brasileira de Psiquiatria, 28*(2), 153–157. http://dx.doi.org/10.1590/S1516-44462006000200015
12 Atakan, Z. (2012). Cannabis, a complex plant: Different compounds and different effects on individuals. *Therapeutic Advances in Psychopharmacology, 2*(6), 241–254. http://doi.org/10.1177/2045125312457586.
13 Project CBD. (2017). *Terpenes and the "entourage effect."* Retrieved from www.projectcbd.org/science/terpenes/terpenes-and-entourage-effect
14 Salema, A. (2002). Proceedings of the Indo-European seminar on Ayurveda held at Arrábida: *Ayurveda at the crossroads of care and cure.* Lisbon, PT: Lisbo & Pune. Retrieved from www.academia.edu/15154551/Ayurveda_at_the_Crossroads_of_Care_and_Cure
15 Booth (2003).
16 ElSohly, M. A., Mehmedic, Z., Foster, S., Gon, C., Chandra, S., & Church, J. C. (2016). Changes in cannabis potency over the last two decades (1995–2014)—analysis of current data in the United States. *Biological Psychiatry, 79*(7), 613–619. http://doi.org/10.1016/j.biopsych.2016.01.004.
17 Abel (1980).
18 Booth (2003).
19 Cohen, J. (2012). Marco Polo went to China after all. *History.* Retrieved from www.history.com/news/marco-polo-went-to-china-after-all-study-suggests
20 Deitch 16.
21 Ibid., 16.
22 Reynolds, J. R. (1890). On the therapeutical uses and toxic effects of cannabis indica. *The Lancet, 135*(3473), 637–638. doi:http://dx.doi.org/10.1016/S0140-6736(02)18723-X
23 Moon, J. B. (1967). Sir William Brooke O'Shaughnessy—the foundations of fluid therapy and the Indian telegraph service. *The New England Journal of Medicine, 276,* 283–284. doi:10.1056/NEJM196702022760509
24 O'Shaughnessy, W. B. (1843). On the preparations of the Indian hemp, or gunjah: Cannabis indica. Their effects on the animal system in health, and their utility in the treatment of tetanus and other convulsive diseases. *Provincial Medical Journal and Retrospect of the Medical Sciences, 5*(123), 363–369. Retrieved from www.ncbi.nlm.nih.gov/pmc/articles/PMC2490264/
25 Schaffer Library of Drug Policy. (n.d.). *Statement of H.J. Anslinger, Commissioner of Narcotics, Bureau of Narcotics of the Treasury Department.* Retrieved from www.druglibrary.org/schaffer/hemp/taxact/t3.htm
26 Lee, M. A. (2012). *Smoke signals, a social history of marijuana-medical, recreational and scientific.* New York, NY: Scribner.
27 Thompson, M. (2013, July 22). The mysterious history of marijuana: Code switch. *National Public Radio.* Retrieved from www.npr.org/sections/codeswitch/2013/07/14/ . . . /the-mysterious-history-of-marijuana
28 Booth (2003).
29 Life in 1937. *Teacher retirement system of Texas.* Retrieved from www.trs.texas.gov/TRS%20Documents/1937_life_in.pdf#search=life%20in%201937

30 Tilem & Associates. (2009, January 10). A brief history of federal mandatory minimum sentencing for federal drug offenses. *New York Criminal Attorney Blog*. Retrieved from www.newyorkcriminalattorneyblog.com/2009/01/a_brief_history_of_federal_man.html

31 Dach, J. (2017). *Bioidentical hormones 101*. Retrieved from www.bioidentical hormones101.com/Cannabis_Miracle_Drug.html

32 Conversation with Raphael Mechoulam. (2007). *Addiction, 102*(6), 887–893. doi:10.1111/j.1360–0443.2007.01795.x

33 Rabelais (1904).

34 Abel (1980).

35 Gaoni, Y., & Mechoulam, R. (1964). Isolation, structure, and partial synthesis of an active constituent of hashish. *Journal of the American Chemical Society, 86*(8), 1646–1647. doi:10.1021/ja01062a046

36 Pertwee, R. G. (2006). Cannabinoid pharmacology: the first 66 years. *British Journal of Pharmacology, 147*(Suppl. 1), S163–S171. http://doi.org/10.1038/sj.bjp.0706406

37 Devane, W. A., Dysarz, F. A., Johnson, M. R., Melvin, L. S., & Howlett, A. C. (1988). Determination and characterization of a cannabinoid receptor in rat brain. *Molecular Pharmacology, 34*(5), 605–613.

38 di Tomaso, E., Beltramo, M., & Piomelli, D. (1996). Brain cannabinoids in chocolate. *Nature, 382*, 677–678. doi:10.1038/382677a0

39 Mechoulam, R., Ben-Shabat, S., Hanus, L., Ligumsky, M., Kaminski, N. E., & Schatz, A. R. et al. (1995). Identification of an endogenous 2-monoglyceride, present in canine gut, that binds to cannabinoid receptors. *Biochemistry Pharmacology, 50*, 83–90. Retrieved from www.csdp.org/research/nixonpot.txt

40 Gardner, F. (2006, December 30). Comes now the ghost of "decrim." *Counter Punch*. Retrieved from www.counterpunch.org/2006/12/30/comes-now-the-ghost-of-quot-decrim-quot/

41 Peters, G., & Wooley, J. (2017, March 21). Richard Nixon: Statement about the drug abuse office and treatment act of 1972. *The American Presidency Project*. Retrieved from www.presidency.ucsb.edu/ws/?pid=3782

42 Transcription of White House tape conversation between Richard Nixon and H.R. Haldeman, May 26, 1971. (n.d.). *Common sense for drug policy*. Retrieved from www.csdp.org/research/nixonpot.txt

43 21 U.S.C. § 812. (2012). Schedules of controlled substances. Retrieved from www.gpo.gov/fdsys/granule/USCODE-2011-title21/USCODE-2011-title21-chap13-subchapI-partB-sec812

44 Booth (2003).

45 Nahas, G. G., & Greenwood, A. (1974). The first report of the National Commission on Marihuana (1972): Signal of misunderstanding or exercise in ambiguity. *Bulletin of the New York Academy of Medicine, 50*(1), 55–75. Retrieved from www.ncbi.nlm.nih.gov/pmc/articles/PMC1749335/?page=20

46 Baum, D. (2016, August 7). Legalize it all, how to win the War on Drugs. *Harper's Magazine*. Retrieved from https://harpers.org/archive/2016/04/legalize-it-all

47 Substance Abuse and Mental Health Services Administration. (1996). *Checklist for monitoring alcohol and other drug confidentiality compliance. Appendix B managed care and client confidentiality technical assistance series. No. 18, (a)*. Retrieved from http://adaiclearinghouse.org/downloads/TAP-18-Checklist-for-Monitoring-Alcohol-and-Other-Drug-Confidentiality-Compliance-108.pdf

48 Peters & Woolley (2017).

49 Zielinski, G. (2001, June 8). Activist Robert C. Randall dies. *The Washington Post*. Retrieved from www.washingtonpost.com/archive/local/2001/06/08/activist-robert-c-randall-dies/c6e832a4-55e2-47fc-a3c8-5e011da66e04/?utm_term=.eee3c228c26c

50 Lee (2012).

51 Hepler, R. S., & Frank, I. R. (1971). Marihuana smoking and intraocular pressure [Abstract]. *Journal of the American Medical Association*, 217(10), 1392. Retrieved from www.ncbi.nlm.nih.gov/pubmed/5109652

52 Hepler, R., Frank, I., & Ungerleider, J. T. (1972). Pupillary constriction after marijuana use. *American Journal of Ophthalmology*, 74(6), 1185–1190. doi:http://dx.doi.org/10.1016/0002-9394(72)90741-6

53 Hepler, R. S., & Petrus, R. J. (1976). Experiences with administration of marihuana to glaucoma patients. In S. Cohen & R. C. Stillman (Eds.), *The therapeutic potential of marihuana* (pp. 63–75). Boston, MA: Springer. https://doi.org/10.1007/978-1-4613-4286-1_5

54 Grinspoon, L., & Bakalar, J. B. (1993). *Marihuana: The forbidden medicine*. New Haven, CT: Yale University Press.

55 Trebach, A. (1987). *The great drug war*. London, UK: Macmillan Publishing.

56 Lee (2012).

57 Randall, R. C., & O'Leary, A. M. (1998). *Marijuana rx: The patients' fight for medicinal pot*. Boston, MA: Da Capo Press.

58 United in Compassion. (2015, December 3). "Robert Randall." *YouTube*. Retrieved from www.youtube.com/watch?v=r0gtvfhTZZI

59 Akchuk. (2014, September 4). Ronald Reagan: "Marijuana . . . is probably the most dangerous drug." *YouTube*. Retrieved from www.youtube.com/watch?v=VxHBx6H-xFo

60 Peters, G., & Woolley, J. T. (2017). Ronald Reagan: Radio address to the nation on federal drug policy October 2, 1982. *The American Presidency Project*. Retrieved from www.presidency.ucsb.edu/ws/?pid=43085

61 Inciardi, J. A. (1990). *Handbook of drug control in the United States*. Westport, CT: Greenwood Publishing Group, Inc.

62 Comprehensive Forfeiture Act of 1984, S.948–98th Congress (1983–1984). Retrieved from www.congress.gov/bill/98th-congress/senate-bill/948

63 Hyde, H. (1995, April 14). *Forfeiting our property rights*. Cato Institute. Retrieved from www.cato.org/articles/forfeting-our-property-rights

64 Rosenberger, L. (1996). *America's drug war debacle*. Brookfield, VT: Ashgate Publishing Company.

65 Boyd, G. (1986, September 14). Reagans advocate "crusade" on drugs. *New York Times*. Retrieved from www.nytimes.com/1986/09/15/us/reagans-advocate-crusade-on-drugs.html

66 U.S. Department of Education. (n.d.). *EDGAR part 86, subpart A, 86.3*. Retrieved from https://ifap.ed.gov/regcomps/attachments/86.pdf

67 Rubin, R. (2005, October 9). Health and behavior. *USA Today*. Retrieved from https://usatoday30.usatoday.com/news/health/2005-10-09-addiction-series-stories_x.htm

68 Snyder, B. (2006). Nora Volkow: Two paths to the future. *Lens: A New Way at Looking at Science*. Retrieved from www.mc.vanderbilt.edu/lens/article/?id=129

69 Ibid.

70 Scientists find link between dopamine and obesity. (2001, February 1). *Brookhaven National Laboratory*. Retrieved from www.bnl.gov/bnlweb/pubaf/pr/2001/bnlpr020101.htm

71 Peele, S. (2015, January 17). *Stop Nora Volkow from taking over the world.* Retrieved from www.substance.com/stop-nora-volkow-late/2720/

72 Toneatto, T., Sobell, L. C., Sobell, M. B., & Eric, R. (1999). Natural recovery from cocaine dependence. *Psychology of Addictive Behaviors, 13*(4), 259–268. Retrieved from nsuworks.nova.edu/cps_facarticles/537/

73 Pickert, K. (2017). Pot Kids: Inside the quasi-legal, science-free world of medical marijuana for children. *Time Inc.* Retrieved from http://time.com/pot-kids/

74 Jones, N. A., Hill, A. J., Smith, I., Bevan, S. A., Williams, C. M., Whalley, B. J., & Stephens, G. J. (2010). Cannabidiol displays antiepileptiform and antiseizure properties in vitro and in vivo. *Journal of Pharmacological and Experimental Therapeutics, 332*(2), 569–577. doi:10.1124/jpet.109.159145

75 Young, S. (2013, August 7). Marijuana stops child's severe seizures. *CNN.* Retrieved from www.cnn.com/2013/08/07/health/charlotte-child-medical-marijuana/index.html

76 Devinsky, O., Marsh, E., Friedman, D., Thiele, E., Laux, L., Sullivan, J., . . . Cilio, M. R. (2016). Cannabidiol in patients with treatment-resistant epilepsy: An open-label interventional trial. *The Lancet Neurology, 15*(3), 270–278. doi:10.1016/S1474-4422(15)00379-8

77 Warner, J. (2014, December 14). *Charlotte's web: Untangling one of Colorado's biggest cannabis success stories.* Westword. Retrieved from www.westword.com/news/charlottes-web-untangling-one-of-colorados-biggest-cannabis-success-stories-6050830

78 Rodgers, J. (2014, December 4). Stanley brothers expanding production of cannabis-based oil to help reduce seizures. *The Gazette.* Retrieved from http://gazette.com/stanley-brothers-expanding-production-of-cannabis-based-oil-to-help-reduce-seizures/article/1542511

79 Industrial Hemp Farming Act of 2015, S.134–114th Congress (2015–2016). Retrieved from www.congress.gov/bill/114th-congress/senate-bill/134

80 Fox, S., Armentano, P., & Tvert, M. (2013). *Marijuana is SAFER, so why are we driving people to drink?* White River Junction, VT: Chelsea Green Publishing.

81 Ibid.

82 Ibid.

83 Martin, A., & Rashidian, N. (2014). *A new leaf: The end of cannabis prohibition.* New York, NY: The New Press.

84 Fox, Armentano, & Tvert (2013).

85 History of Colorado's medical marijuana laws. (2013). *Sensible Colorado.* Retrieved from http://sensiblecolorado.org/history-of-co-medical-marijuana-laws

86 The facts on DC marijuana laws. *Metropolitan Police Department.* Retrieved from https://mpdc.dc.gov/marijuana

87 Nelson, S. (2015, June 22). Major pot research barrier goes up in smoke. *U.S. News and World Report.* Retrieved from www.usnews.com/news/articles/2015/06/22/major-pot-research-barrier-goes-up-in-smoke

88 Sailor, C. (2016, August 11). In South Sound, collective shrug over feds' decision to keep pot on most dangerous list. *Tribune News Services.* Retrieved from www.thenewstribune.com/news/local/marijuana/article95211422.html

89 Barro, J. (2015, April 9). Marijuana taxes won't save state budgets. *NY Times.* Retrieved from www.nytimes.com/2015/04/09/upshot/09up-marijuana.html

90 La Corte, R. (2014, April 11). Legal pot bringing in even more tax revenue than predicted. *Huffington Post.* Retrieved from www.huffingtonpost.com/2014/11/20

Chapter 3

Jack

The coffee shop is busy and noisy, a poor choice to do an interview. The coffee, however, is very good—an attribute that is lost on Jack, who does not drink coffee or tea. He does not ask many questions when presented with the format of the interview. He wants to get started, but not because he is in a rush to get somewhere else. When he starts speaking it comes in near streams of consciousness. He wanted to talk about this.

"My parents are neuroscientists. . . . I was familiar with addictions early, because my mom drank when I was very young. My dad would say she was an alcoholic, but she has not drunk in over ten years. So I grew up with this fear of addiction. I think that the word is so powerful that when you say to someone, like, 'you have an addiction,' just by saying that, you can cause them to develop one." Despite this fear, his first experimentation with marijuana was early. He states: "It's funny; the first time I tried it, I pretended to smoke. I was age 13 and with my neighbors. We were in the woods. I was scared shit, so I pretended and I was, like, 'yeah, I smoke sometimes too,' then faked taking a hit. I actually didn't get high for the first time until months later."

Jack clearly identifies middle school as the main rallying point for the future stoners of his class. School allowed several free periods for students to sneak off grounds and do secret things kids of that age do. He and his friends would go behind a grocery store nearby. "It was weird at first, having to go back to class. There was intense paranoia. I felt different, though. I remember my friend bringing me a sandwich one time after I had smoked. Just two pieces of bread with ham in between. But a sandwich never looked or tasted so good."

"There's this stigma where you hear that marijuana is addictive, yet there is this other thing you keep hearing that marijuana is not, it's just a plant. And on some level that is true, it is a plant." Throughout the next couple of years in junior high, Jack would leave the school and go out with his friends into the snow or whatever weather and smoke, then come back to class. "Then we'd go out and smoke again and that would be the activity."

Jack then confides that when he was in his junior year of high school, he was arrested for possession under age 18. "Because I was under 18, it wasn't too bad, but it affected my future." He adds with residual outrage: "In my view it's like a victimless crime, like prostitution." In his home state, underage marijuana arrests often resulted in youths being referred to an outpatient program where every week they would have to come in once with parents and once alone. Jack was required to participate in such a program and was drug tested every visit. "I was treated like some crack head!" As part of the program, Jack had to attend AA meetings, and he disliked them. "They make you feel like you can't control it. If you slip up in AA, there is this sense of 'fuck it!' I fucked up so I might as well go wild." The program, nevertheless, introduced new concepts that have stuck with him. "They talked about the gateway theory, and I kind of agree with the gateway theory. Some people say it isn't . . . because marijuana is seen as so harmless, then once you've tried that you are more prone to try something else. Like in freshman year of college, I tried a lot of stuff. I never tried heroin, or crack or meth or anything, but I did do stuff like painkillers." He backtracks: "After the program—I had been good during it, I didn't smoke the whole time—when I got done with it I just went back to it. I would be dropped off at school, meet with my friends, then go out and smoke. I began to realize that when not at school, we wouldn't do anything. We would just be in one of our rooms doing nothing, just staring at the computer. After a while I tried to get us to go out and do stuff, like go hiking." Jack was asked if this led to him reconsidering his use. He did slow down for a while, but eventually resumed regular smoking. Asked if his return to marijuana smoking was simply a series of decisions to resume his previous patterns of behavior or if there was an element of anger and defiance from being compelled into treatment by the system, he becomes introspective. "When I was that age, 15, I felt like I knew everything. The way they treated weed was like, it will ruin your life, and I said, 'fuck you, no it won't.'" He began to engage in lively conversations with his father, who was against marijuana and did not even drink. "On the other side were my friends, and what I was learning in classes about the War on Drugs and how weed became illegal." Jack begins to step up to the pulpit at this point. "I'm taking this class now on this subject and they're talking about how if it is regulated, it will end up branded out to the pharmaceutical companies. It's ridiculous. Like when tobacco became regulated the tobacco companies began to add chemicals to make it more addictive. Then it will be found at stores just like alcohol and cigarettes. People will become used to it—I don't want to say addicted, that's too powerful a word. But, it's just like a person who goes to a bar after work and has a drink, versus someone who goes home after work and smokes a joint. One is seen as legal, the other illegal."

It becomes clear that his mother's past drinking problem remains a major factor in how he views his own use of substances. Jack views her compulsion to drink as something quite different from what marijuana use can create. "She can't be near it, it is like it is out of her control. Pot isn't like that. I'll go days without smoking and not think about it. I don't need it." He shifts once again. "My mom was looking into the whole addiction thing. She was looking into AA and abstinence as compared to a group of controlled drinking. To me it's a mental thing. In AA, they're saying, 'I have no control over drinking,' where the other states, 'I have control.' I was talking with a professor, and he said that it's stigmatizing saying it's an addiction and that by saying that it's more likely to become true." Jack does, however, concede that some people may be predisposed to developing the "A" word. "My friend who was in school freshman year, now he is in rehab. He was into everything, including heroin—now he's clean. But he had to drop out of school. That's like what a true addict is, and it was getting worse and worse."

He delves more into his own journey with cannabis. "I started waking and baking. You're not physically addicted, but you get into a cycle. It is about control, over your own life and you are responsible. I didn't want to wake up every morning and smoke. Last summer I ended up working at school and—have you heard of dabs?" Jack describes himself as a "regular smoker" until that summer when introduced to dabs. "A friend on my floor was doing them, so I would go visit him in his room and we'd do a dab. It was so much more potent and my tolerance grew higher." He began to purchase his own. "I started to buy more dabs, less weed. I was waking up and dabbing."

He identifies a turning point in his use: "It was my birthday and my parents came up to visit, so I couldn't do any. After the first day, I felt it. It was the first time I had ever felt a withdrawal from something. I was feeling depressed. Dabs really amplified it. It was the first time I felt like I really didn't have control." He acknowledges feeling depressed for two to three weeks. He began to look at dabs differently from marijuana. "It's like those people who chew coca leaves, then they take it and make cocaine or crack out of it. I began to see dabs as a drug. It crossed the line for me, it wasn't a recreational thing anymore." On occasions when he smelled dabs weeks afterward, he felt sick: "You start to smell the butane, or maybe it's the other stuff in it." Despite this routine, he denies that his experience impacted his academic performance. "I was on the Dean's list all last year while I was smoking it."

Jack's decision to try to change was based on a growing self-awareness. "The whole problem with weed is that I was relying on it. I don't want to be reliant on anything. After using dabs, when I was away from home I would just drive around and smoke a blunt. After a while I began to realize that all I was doing was wasting gas and getting stoned. I had been smoking a lot last fall to compensate for the heavy use of dabs. I then decided that I really needed to stop. So, I didn't smoke for a month. The first day I couldn't even eat, then, I gradually began to feel better. At first, I didn't know what to do. I began to go on walks. You forget how much stuff there is to do. I found out about this club on campus that promotes recovery from drugs. I was just walking around the student union building, thinking about maybe joining a club or activity or something and saw this poster. It said something, like 'Are you tired of relying on drugs and alcohol for a good time?' and I thought, 'that's perfect.' So, I checked it out. It was not like AA where you go in and say something like, my name is Jack, and I'm an addict. We do stuff like talk about how we're doing. We've done meditation." Over time, he started to change some of his routines, especially the recreational ones. He began to go fishing with new friends. He has not, however, embraced a life of abstinence. "I made some rules for myself. I won't smoke if I have to go to class the next day. I still smoke on some weekends and occasionally one night a week, just to show that I can do that."

As the summer is approaching, he is now thinking about how he can maintain these changes in the face of a less structured schedule. "I'm going to try to increase my activities, thereby decreasing my opportunities to smoke." He is also trying to get an internship and may stop smoking entirely in case he is drug tested.

Jack is asked about what he thought his future relationship with marijuana might look like. He is adamant in his reply. "I do *not* want to be a stoner, because I don't want society to look at me that way, and I don't want to look at myself that way." When asked about how he will view cannabis as a future parent, he explains, "When I was younger, my parents always talked to me about weed being bad. I had friends whose parents were cool with it. Some even smoked with them. Now, I go back and those kids are still there. One still lives in his home and gets high with high school kids. Teens don't know what moderation is. When you're doing it more than once a day, what are you doing? When we are younger, we're not thinking about our health. I don't want my kids to go through it. What it comes down to, though, is listening and understanding what they are going through."

For now, Jack insists that he likes where he is at and where he is going. He will continue to smoke weed on occasion, since he believes he has learned valuable truths about how to control it and to not allow it to control him. He finally runs out of things to say and expresses thanks for being afforded the opportunity to talk about this subject. He leaves the shop with a charge in his walk, even triumphant, perhaps.

Chapter 4

The Culture on Campus

Hasheesh is indeed an accursed drug, and the soul at last pays a most bitter price for all its ecstasies; moreover, the use of it is not the proper means of gaining any insight. . . . In the jubilance of hashish, we have only arrived by an improper pathway at the secret of that infinity of beauty which shall be beheld in heaven and earth when the veil of the corporeal drops off, and we know as we are known.
—Fitz Hugh Ludlow, *The Hashish Eater* (1857)[1]

Fitz Hugh Ludlow was, by most accounts, an odd character. Though superficially agreeable, he was not particularly well-liked by his peers.[2] Despite his social deficits, he managed to get inducted into the Kappa Alpha Society, the oldest established fraternity, second to Phi Beta Kappa, in the United States, founded in 1825. He brought with him to college more than his academic potential. The year before his arrival, he had been introduced by an apothecary to a tincture of hashish labeled *cannabis indica*—a medicine new to the pharmacopeia of the United States. Ludlow began experimenting with this elixir and wrote down his experiences, many of which were chronicled in his book, *The Hashish Eater* (1857).

Ludlow's descriptions of the psychoactive effects of hashish include florid hallucinations—depictions amplified further by an extravagant writing style, even by mid-nineteenth century standards. His autobiographical account includes some of the earliest depictions in English literature about the mind-expansion qualities of hashish. He also let some of his fellow students in on his secret, even "turning on" some of them to cannabis, noting the varying effect it had on different individuals. He eventually recognized that he was becoming enslaved to this drug and sought to free himself from it. His description of his withdrawal is horrific, at least from a psychological standpoint, and far beyond the characteristic abstinence syndrome that is reported by most people who are cannabis dependent.

Marijuana use in college, for decades of this country's history, commonly involved already experienced students like Ludlow introducing others to the seductiveness of the drug. They had the reefers, joints, bowls, blunts, bongs, nails, or vapes. They knew how to smoke it, how to hold it in as long as possible, and how to mentor others through the initial high. In many ways, marijuana smoking, especially at first, is a very intimate act. There can be a sense of daring in it and so demands a leap of trust and faith. It can signify severing ties with rules, norms, and expectations of the parents' culture. For some students, it may be the first time they have knowingly broken the law. By comparison, collegiate drinking is a mass convivial rite—mindless in aim with any meaning lost in its raucous and anonymous character. Even now, marijuana smoking remains (outside of 4/20 celebrations) a mostly exclusive social bond. Faculty members have also undoubtedly, if infrequently, played the role of initiator. Consider Donald Sutherland's subversive, even creepy, Professor David Jennings introducing some of the Delta Tau Chi members to grass in the movie *Animal House* (1978):[3]

Pinto (Tim Hulce) being passed the joint:	"I won't go schizo, will I?"
Professor Jennings:	"It's a distinct possibility."

Historically, university served as the jump-off point for cannabis use as well as many other forms of experimentation during this period of a student's life. Not so anymore: many students come to college having used marijuana since high school or even middle school. According to the National Survey on Drug Use and Health, the age of first use by adolescents actually increased from 17 to 18 years old between 2002 and 2013.[4] Presently, around 30% of all college entrants report use of marijuana prior to coming to school.[5] This reality is one of the prime factors in the rise of cannabis use we see in the collegiate environment.

Evolving Attitudes

Not surprisingly, marijuana use among university students began to bloom during the mid-to-late 1960s. Smoking grass became emblematic of the growing counterculture that had largely become rooted on college campuses. For a generation that was distinguishing itself from the society of their parents, the act of lighting up a joint was one of not merely igniting self-definition but defying a culture they perceived as enslaved by the military-industrial complex.

By the 1970s, cannabis use was seen as an acceptable and safer recreational high than other drugs. Also, it was no longer so much a social statement as the times had shifted from political awareness and social change to individualism. The rate of marijuana use remained constant throughout the 1970s to 1980, followed by a gradual decline in overall use through the 1990s and into the new millennium. Since that lull, however, we are again seeing a steady rise in cannabis use among college students as well as other demographic groups. Associated with this increase is the growing student perception of marijuana as a benign drug. In 2013, the Monitoring the Future Survey asked high school students if they see "great harm" in smoking regularly: 60% did not—the lowest this has been since 1979.[6] Moreover, in a 2014 survey, almost 6% of college students said they smoked marijuana over 20 days of the prior month. This was the highest rate ever reported since the survey began close to a quarter of a century ago.[7] Some suggest that this shift began not with recreational legalization but with the emergence of medical marijuana laws, starting with the Compassionate Care Act (1996) in California. To the millennial generation, who may not remember a time without the existence of medical marijuana, the association of cannabis with medicine may have engendered a sense that the plant is not merely safe but therapeutic. However, research has not yet observed that this shift in belief leads directly to increased use,[8] despite data showing that the perception of marijuana being safer is growing among youth. Coincidently, this generation has no collective memory of pharmaceutical drugs not being marketed on television as well. In 1997, the Food and Drug Administration (FDA) cleared the way for pharmaceutical companies to advertise directly to consumers through the media, including one that even small children paid attention to—television. The millennial generation students have been raised on a steady diet of commercials that often convey a warm and safe emotional message through visual images and music, a canny slight-of-hand that distracts viewers from the FDA-required litany of potentially harmful side effects being rattled off with the rapidity of a tobacco auctioneer. This recent leap in the "medicalization" of our culture, a concept first voiced in alarm by Thomas Szasz and Barbara Wootten in the 1950s, may have culminated in the opioid abuse epidemic we are now combatting.[9] Many adolescents began to use with prescription medications in middle and high school, often taken from family medicine cabinets, then sharing them with friends, some of whom were unaware of the addictive potential. However, this was but one of several influences on youth and young adults.

The ubiquitous presence of medicine marketed as safe may interplay with the growing existence of medical marijuana to increase overall attitudes that marijuana is therapeutic. Consequently, medicalization of our culture has laid the groundwork for rapidly evolving attitudes toward marijuana as a safe substance.

Medicinal marijuana was one way the plant entered public consciousness, but not the first. Music was a primary means by which marijuana use was slipped into the awareness of the American public. Early on, jazz musicians such as Louis Armstrong and Cab Calloway alluded to cannabis in tunes such as "Muggles" and "The Reefer Man." Of course, the music of the 1960s brought pot into the forefront, starting with songs such as Dylan's "Everybody Must Get Stoned." That list is almost too long to try to represent here. Pot was a regular topic in the music of the times because it was a major symbol of the times. Sex, drugs, and rock and roll. In the 1970s, a previously little-known music with a political message emerged from the island of Jamaica—reggae—that became increasingly popular due primarily to the personage of Bob Marley. Marley, a devotee of Rastafarianism (a belief system indigenous to the island nation that grew out of the Afro-Jamaican experience), was the minstrel who spread the spirit of Rasta through his words and the distinct rhythms of reggae. He sung of peace and ending poverty but also of regular use of *ganga*—prescribed by the movement not merely as recreation but as sacrament. Marley died in 1981 of cancer, yet despite his relatively brief time in the international limelight and the fact that he never had a hit record, he has left an enduring influence on the college community, resonating chiefly with students who use marijuana. It is commonplace to go into the dorm rooms of students and find posters of Marley, a man who left this earth long before they were born yet who remains an icon to the cannabis culture.

With the coming of the millennial generation, one that has grown up with hip-hop as a fundamental force in the culture, references to marijuana use are commonplace. No longer political in tone or an ingredient in spiritual self-awareness, weed is more about an image, a lifestyle. Going all the way back to "old school," such as Cypress Hill (with "Hit from the Bong") and the Beastie Boys ("Hold It Now Hit It"), the list includes the pantheon of hip-hop royalty: Dr. Dre, Kid Cudi, Ludacris, Lil' Wayne, Tupac, Outkast, Wiz Khalifa, 50 Cent, and, of course, Snoop Dogg. There is less allusion to marijuana in these lyrics; like the art form, it is in-your-face with attitude. To a college student plugged in with ear- or headphones, the praise of weed becomes a constant backbeat. The pervasiveness of marijuana in the millennial experience has made conceptualizing a society with legalized weed a natural evolution.

A Rapidly Expanding World

With the advent of legalized marijuana, this rapidly growing industry saw the creation of a wide range of cannabis products. Strains of marijuana, many very potent, have been given colorful and inventive brand names such as Bubba and Purple Kush, Girl Scout Cookies, Blue Dream, Train Wreck, Northern Lights, and White Rhino. These are either sativa, indica, or hybrid strains, and each is marketed as being endowed with distinct properties and blends of THC and CBD. Although legally securing the rights over a brand of cannabis is difficult—it cannot be registered through the United States Patent and Trademark Office (USPTO), as it remains a Schedule I substance—states with legal recreational and medical laws are trying to create paths to guaranteeing intellectual property. Celebrities are now starting to market their own name brands of pot, such as Snoop Lion (also Snoop Dogg and Snoopzilla, among other aliases) and Willie Nelson. Melissa Etheridge has launched her own cannabis-infused vino.[10]

Other marijuana products, such as edibles, are now the focus of a growing number of food-weed-critic reviewers. All things marijuana are now regular offerings of major publications like the *Denver Post*, which employs its own cannabis critics to review the cannabis culture. Products are described with sensuous language previously reserved for wine connoisseurs. And college students do read these, as they might restaurant reviews on Yelp.

The effect of any marijuana product is mediated by its delivery system. Marijuana was more commonly ingested before tobacco smoking was introduced from the New World. Smoking became the primary mode of use in the United States during the twentieth century, where it was rolled into cigarettes called "muggles," "reefers," and then "joints," prominently in the 1960s. The term "spliff" is typically a mixture of cannabis and tobacco, though it can refer to any marijuana cigarette, especially in Europe. Regular spliff smokers can also experience tobacco withdrawal when they decide to quit. The term "blunt" entered our lexicon in the early 1980s, introduced by African Americans, and was emblematic of growing hip-hop culture.[11] A "blunt" is a small cigar—a "Philly Blunt" for an eponymous example—where the tobacco has been emptied from it and replaced with marijuana. Because the wrapper is tobacco, not paper, nicotine is also inhaled.

Marijuana is also smoked through a pipe, often a simple device with a screen—this is known as "doing a bowl." Pipes can also vary greatly in shapes, sizes, and the materials from which they are made. A bong is a pipe with a wide mouth and a water chamber; the smoke is cooled by whatever liquid is used, allowing for deeper inhaling ("hits") and a quicker, more powerful intoxication. College students who are real aficionados of marijuana consumption may proudly own collections of "glassware"—various pipes, bongs, and other smoking devices. Some of these can be unused *objets d'art* and visually attractive independent of their utility. Smoking marijuana provides a swift and predictable effect, but, as mentioned in the previous chapter, a lot of the cannabinoids are lost to pyrolysis, destroyed by the heat. Further, consumers are breathing hot gasses, carcinogens, and particulate matter into their lungs. *Vaping* is a process by which cannabis, either the flower or hash oil, is heated by a vaporizing apparatus—an electronic pen or plug-in—but to a temperature lower than the point of combustion. This prevents the release of irritants and noxious chemicals caused by smoking. High-THC butane oils, waxes, "shatter," or "dabs" require a surface often referred to as a "nail" being super-heated before the dab is placed on it and the resulting vapor inhaled. Nails are heated with torches, or e-nails can be purchased. The concentration of THC resulting from dabs creates an intense high, preferred by many regular marijuana users with already high tolerances, but likely too powerful for students who are recent initiates. In addition to the extremely unpleasant experience of overdose by some, a potential danger with "dabs" lies in the preparation, a process that involves butane to extract the THC from the plant. Butane, commonly used in lighter fluid, is, obviously, combustible.

Edibles are becoming big business in states with legal recreational use and easily found on campuses, especially in states with legalized recreational cannabis laws. They are also marketed through medical marijuana dispensaries as an alternative to smoking. The creation of the iconic hash brownie is loosely attributed to Alice B. Toklas, otherwise famous for being the lover of writer Gertrude Stein. The hash brownie did not become popular until the 1960s and was associated with the youth counterculture. That changed dramatically in the new millennium with legalization in Colorado and Washington. Companies are now infusing all types of foods with either pure THC extracts or in combination with other cannabinoids, making baked goods, chocolates, coffees, candies, sodas, coffees, butters, and gummies. Restaurants in legal states have begun to pair cannabis strains with meals as one might with a fine wine and the right course. Chefs are using cannabis in their dishes as they might use tarragon or dill. In fact, the packaging of cannabis edibles became so mainstream that children began ingesting them, thinking they were candy or soda, resulting in terrifying trips to the emergency room in some cases.[12]

Cannabis use cuts across all gender, racial, and ethnic groups and socioeconomic classes. Males use more than females in all age groups. Students from Asian backgrounds tend to use all substances less;[13] this can be particularly true with international students from Asian countries, probably because most lack the connections to obtain it. What may also vary is the type of product used and by what means, but there is insufficient data on this. Not surprisingly, there is little data on use by faculty and staff, an area demanding more research as well.

Students who are regular users of marijuana have a wide range of associated habits. Smoking a joint or taking a hit from a bong can be a very social activity or an intentionally solitary activity. Preparation for consuming is itself a significant component of the experience. The right amount of marijuana must be selected and may be processed with a grinder for easier smoking or vaping.

Meanwhile, the brain prepares for the ensuing intoxication; the expectation of the high and its reward is one aspect of intoxication that cannot be overstated.[14] In anticipation, areas of the brain experience upsurges in neurotransmitter activity, excitatory ones—such as *glutamate* and *dopamine*.[15] The brain is getting high even before use: the placebo effect in full flourish. This activity is common to all substances of abuse and may even become the primary motivator and reward for using when tolerance to a drug develops. The experience of marijuana use is not just intrapersonal but collective and galvanizing. Watch college students gather on campuses late Friday afternoons or early evening as they begin to migrate toward the chosen watering hole, bar, or party. There is electricity in the air. Within the intimate confines of their rooms or apartments, students grinding, packing, or rolling their weed engage in a ritualism, like a Mass—for what they do is a form of communal worship, one that humans have been engaging in for millennia long before the rise of Christianity.

The effects of marijuana can be dramatic to recent initiates and distinctly different from one person to another. Inhaled marijuana works within seconds, and intoxication peaks variably from 15 minutes to a half hour, then recedes over the next several. There can be an initial rise in blood pressure and heart rate, a cardiovascular effect adding to the sense of the "rush" experienced in the head and throughout the body. The intensity of the high is dependent on how much is inhaled and by what method (e.g., a bong hit is generally more powerful than one off a joint due to the volume of smoke and THC). Sensation is experienced as more acute: sounds, smells, and taste heighten, or at least the subjective experience of these senses, and listening to music, eating, or having sex may be felt more intensely. Focus seems to increase, but not necessarily on what may have been important prior to getting high. Thoughts may arise that seem like leaps of insight, as though some curtain within the universe were suddenly pulled away revealing a hidden truth. Things previously mundane can suddenly become interesting, distracting. On occasion, the opposite occurs: anything that the student was worried about or preoccupied with can become an obsessive fixation leading to an unpleasant high. Another common disagreeable sensation is one of mild paranoia—not necessarily psychotic, but a discomfort around others who are not high as well. The experience of time is distorted and usually seems to slow down or elongate. As students use more regularly they may become desensitized and skilled at being high in public-like classrooms. Eye drops are kept handy to eliminate bloodshot. Like anything else, being stoned is a learned behavior.

Eating cannabis is distinct from other modes of use. The effects last longer due to the path cannabinoids take to the brain. What happens for some who are not edible-savvy is that they will take a small piece of a THC-infused cookie as prescribed by a friend, but nothing seems to happen even after waiting half an hour. Impatient, they might then eat more or all of it believing they have not ingested enough. What they do not grasp is that THC, when eaten, passes through the liver and is metabolized into 11-hydroxy-delta-9-THC. Due to THC and its metabolites' high lipid-solubility, it is immediately absorbed into the fat surrounding the liver where it is released slowly back into the bloodstream starting around a half hour after ingestion, so the peak effect is not experienced until anywhere from one to four hours.[16] For impatient students who proceed to eat the entire edible, they now have consumed up to 100mg of THC. The recommended serving amount of an edible in Colorado is 10mg,[17] so they have exceeded the recommended amount ten-fold. The result can be a harrowing high characterized by extreme panic, paranoia, and even hallucinations that can last up to 12 hours. Individuals who may have gone through such an experience sometimes suffer lingering symptoms including severe panic and even dissociation.

Ask any college students who are marijuana consumers how they obtain their marijuana in a state where it remains illegal, and their answers will sound like several friends going in on a pizza—except this pie is bought from an exclusive pizzeria that only a handful of other students know about. At least one member of the group has a contact from home or elsewhere—they could be friends from the same hometown or more recent relationships like roommates in the dormitories. The students pool their money together, and the member with the dealer connection either drives to meet this contact or sees that person at home on break or on a weekend. Cellphones and texting have made these deals accomplished much more easily. Often the contact, if living within driving distance, will deliver the "pizza" personally. This contact is not some sketchy character lurking in a dark alley somewhere, but could be just an entrepreneurial friend or a fellow student trying to finance college via illicit means. Not uncommonly, the dealer is a former student who dropped out as his side-business gradually impeded his academic career yet remained on campus near his client base. Dealing may be illegal and risky but is much more profitable per hour than a part-time job flipping burgers or waiting on tables. Small-time suppliers usually sell by dime bags ($10–$20 each), eighths of an ounce (at $30–$60), and up to a quarter ounce (which commands $100, on average). There is no established price list for marijuana by weight or strain, no "Blue-Book values"; the cost is subject to what the market will bear and can be affected by several factors, quality being foremost among them. Low-grade weed, often referred to as "shwag" or "dirt" among other names, obviously comes at a lower price than higher mid-grades such as "high-mids" or "headies" that command more. "Dank" or "skunk," strains with the highest THC content, are priced more accordingly.

Buyers prefer a dependable supplier or risk getting beat—spending too much money on marijuana of poor potency or cheated by weight. While this is true, that need for a trustworthy relationship flows both ways. Customers who feel they were cheated either by amount or by grade are more likely to spread ill will within the market if the situation demands it. And authorities have their ears to this scuttlebutt. Dealers often prefer to sell to known persons for several very important reasons. While small-time suppliers are not at great risk for being beaten or robbed of their money and drugs-on-hand, it does happen. An even greater peril exists when customers are caught in possession of enough marijuana that the police can exert legal leverage, such as being willing to drop the charges in exchange for the name of the dealer. Some marijuana dealers will take on a new customer only if that person is referred by an acquaintance and only in small amounts at first. Often, credit is extended, not only to increase the amount that can be sold, but also to test a customer's reliability and to ensure future business. The further up the criminal echelon student-dealers go, the more money they can make and the more personal liability they assume. Small-time dealers can generally make $100–$300 in a day. With a steady, dependable clientele, a college student-dealer can make up to $40,000 in a year part-time, paying off that year's tuition and other expenses. The problem that can arise is eventually setting limits on such a growing, lucrative enterprise. Customers talk with other potential buyers, and the demand swells if the product is good. The allure of soaring profits becomes increasingly tantalizing. There may be requests for other drugs that are more difficult to obtain and thus have a greater profit margin. Small-time weed dealers may now find themselves procuring substances such as MDMA, LSD, meth, ketamine, cocaine, opioid painkillers, and even heroin for their growing market. Once they have breached that line, it is often difficult to dial back the scope of their business, and they find themselves increasingly consumed by their erstwhile part-time endeavor. Another common potential pitfall is becoming one's own best customer, dipping into the inventory and eating into the profits. Unlike those who deal harder drugs such as heroin or cocaine and know that sampling one's wares too often can lead to disaster, weed dealers generally do not abstain from their product.

Many college students who deal come from upper-middle to upper class socioeconomic backgrounds and would not seem to need the money. They are not working their way through college by means outside the norm but engage in this venture for several other reasons. They may be dealing just to afford their own stash of drugs or to increase discretionary cash. Some become fascinated with the unlimited potential of the marketplace, filled with an entrepreneurial spirit. Others are motivated by the promise of increased social status, thrills, and a sense of self-directed individuation from their backgrounds of privilege.[18]

Campus Housing

Although obtaining marijuana is easy in states that have legalized its recreational use for adults 21 and older, college students still need to consume it off-campus or hidden from residence hall staff and authorities. Students are bound legally only by how much they can have. In Colorado, for example, with the passing of a new law on October 1, 2016, both state residents and out-of-state students 21 and over can possess up to 1 ounce of cannabis plant and up to 1 ounce of THC product such as wax, oil, or edibles. A person with government-issued identification can buy an ounce of marijuana flower or up to 8 grams of THC concentrate (wax, oil, shatter, etc.) or 800 milligrams of THC-infused edibles per transaction. Those states that have been part of a second wave of legalization—Nevada, Massachusetts, Maine, and California—have adopted laws that vary in restrictiveness. For example, Massachusetts passed a law making it legal for adults to possess 10 ounces of marijuana, a substantial amount of plant. California, which launched the revolution in cannabis legality with the Compassionate Care Act in 1996, now has made it legal to possess, obtain, or give an adult 21 or older up to 1 ounce of marijuana. Though the laws vary, one common denominator between the states is the prohibition against use in public places.

Given that on-campus marijuana use remains a clandestine activity in all states, students employ a variety of stratagems to consume their plant. When it comes to smoking, they will often exit their dormitories to find a secluded spot to light up. The problem is that the campus police and other authorities know of these favorite places as well, having busted generations of students there. The distinct aroma of marijuana smoke can make it easy for authorities to track the students down, and some of the high-potency cannabis available these days smells so extraordinarily "skunky" that detection even without lighting up is possible. Some students regularly throw caution to the wind and smoke in their rooms, employing the tried and (usually) true method of stuffing a damp towel under the crack of the door to block any odors from escaping, a method that becomes problematic when visitors show up knocking on the door: once the door is opened, even for a second, the genie is out of the bottle. And when the smell of weed begins wafting down the hallway, there are some non-using students that have no problem immediately complaining to the floor residence assistant (RA)—a fellow student, who is mandated to report it. RAs may feel conflicted in enforcing university drug policies that may end up in fellow students suffering possible damaging consequences.[19] Marijuana violations vary from school to school, but, in addition to criminal charges in instances of large amounts and expulsion, smaller amounts may lead to removal from campus housing. Some RAs forge an agreement with the students on their floor early on in which they agree not to come looking for marijuana violations if it is done discretely. In other words: *don't make me have to come knocking on your door*. When notified, campus police will come to investigate, sniffing their way to the source. They also occasionally use this opportunity to sweep the whole floor or even the entire dorm, often catching more than the reported offenders. If discovered by police, the officers will usually use their own discretion as to how they want to handle it, often depending on the laws of the state. Vaping cannabis has an advantage in this respect—while it does give off an aroma, the fumes are less voluminous and pungent. Edibles are virtually undetectable—barring chance discovery by an authority—but are harder to obtain in non-legal states.

Off campus, the need for secrecy decreases markedly, and many avid cannabis consumers opt for living off-campus as soon as possible for that very reason. Students who live off-campus are often older—upperclassmen or even graduate students—and may have known each other and shared weed together longer. In such a favorable environment, students may then find their frequency of consumption snowballing from intermittent to constant.

Greek Life

Although alcohol remains the intoxicant of choice among fraternities and sororities, marijuana is not far behind. College prevention professionals identify fraternity membership as a high-risk group for substance-use issues, along with athletes.[20] Marijuana use among fraternity members increases with age at a higher rate than in other groups. While substance use increases when students join Greek life, there is evidence that their higher use predates joining these organizations; therefore, the fraternities known for partying seem to attract established weed lovers.[21] However, members can see themselves as reflections of the wider campus society, yet subject to more scrutiny. States a former member of one of the more notorious fraternities at his school, "When someone goes to the hospital because of their drinking, schools don't have to look at the behavior of the individual because they can look at the entity as a whole." He contends that this was also true in his fraternity with marijuana use; rather than an entire chapter being into alcohol or weed or psychedelics, it was comprised of different subgroups. Some would consume cannabis more regularly; others preferred alcohol. And there were smaller coalitions who were more interested in other substances. As he describes it, each group was privy to a campus-wide network of students who were into the same illicit substance and, being part of that intelligentsia, knew where to go to purchase their drug. Even though there might be a fraternity brother with a contact at home, just as frequently a member had connections on campus. What happens within a fraternity house is also mediated by whether or not it is part of university housing. On-campus housing is generally under the administration of that school's residential life department, so the quarters are monitored by school employees. Off-campus fraternity houses are a different situation. While no national fraternity organization condones the use of drugs such as marijuana, the unwritten rules within the house of an individual chapter can be otherwise. It is fluid as well, changing as peer groups graduate and are replaced by new ones. "When I first joined," one member revealed, "the older brothers had connections to get cocaine for those who wanted it. After they left, that connection was lost." Whether done openly in communal areas or more discretely behind a closed door with an enclave of consenting brothers, marijuana consumption is subject to ongoing negotiation and renegotiation within the house. One year you might be able to light up in the dining room; the next year the behavior is frowned-upon.

The relationship between a sorority and marijuana may be, in a large part, a reflection of their relationship with a given fraternity. These connections can be even more deeply etched in Greek life whenever there are Big Brother / Little Sister or Big Sister / Little Brother relationships between the two groups. Although there are exceptions, sororities are generally more image-conscious than their male counterparts. As one sister explained, "It's understood that we are always recruiting." The expectation to present as an admirable representative of that organization is constant. There are pressures within some sororities to look and behave certain ways, and these mandates are not necessarily compatible with each other or easily negotiated: there is a fine line between successfully finessing that narrow distinction and failure. Members are expected to take part in social events, often in concert with a "Big Brother" fraternity. This can include an expectation surrounding dress or drinking alcohol to be requisitely fashionable. Woe to the sister who, in attempting to keep with this dictate, crosses the line in her drunken behavior that results in anything to discredit the sorority, like sleeping with the wrong person or creating a dramatic scene. She might find herself being summoned before the chapter's officers and reprimanded by fellow sisters—the same ones she witnessed at the party so inebriated they were vomiting in the restroom. Depending on the norms of her chapter then, the use of marijuana can be a delicate tightrope walk. It comes as no surprise that little research exists on marijuana use within sororities, and what information we do have lumps them together with fraternities.

Athletics

One area in which there has been a spotlight on marijuana use has been in college sports. Ricky Williams, former Heisman Trophy–winning running back from the University of Texas, had his professional career negatively impacted by his regular—and at times unrepentant—use of cannabis. Other high-profile athletes are occasionally in the headlines, suspended or worse because of their attachment to the drug. Marijuana is among the list of banned substances under National Collegiate Athletic Association (NCAA) and the National Association of Intercollegiate Athletics (NAIA).

Marijuana has become an increasingly popular drug for student athletes, although the rates of reported use are still less than those of the general student population: 22%[22] versus the 33% of the general student population in 2014. This makes sense as athletes are subject to mandatory drug tests, and marijuana is among the easiest drugs to test for. When used in any fashion, a metabolite of THC (THC-COOH) is stored in body fat, resulting in a longer time for marijuana to be eliminated from the body in comparison to other substances. In frequent users, especially those with higher body fat, cannabis can be detected at 50ng/ml up to ten days after their last use and in extreme cases even up to 67 days.[23] The number of positive marijuana tests in post-season events in all three divisions almost tripled from academic years 2008–9 (28 tests) to 2009–10 (71 tests).[24] This can be a reflection of the student-athlete's previous experience with cannabis in high school, where use has also been increasing among all students.[25] Athletes are often recruited from schools or geographic areas where regular cannabis use was commonplace among their peer groups and part of the daily routine. As one athlete put it, "It's what me and my boys did, you know. It was an everyday thing." Another perceived benefit: "Weed helps me slow down at night." Even though there are frequent drug tests for student athletes, rates of marijuana use may be powerfully affected by the peer-group culture that athletes had prior to college.

Why is marijuana a banned substance to NCAA athletes when it has no proven performance-enhancing properties? Perhaps the key word is *proven*. While there are studies showing that cannabis has a negative effect on elements of athletic performance, such as maximal exercise levels,[26, 27] it is not generally considered a performance-enhancing drug (PED). Recently, endurance athletes like long-distance runners and triathletes have publicly extolled the benefits of a regular cannabis regimen. They claim that marijuana helps them relax and alleviate pain from pushing their bodies so hard.[28] There are little or no controlled studies demonstrating that marijuana helps improve training or athletic prowess—except for maybe assisting with relaxation and sleep at the end of the day. So, we come back to the original question: why the ban?

According to Dr. Jeff Anderson—from 2009 to 2013, the chairman of the NCAA Competitive Safeguards and Medical Aspects of Sports Committee (CSMAS)—the NCAA just wanted "clean championships." The CSMAS is a body that makes recommendations to the NCAA about matters regarding health and best medical practices, and it is instrumental in assisting with policy on drug testing, such as what substances, frequency, and penalties. These are recommendations only; the NCAA sets the final policy. When the ruling was made back in 1999, it placed marijuana on the banned list of recreational drugs, including it along with other illicit narcotics such as heroin and LSD as it was and still is a Schedule I substance. When athletes have positive results for banned substances in an NCAA test, they can lose eligibility to play for a year, not just be kept out of a championship. Individual schools have their own drug-testing policies and procedures in addition to this and can set their own consequences for violations, independent of NCAA policy. Does the NCAA set up guidelines to advise schools? "I don't believe there is a 'best practices' document that is distributed by the NCAA to the schools," Dr. Anderson states.

In August 2015, the NCAA toughened the testing threshold for a positive cannabinoid screen, from 15ng/ml down to 5ng/ml. Yet, conversely, there has been evidence that the NCAA is also beginning to soften its stance of marijuana infractions. More recently, while the NCAA still tests year-round, it tests for marijuana only in the case of impending championships. If an athlete does come up positive for cannabis, he or she may not participate in that event and must sit out half of the following year. Further, there are those within the organization who are pushing for the NCAA to bow out of policing athletes for recreational drugs entirely. Mary Wilfert, the associate director of the NCAA's Sports Science Institute, was one such voice, advocating for a major change in the long-standing policy: "In December of 2014, the committee determined that a best-practice approach would be for the NCAA to no longer test for marijuana in its championships-testing program—which is when we do test as far as the NCAA testing goes—and that it would make more sense for institutions to focus in on the deterrents and intervention at the local level. In other words, an educational intervention, counseling, whatever approach made more sense on recreational drug use than a punitive approach, which is all the NCAA program does right now."[29] Dr. Anderson, along with other fellow committee members, may have been part of that early movement toward changing how the NCAA views marijuana:

> I was actually a big proponent of this. I felt the penalties for a positive marijuana test, as were other members of the committee, for an entire calendar year suspension was too punitive [for a positive test]. And as a result, our concern was that we were losing student athletes who were facing a full calendar year [suspension] and would potentially leave school. When we saw that was the case, it augmented our argument that we should dial back. There is no institution on the planet that has a full calendar year suspension for a first positive test

for marijuana for a student athlete. So, from an over-arching stand-point with the NCAA, we were inconsistent with what the institutions were doing.

Another situation created by the marijuana ban in athletics was that more and more athletes started using synthetic THC products, at one time legal, as a way to circumvent the testing system and still get high throughout the year. These substances, variably known as K2 or Spice among 500 or so street names, are essentially a potpourri laced with synthetic cannabinoids, mostly created in laboratories in China. Originally marketed as an herbal blend, they were anything but natural, containing chemicals that fall into seven structural categories such as Napthoylindoles, napthylmethylindenes, and phenylacetylindoles. K2 was sold in gas stations, head shops, and 24-hour markets or available online until state governments began to outlaw their legal distribution and President Barack Obama signed the Synthetic Drug Abuse Prevention Act in 2012, making all such chemicals Schedule I substances. Most had typical cannabis-like effects, but others were potentially dangerous. The problem came to the attention of the NCAA, but most of the direct actions were taken by universities themselves—a response that became even more necessary in 2012 when a college basketball player collapsed and died in practice of acute toxicity from JWH-018, one of the most common chemicals found in synthetic marijuana. Louisiana State University, among the first of the schools to test their athletes for these chemicals, suspended three football players who tested positive before a game.[30]

Dr. Anderson explains that the NCAA initially investigated the feasibility of testing for synthetic marijuana (the NCAA even added K2, Spice, JWH-018, and JWH-073 to the list of banned substances in 2011), but adding it to their testing protocol was challenging. "The lab that the NCAA uses, the UCLA lab, felt that, at that time, the tests were not up to the quality that the results could be used in a forensic setting." A testing protocol was finally implemented in August 2013.[31]

College football is a multi-billion-dollar enterprise. For a big-name school such as Alabama or Ohio State, losing its star quarterback for a bowl game due to a marijuana urine-test violation could have enormous financial repercussions. Did the NCAA experience any pushback from some of the power football conferences, such as the SEC or Big 10? Dr. Anderson claims that the opposite was, in fact, true: "We as a committee thought it was more appropriate to have a shorter penalty, and we got institutional (schools) push back because they didn't want the NCAA to appear to be soft on drugs. I never once heard a conference or an institution say that they were uncomfortable with the penalties."

Surprisingly, until thought through, the arrival of legalization in some states ended up having little impact on the NCAA view of testing for cannabis. "It was something we knew was coming. And we had questions, like if marijuana gets legalized, how do you test for it and ban it? The answer was relatively simple. There is a difference between a legal drug and a banned drug. And this is true with performance enhancing drugs all the time. It is legal to take Adderall (a stimulant prescribed for Attention-Deficit Disorder), but Adderall is banned unless you have a therapeutic use exemption in competitive sports, because it is a performance-enhancer. So just because something is legal doesn't mean it can't be banned."

Legal Tangles and Administrative Headaches

It would seem that this is an important time for universities to step up prevention education and intervention around cannabis use on campus. However, this has not been the case overall even though there have been such efforts by many higher-education institutions. Resources spent on marijuana and other drug prevention pale in comparison to the collegiate prevention culture devoted to deterring student alcohol use. Many colleges lack the financial resources to tackle both substances adequately. Alcohol use is still much more prevalent, though binge drinking this century has trended slightly downward from a high point of 45.6% in 2006 to 39% in 2013.[32] Alcohol has also been responsible for student accidental deaths and occasionally lethal violence, destruction of university property, sexual assaults, administrative expulsions, loss of revenue due to attrition, and really bad press. In contrast, marijuana's damage is subtler, more difficult to identify and quantify. The financial fallout from binge drinking and other forms of alcohol misuse on campus is estimated to be enormous. While there are no data demonstrating this number specific to colleges, the annual overall costs of alcohol use by persons under age 21 has been estimated by the National Institute of Alcohol Abuse and Alcoholism (NIAAA) to be more than $62 billion.[33] This number was based on current health and criminal justice data that assign costs associated with violent crime, traffic crashes, treatment, sexual assaults, and alcohol poisonings, among other variables. Within colleges specifically, there are also factors such as loss of revenue due to alcohol-related attrition as well as administrative costs related to the time spent in student affairs offices dealing with the management of this problem. This includes handling housing conflicts, intervention/screening programming, legal costs, counseling (if done internally), and judiciary processes, to name but a few.

With the exception that it is still illegal in most states and in violation of university policies, marijuana does not lead to the mayhem generally associated with drunkenness. Cannabis misuse also creates problems, but ones that are less dramatic and more difficult to connect directly to costs—financial or otherwise. Except for those students who get arrested for possession or intent to distribute, the consequences of marijuana use on campus are less prominent and more difficult to attribute directly to the drug. No students die from marijuana overdose, although we are seeing more incidents of panic attacks and psychotic events associated with heavy THC ingestion. Another phenomenon being seen more frequently in emergency rooms is complaints by heavy consumers of severe nausea and vomiting attributed to *Cannabinoid Hyperemesis Syndrome*.[34] The exact mechanism of this condition remains unknown, but cessation of use does not always result in immediate symptom relief, with only hot showers being reported as helpful.

During certain celebratory occasions on campus, such as after major sports events (especially if the home team triumphs) or the ubiquitous rites of spring that are commonplace at schools, local emergency departments are often inundated with waves of ambulance transports bearing students suffering from alcohol overdoses or associated traumas—not so much with marijuana, even with the massive 4/20 celebrations witnessed in Colorado and Washington State in recent years.[35] But this should not nullify the damage that it does cause for those students who abuse or become dependent on it. Marijuana's primary deleterious effect is on the academic and social functioning of the student population who consume it. Elaborated further in Chapter 7, these effects include disruptions to memory and cognition, though the exact nature of this causality is not yet fully understood. These disruptions harm academic performance and can lead to decreased retention of students—something that should grab college administrators' attention. However, the direct impact cannabis plays in student dropout rates is difficult to quantify. We cannot say with certainty that marijuana is primarily responsible for a given percentage of attrition, even though most people in student affairs recognize that it is a problem needing a response. The data are just not available to a data-driven field. The reality is that universities have not yet demonstrated motivation to perform such assessments or adequately invest in addressing cannabis-use disorders. With more states embracing legalization, that may soon change.

And then there are some schools that play hardball, like Liberty University, Brigham Young University, and, of course, West Point.[36] Liberty University maintains a policy that students can be drug tested through urine, blood, or hair. Harding University, a small Christian college located in Searcy, Arkansas, does that even better, reserving the right to polygraph students anytime; refuse and they face expulsion. A surprising addition to that list is the University of Houston, also the home of the Center for Drug and Social Policy Research. Notably, Houston has had no significant drug-abuse-related incidents in recent years. San Diego State University, though not the strictest by a wide margin, nevertheless wins the prize for the most ambitious anti-drug sting. Named "Operation Sudden Fall," it involved a joint effort between campus police and DEA agents that was executed over six months. Several undercover "students" were planted into the party scene within seven of San Diego State's fraternities. By the end of the investigation, 96 people—75 of them university students—were arrested for selling and possessing marijuana, methamphetamine, cocaine, and ecstasy. One was a criminal justice major with comically bad timing: while being taken into custody, he asked one of the officers if his arrest would damage his chances in a law enforcement career.[37]

In states with legalized recreational use for adult students over age 21, university police find themselves enforcing not statutory violations but university conduct codes that are there to protect the school's federal funding under the Drug Free Schools and Communities Act Amendment. Within the university they have to coordinate with the student conduct and student housing offices, as marijuana use is technically not a violation of the law. Within all states, collaboration with local authorities where the campus police may have no jurisdiction is also essential to keep abreast of students who may be struggling with cannabis abuse problems. As a result, there are often distinct judiciary processes that students must go through concurrently when they have been arrested off-campus for a marijuana-related offense. Even though a drug-related incident occurred off-campus, the behavior can still be in violation of the school's code of conduct, and the university can maintain the right to apply disciplinary measures above any legal consequences. The courts may order drug-education programs in lieu of other punishment, such as incarceration, since most states have decriminalized possession charges involving small amounts. A university's own student conduct procedure may also require an educational intervention. Of course, dismissal remains a possibility in more egregious cases or instances where there has been a history of multiple infractions.

Another legal issue for campus police and student conduct personnel is that of DUI resulting from cannabis intoxication. There has been some controversy surrounding DUI laws and how accurate they are in determining actual driver impairment. If so, how can that determination be established objectively, independent of failing a field sobriety test? In general, DUI laws from state to state include any apparent form of intoxication: if a police officer evaluates a driver and concludes that the person is impaired, an arrest can be made regardless of whether the inebriant is known. Some states have *per se* laws where prosecution can result from any amount of THC detected, including its metabolites. While most states with medical marijuana laws have made provisions for registered patients, others with *per se* laws have not. Critics of such laws argue that they establish a legal prohibition against anyone legally on medical marijuana so that under a state's own law that person would be unable to legally drive.

Individuals under the influence of cannabis can demonstrate a wide range of performance, leading to the following question: are regular consumers more practiced, more experienced behind the wheel than occasional users under the influence? The results of studies are inconclusive. A number have demonstrated that cannabis negatively affects reaction time in drivers.[38, 39, 40] The effects of cannabis seem to vary in individuals, and these effects are dose-related. They are also more obvious in automatic driving functions like reaction time, "but more complex tasks that require conscious control are less affected, which is the opposite pattern from that seen with alcohol."[41] In driving tasks that require conscious control, marijuana users tend to compensate by exerting more focused attention. They may drive more slowly or employ other ways to compensate for their impairment—hence the now-cliché reference to Cheech and Chong being pulled over on the Los Angeles freeway for driving 20 miles per hour. But 40 years ago, Cheech and Chong were not doing dabs of 60% THC oil, though many of these studies have utilized dronabinol, synthetic THC, for more precise dosing. The results to date of crash culpability studies have failed to demonstrate that drivers with cannabinoids in the blood are significantly more likely than drug-free drivers to be responsible for road crashes: "[C]ases in which THC was the only drug present were analyzed, [and] the culpability ratio was found to be not significantly different from the no-drug group."[42] Another confounding variable may be that the demographic group most responsible for car accidents—males under age 25—are also the greater risk-takers and marijuana consumers.[43]

A 2002 Canadian report summed up their findings on the hazards of driving stoned in a way that both sides of the debate could find some validation:

> Cannabis leads to a more cautious style of driving, [but] it has a negative impact on decision time and trajectory. [However,] this in itself does not mean that drivers under the influence of cannabis represent a traffic safety risk. . . . Cannabis alone, particularly in low doses, has little effect on the skills involved in automobile driving.[44]

———

Regardless of legalization, cannabis brings with it consequences for school and public sectors. This can be seen played out in campus conduct policies, emergency departments, and DUI laws. It is certainly a different landscape for collegiate life with marijuana having an impact particularly on campus housing, Greek life, and athletics. Attitudes continue to evolve as marijuana is increasingly accepted in the cultural mainstream and as new cannabis products proliferate.

Notes

1 Ludlow, F. H. (1857). *The Hasheesh eater: Being passages from the life of a Pythagorean*. New York, NY: Harper & Bros. Retrieved from http://public-domainreview.org/collections/the-hasheesh-eater-1857
2 Booth, M. (2003). *Cannabis: A history*. New York, NY: St. Martin's Press.
3 Reitman, I., & Simmons, S. (Producers), & Landis, J. (Director). (1978). *Animal house* [Motion Picture]. United States: Universal Pictures.
4 Substance Abuse and Mental Health Services Administration. (2014). *Results from the 2013 National survey on drug use and health: Summary of national findings*. (NSDUH Series H-48, HHS Publication No. (SMA) 14–4863). Rockville, MD: Author. Retrieved from www.samhsa.gov/data/sites/default/files/NSDUHresultsPDFWHTML2013/Web/NSDUHresults2013.pdf
5 Suerken, C. K., Reboussin, B. A., Sutfin, E. L., Wagoner, K. G., Spangler, J., & Wolfson, M. (2014). Prevalence of marijuana use at college entry and risk factors for initiation during freshman year. *Addictive Behaviors*, 39(1), 302–307. Retrieved from www.ncbi.nlm.nih.gov/pubmed/24455784
6 National Institute of Drug Abuse. (2013). *Monitoring the future survey, overview of findings 2013*. Retrieved from www.drugabuse.gov/related-topics/trends-statistics/monitoring-future/monitoring-future-survey-overview-findings-2013
7 Rettner. R. (2015, September 1). Daily marijuana use among college students reaches 30-year high. *Live Science*. Retrieved from www.livescience.com
8 Lynne-Landsman, S. D., Livingston, M. D., & Wagenaar, A. C. (2013, August). Effects of state medical marijuana laws on adolescent marijuana use [Abstract]. *American Journal of Public Health*, 103(8), 1500–1506. doi:10.2105/AJPH.2012.301117
9 Poitras, G. (2012, November 19). OxyContin, prescription opioid abuse and economic medicalization. *Medicolegal and Bioethics*, 2, 1–13. Retrieved from www.sfu.ca/~poitras/MB_final.pdf
10 Wyatt, K. (2015, December 30). Celebrity endorsements to branded logos, marijuana industry building brands. *The Associated Press*. Retrieved from http://globalnews.ca/news/2427449/celebrity-endorsements-to-branded-logos-marijuana-industry-building-brands
11 Ream, G. L., Johnson, B. D., Sifaneck, S. J., & Dunlap, E. (2006). Distinguishing blunt users from joint users: A comparison of marijuana use subcultures. In S. M. Cole (Ed.), *New research on street drugs* (pp. 245–273). New York, NY: Nova Science Publishers, Inc. Retrieved from www.drugpolicy.org/docUploads/nymmj_bluntsjoints.pdf
12 Ingold, J. (2016, July 25). Kids' emergency room visits for marijuana increased in Colorado after legalization, study finds: Edibles account for nearly half of accidental exposures. *Denver Post*. Retrieved from www.thecannabist.co/2016/07/25/marijuana-safety-kids-er-visits/59291/
13 Substance Abuse and Mental Health Services Administration (2014).
14 Metrik, J., Rohsenow, D. J., Monti, P. M., McGeary, J., Cook, T. A. R., de Wit, H., . . . Kahler, C. W. (2009). Effectiveness of a marijuana expectancy manipulation: Piloting the balanced-placebo design for marijuana. *Experimental and Clinical Psychopharmacology*, 17(4), 217–225. http://doi.org/10.1037/a0016502.
15 Adinoff, B. (2004). Neurobiologic processes in drug reward and addiction. *Harvard Review of Psychiatry*, 12(6), 305–320. http://doi.org/10.1080/10673220490910844.

16 Hart, C. L., & Ksir, C. (2011). *Drugs, society, and human behavior* (15th ed.). New York, NY: McGraw-Hill.

17 Barrus, D. G., Capogrossi, K. L., Cates, S. C., Gourdet, C. K., Peiper, N. C., Novak, S. P., . . . Wiley, J. L. (2016). *Tasty THC: Promises and challenges of cannabis edibles.* Research Triangle Park, NC: RTI Press. http://dx.doi.org/10.3768/rtipress.2016.op.0035.1611

18 Mohamed, A. R., & Fritsvold, E. D. (2010). *Dorm room dealer: Drugs and the privileges of race and class.* Boulder, CO: Lynne Rienner Publishers, Inc.

19 Guess, A. (2007, October 10). Between a rock and a hard place. *Inside Higher Ed.* Retrieved from www.insidehighered.com/news/2007/10/10/marijuana

20 Capone, C., Wood, M. D., Borsari, B., & Laird, R. D. (2007). Fraternity and sorority involvement, social influences, and alcohol use among college students: A prospective examination. *Psychology of Addictive Behaviors, 21*(3), 316–327. doi:10.1037/0893-164X.21.3.316

21 McCabe, S. E., Schulenberg, J. E., Johnston, L. D., O'Malley, P. M., Bachman, J. G., & Kloska, D. D. (2005). Selection and socialization effects of fraternities and sororities on US college student substance use: A multi-cohort national longitudinal study. *Addiction, 100*(4), 512–524. doi:10.1111/j.1360-0443.2005.01038.x

22 National Collegiate Athletic Association. (2014, August). *NCAA student-athlete substance use study: Executive summary.* Retrieved from www.ncaa.org/about/resources/research/ncaa-student-athlete-substance-use-study-executive-summary-august-2014

23 Cary, P. L. (2006, April). The marijuana detection window: Determining the length of time cannabinoids will remain detectable in urine following smoking. *National Drug Court Institute, 4*(2T), 1–16. Retrieved from www.ndci.org/sites/default/files/ndci/THC_Detection_Window_0.pdf

24 Carey, J. (2011, June 22). NCAA drug testing shows increase in pot use. *USA Today.* Retrieved from www.usatoday.com/sports/college/2011-06-21-ncaa-drug-testing-marijuana_n.htm

25 National Institute of Drug Abuse (2013).

26 Menetrey, A., Augsburger, M., Favrat, B., Pin, M.A., Rothuizen, L. E., Appenzeller, M., . . . Giroud, C. (2005). Assessment of driving capability through the use of clinical and psychomotor tests in relation to blood cannabinoids levels following oral administration of 20 mg dronabinol or of a cannabis decoction made with 20 or 60 mg delta9 THC [Abstract]. *Journal of Analytical Toxicology, 29*(5), 327–338. Retrieved from www.ncbi.nlm.nih.gov/pubmed/16105257

27 Renaud, A. M., & Cormier, Y. (1986). Acute effects of marihuana smoking on maximal exercise performance and driving/piloting skills. *Medicine & Science in Sports & Exercise, 18*(6), 685–689. Retrieved from www.ncbi.nlm.nih.gov/pubmed/3097453

28 Warner, J. (2014, November 13). Get high, train harder. *Men's Journal.* Retrieved from www.mensjournal.com/health-fitness/exercise/get-high-train-harder-20141113

29 Murshel, M. (2015, October 19). NCAA pushes to end marijuana testing, suspensions in favor of treatment. *The Orlando Sentinel.* Retrieved from www.orlandosentinel.com/sports/nfl/os-ncaa-pushes-end-marijuana-testing-20151018-story.html

30 Scarbinsky, K. (2012, July 29). The spread of Spice: Colleges, NCAA deal with the problem of synthetic marijuana. *AL.com.* Retrieved from www.al.com/sports/index.ssf/2012/07/the_spread_of_spice_colleges_n.html

31 Payne, M. (2016, January 15). Synthetic marijuana has a short but ugly history in sports. *The Washington Post.* Retrieved from www.washington-post.com/news/early-lead/wp/2016/01/15/synthetic-marijuana-has-a-short-but-ugly-history-in-sports/?utm_term=.f22d4cc6b0c4

32 Substance Abuse and Mental Health Services Administration (2014).

33 Harwood, H. (2000). Updating estimates of the economic costs of alcohol abuse in the United States: Estimates, update methods, and data. National Institute on Alcohol Abuse and Alcoholism. Rockville, MD: National Institutes of Health. Retrieved from https://pubs.niaaa.nih.gov/publications/economic-2000/alcoholcost.PD

34 Galli, J. A., Sawaya, R. A., & Friedenberg, F. K. (2011). Cannabinoid hyperemesis syndrome. *Current Drug Abuse Reviews, 4*(4), 241–249. Retrieved from www.ncbi.nlm.nih.gov/pmc/articles/PMC3576702

35 Coffman, K. & Cohen, B. (2014, April 20). *Reuters.* Retrieved from The *Huffington Post.* www.huffingtonpost.com/2014/04/20/washington-420_n_5182906.html

36 Knock, A. (2012, April 20). CM's top 10 anti-marijuana friendly schools. *College Magazine.* Retrieved from www.collegemagazine.com/cms-top-10-anti-marijuana-friendly-schools

37 Perry, T. (2008, May 7). How the police busted a drug crime scene. *Los Angeles Times.* Retrieved from http://articles.latimes.com/2008/may/07/local/me-drugbust7

38 Hartman, R. L., Brown, T. L., Milavetz, G., Spurgin, A., Pierce, R. S., Gorelick, D. A., . . . Huestis, M. A. (2015). Cannabis effects on driving lateral control with and without alcohol. *Drug and Alcohol Dependence, 154,* 25–37. doi:10.1016/j.drugalcdep.2015.06.015

39 Hartman, R. L., & Huestis, M. A. (2012). Cannabis effects on driving skills. *Clinical Chemistry, 59*(3), 478–492. doi:10.1373/clinchem.2012.194381

40 Lenné, M. G., Dietze, P. M., Triggs, T. J., Walmsley, S., Murphy, B., & Redman, J. R. (2010). The effects of cannabis and alcohol on simulated arterial driving: Influences of driving experience and task demand. *Accident Analysis Prevention, 42*(3), 859–866. doi:10.1016/j.aap.2009.04.021

41 Sewell, R., Poling, J., & Sofuoglu, M. (2009). The effect of cannabis compared with alcohol driving. *American Journal of Addiction, 18*(3), 185–193. doi:10.1080/10550490902786934

42 Chesher, G., & Longo, M. (2002). Cannabis and alcohol in motor vehicle accidents. In F. Grotenhermen & E. Russo (Eds.), *Cannabis and Cannabinoids: Pharmacology, toxicology, and therapeutic potential* (pp. 313–323). New York, NY: Haworth Press.

43 Ibid.

44 Canadian Senate Special Committee on Illegal Drugs. (2002). *Cannabis: Our position for a Canadian public policy, 1*(1–2). Retrieved from https://sencanada.ca/content/sen/committee/371/ille/rep/repfinalvol1part4-e.htm#Chapter%208

Chapter 5

Nora

The conference room where the Students for Sensible Drug Policy (SSDP) generally meet is set up tonight for a speaker from LEAP—Law Enforcement Against Prohibition. LEAP (since renamed Law Enforcement Action Partnership), according to its website, is a "nonprofit organization made up of current and former members of the law enforcement and criminal justice communities who are speaking out about the failures of our existing drug policies."[1] The presenter, a retired policeman, shows a PowerPoint program, advancing slide after slide, making the occasional droll comment and obviously playing to his audience; he clearly knows he is preaching to the choir here. Each frame, full of statistics from various sources, is another count in his indictment against the War on Drugs. He shares personal insights from his experiences as a law enforcement officer (and, at one time, an undercover cop) about the futility of our system of criminalizing substance use. He takes a step beyond, blaming the drug problem in the United States and elsewhere on our disastrous policies, declaring that the present state of addiction is a socio-economic condition that arose from the prohibition itself. With each slide that appears with the clicking of his remote, he smiles knowingly, as though he is letting them in on a secret most of them already suspected but that only now is being confirmed. He starts by giving them the earliest-known estimate nationally of citizens with addiction—around 10%. He shows how the federal expenditures for interdiction swelled over time and into the 1970s and 1980s. He interrupts with another slide showing the rate of addiction during this period as unchanged. He caps off his presentation showing the percentages of persons incarcerated for drug-related crimes—disproportionately minorities—and the unfathomable cost to taxpayers for this. And one final slide: the present rate of addiction still holding steady at 10%. His presentation is uniformly well received, and there are no challenging questions, his facts and statistics seemingly admitted a priori.

Nora is co-chairperson of this chapter of the SSDP, which was started in 1985 by college students in response to the reauthorization that year of the Higher Education Act, which contained the provision that eliminated students arrested for drug possession—marijuana included—from federal aid for college loans. She proudly adds that SSDP is the result of a grassroots initiative, the only student-run international organization of its kind. She explains that their focus is on changing the present drug laws, not to advocate for drug use, and though she allows that many of her group members are also consumers, they also dislike being known on campus as the "drug club." She states that their focus is on harm reduction, a policy that advocates for practical policies that decrease the potential damage by psychoactive substance use to individuals and society, not to punish use. Beneath this lies a belief that people have and always will seek intoxication in some form and that our historical attempts to intercede have not only proven ineffective but actually caused harm.

When asked why SSDP and how marijuana, if in any way, was part of her process, she offers something surprising. "I grew up seeing marijuana only in medicinal terms. I was actually confused at first to find out that people were smoking it for fun. I didn't know it did anything. I was brought up in California where my father qualified for medical marijuana. He was able to use cannabis and grow small amounts for his personal use. He would only have a tiny amount at any time, when he was going through chemotherapy, and it was never in my face." So there was never a bong on the coffee table? "No," she laughs, "he would use just a small pipe, so I didn't grow up around huge glassware or anything." When I moved to New England with my mother, initially it was a very, very stark contrast and I didn't understand why it was so heavily demonized."

She describes developing political awareness in seventh or eighth grade: "Someone very close struggled with substance use issues for most of their life. I witnessed their falling into addiction when I was just 5 years old and those issues remained for many years. I became aware of the politics behind substance use and abuse at a young age." Her views of marijuana came into conflict as she came into adolescence. "At that age, I wasn't sure of how I felt about it in terms of recreational use, I still only thought of it medicinally. People started smoking regularly at 11 or 12 years old, for me that was not the case, but I knew people like that."

To illustrate how rigidly against recreational drug use she was when younger, she shares an incident in middle school that stands out for her. "I had a friend whose sister also had an opiate problem, just like my loved one. One time she took out a Percocet and showed it to me and I told her if she used it I wouldn't be her friend. In hindsight, it's not the way I should have approached the issue and wouldn't now, but at age 12, I was already acutely aware of how opiates could destroy lives because they had in my family for years." She laughs, "I definitely didn't approach that situation through a compassionate care lens, though, or even a realistic one. But I cut myself a break because I was only 12."

"In high school, I saw marijuana being used more and more recreationally, and I was curious as to why it was being used that way and by so many. In high school, I probably used—maybe five or six times: I didn't use it much. I tried it purely out of curiosity, and I knew it wouldn't hurt me because I was aware of my father's prescriptions. I would read his prescriptions when I was little, because it would come in all the big packets with stuff about what it does. I knew that, at the very least, I wouldn't die or freak out or that my mother wouldn't find me all messed up or anything like that. But I definitely didn't know what else it would do. When I first tried it, freshman year, I was like, 'okay, that was cool, that's fine.' I didn't try it again until my junior year; the same with alcohol. I didn't really get why people used it recreationally so much. I don't think I used it the correct way, how I inhaled it, but I definitely felt calm. I felt kind of sleepy, so I got why my dad was doing it before bed, but I didn't think it would be too fun recreationally. I never considered that maybe it was medicinal for them as well."

Nora is asked about her experience in college and what events led to her becoming politically active. "In college I still didn't smoke, really; it wasn't until I studied abroad where it was more common. In southern Germany, they smoked mostly hash, which was different, and for me it was purely because of the people I was around. It was very different than anything I had ever done. I was with deep thinking, empathetic, artsy people who did things like paint murals or did sculptures or wrote poetry. It was nothing at all like my home town in New England. So, I just took it all in and was amazed that these people would think I had something to contribute. I would only smoke socially and it was always followed by great expressions of creativity or intense philosophical discussions. I had a very framed relationship with cannabis. From the beginning, I have always had good experiences with it, but a lot of it was based on who I was around, where and certain things like that." When asked if she thought if her Bohemian companions had a similar relationship with cannabis, or if they were much more regular users, she expands on the point: "They were more regular, but at that time when I began to see people using in a way that seemed almost spiritual to them. They had a really big appreciation for the plant, what it did for them, that it was very creative and calming for them. It allowed them to connect more easily, and they treated it with respect, and I hadn't seen that up to then. It gave me more respect and appreciation for substance usage; understanding that you could use a substance, and it would do something for you and you could do something for it at the same time—definitely not common back in college, how it is seen here. All those people [in Germany] were from other places; many of them were refugees from Turkey. It was just very communal."

When asked how it was used, she responded that it was invariably rolled up into cigarettes with tobacco, smoked as "spliffs." Asked if she had a problem with the tobacco part of it, she answers quickly. "Yes! Both my parents smoked tobacco, and I definitely hated the smell of it. I remember being very embarrassed when I was young, going over to my friends' houses, my clothes, all smelling like tobacco. At first I didn't know there was tobacco. I was told there was just hashish, but I noticed a certain sweet taste. I got more—no, I'm not going to lie—I definitely ended up liking tobacco. Luckily, I never developed an addiction to nicotine and I have been able to smoke for a bit at a time, be halfway through and I'm done and not smoke for months." She admits to still smoking on occasion, in particular social situations.

Coming back to school, she felt she had to establish more connections. "I joined when I came to school because I needed something more to do. At first, I was just looking for service work, but I was also interested in sexual assault awareness, which sparked the political fire for me. Then I heard about [a] rally against police brutality and mass incarceration, but not necessarily the drug war end of it. More so out of a compassionate care angle for people like my loved one, who isn't a bad person but didn't always make the best choices. Having seen that growing up in my household and having a terminally ill parent, it made me more understanding of how people could do things that other people wouldn't understand or deem as unacceptable. That maybe some people just didn't have access to resources to help them. So when I went there—I had a car—and I volunteered to shuttle people there and one of those people was the then president of SSDP. He now works for them nationally as an outreach coordinator."

She asked what SSDP does to further change things. "They like to look at the impact of substance usage on different communities, but more so how the present War on Drugs has impacted our society as a whole, how it has failed us. Not just fiscally, but in terms of oppression and prejudice. They are really big on peer education and holistic drug knowledge, not just skewing the drug knowledge into 'yeah, we want to legalize cannabis, so we're only going to talk about it in this way.' You need to talk about how it can be good, and how it can be bad. An honest approach to it."

Nora launches into her fervent belief in the harm-reduction approach, a held value, a value influenced by watching the struggles and losses suffered by her loved one that suffered with addiction to heroin. "What can we do to reduce the harm of these situations? Although we wish people wouldn't do heroin, people are going to do heroin. It doesn't mean that these people deserve to die or be incarcerated and be disenfranchised by being incarcerated. So, SSDP is very multi-faceted. I expected it to be very skewed; I was worried that it was going to focus on 'just legalize pot because we all smoke.' That was not at all what I wanted. It ended up not being like that."

SSDP, Nora states, partners with other in-kind organizations, such as National Organization for the Reform of Marijuana Laws (NORML) and the Drug Policy Alliance. "We do a lot with the Open Society [an international organization funded by billionaire George Soros]. We work a lot with attorneys to affect policy. Members and alumni do things like lobbying and podcasts. Many of our alumni have gone on to law school. We do a lot. They hook you up with elected officials and law firms so you can get more ground on how you're approaching this." The impact the present policies have on racial minorities, in particular, is a sore point for Nora. "We see a lot of money being thrown at the DEA, towards the militarization of the police force, and at housing a bunch of inmates for non-violent drug offenses. When you do that you create this vicious cycle where, when people from low-income areas get out, and their family comes from government-funded housing, well they can't live with them in Section 8 housing with a drug offense. They can't get federal financial aid, so there goes access to higher education. They can't vote or find jobs. Where is their voice?"

She is asked this final question: "When considering ending the War on Drugs—usually when we win a war, the other side surrenders. There is no other side in this case. How do we, after 80 years, actually, and a trillion dollars later, dismantle the apparatus we have built? There is an infrastructure here, many people have jobs and careers, their whole lives are dependent on interdicting substances, and the most prominent one, because it is the most used and easiest to get, is marijuana." She responds by admitting that she does not necessarily believe that all drugs should be legal: "Because you have to have the separation between what is prescribed and what is used recreationally. The problem is that a lot of drugs that are illegal have prescription substances that are very similar. We aren't proposing a free-for-all where everything is accessible and legal to all. The reality is that we have people who abuse substances no matter what the legal status is. It doesn't mean they have to be incarcerated for it or that they should be seen as lesser than. That doesn't mean that people who use substances don't do other things—both good and bad. There is no moral absolution."

"As we move toward cannabis legalization, we need to be very careful about dosages. A problem they have in Colorado is that they have these cookies with 100mg of THC, which is absurd. You're supposed to be breaking it up into pieces, but people are eating the entire cookie and freaking out because they're stoned for 12 hours. Also, cannabis isn't for everyone, and people need to have access to being educated about dosages and possible reactions."

Nora believes in practical change extending beyond marijuana and shifting the way society approaches all substance use. She does not see this desired change as merely about marijuana and talks about an eventual shift in how we, as a society, need to approach all substance use, denying that it is utopian, but instead practical. She is an avid proponent of harm-reduction policies, some of them already implemented in certain European countries. "I'm really for safe injection sites that would have medical personnel available and people can be provided with clean needles. They can monitor users for safety, provide drug education, but also help people with accessibility to rehabilitation programs, to therapists and doctors. They would have rapid HIV and Hep C testing there. Ensure access to testing kits so that they know what they're putting into their body—so that they don't die because someone laced their bag with Fentanyl. The message would be this, that is a judgment-free zone, we're not going to call people junkie trash, and you're not going to be thought of as such. We're going to give people all the tools needed to quit or do whatever is best for them, and we don't believe that people deserve to die because they didn't 'get sober.' We'll keep them safe. This is not a popular belief in the U.S., I know, because other people will think we would be condoning it. But this is a belief that has been successfully applied in other countries. We focus on condoning the usage, yet we ended alcohol prohibition. We still run commercials for alcohol. Doesn't that condone the usage? We are the only country that has commercials for pharmaceuticals, substances that are supposed to be prescribed for us. Do you really believe that those things don't condone substance usage to folks?"

One final salvo: "For people who think that marijuana is useless across the board, I think they are being willfully ignorant because they want to be. For those who are for medical marijuana only, I see where you're coming from, but not everyone has the resources to obtain a medical card, and states are incredibly strict on what qualifies. Why do we prescribe harsher pharmaceuticals for things like PTSD and anxiety that could kill you from withdrawal, instead of allowing people to use a plant that has minimal side effects? I think that a lot of people haven't had access to enough information about drugs in an honest approach or haven't had experiences listening to people's encounters with different substances, including abuse. Without that accessibility to those things, how are they supposed to think any differently?"

Note

1 Law Enforcement Action Partnership. (n.d.). Who we are. Retrieved from https://lawenforcementactionpartnership.org/about-us/who-we-are/

Chapter 6

The Widening Schism

The most difficult subjects can be explained to the most slow-witted man if he has not formed any idea of them already; but the simplest thing cannot be made clear to the most intelligent man if he is firmly persuaded that he knows already, without a shadow of a doubt, what is laid before him.
—Leo Tolstoy, *The Kingdom of God Is Within You* (1894)

Do any internet search on cannabis, and the polarity of information about this drug becomes abundantly clear from hits on the first page or two. On one side, there are articles from government agencies or prevention/treatment organizations describing the dangers of marijuana use, particularly to youth. In stark contrast, there will be articles, blogs, and websites from the anti-prohibition contingent—many attempting to discredit the science behind government-funded studies or others focusing on the desirable characteristics of cannabis while ignoring research entirely. In this age when students can instantly look up almost anything, this is now the central arena.

This conflict is plainly visible when researching a topic such as "cannabis and mental health disorders." An initial search reveals literature from government agencies such as the National Institute on Drug Abuse and from online news agencies publicizing studies demonstrating a correlation between cannabis use and serious psychiatric disorders. Other hits will be articles, blogs, and, yes, research from the pro-legalization bloc, all with arguments in pointed refutation. The research studies, usually initially published in professional journals, are not breezy reads. They are highly technical, having been through a rigorous scientific process involving intensive peer reviews to approve publication. Some do not include experimental designs but are instead assiduous reviews of the literature or meta-analyses of research to assess the effect size of a body of replicated studies. They may evaluate available research in an attempt to resolve contradiction between incongruent findings on a marijuana-related subject.

Articles in journals can be difficult for average readers to slog through. Almost every line or statement is tattooed with references to other research, chopping up the flow of the text. They are deliberate and precise but less readable and not very compelling for most people, despite the trove of information contained within. Researchers are drilled to be cautious with their conclusions and clearly delineate the limits of their results so as not to breach the line into unsupported opinion.

This rigorous standard can change once the media gets a hold of research. Media journalists attend conferences where studies are presented, or sometimes the research funding source makes a press release to trumpet newsworthy findings. Some journalists in need of a topic, or who are assigned to one (e.g., science news), will scour the internet for recent journal articles. Such articles are sometimes transformed by mainstream media into eye-catching headlines. This is particularly the case when the more sensationalistic tabloids decide to report on these findings— perhaps out of a momentary lack of available more shock-worthy news. Unlike researchers, their goal is to grab the reader.

On sporadic yet striking instances, misinterpreted research results can lead to subsequent inexplicable actions by the government and public. For example, in 1996, a federal agency published data from a survey that year showing that 32 out of 4,500 teenagers polled reported heroin use.[1] In the same survey the previous year, only 14 teens out of the same number admitted using this drug. How was this change spun by the agency and interpreted by the media? Heroin use had more than *doubled* from the previous year. Such a staggering reality could not be ignored by conservative Congress members, and Democrat President Clinton was attacked by the right as being soft on drugs—a label no politician can long endure. In response, Clinton increased funding to the sum of $112 million to Latin American governments to heighten their drug-interdiction efforts. To those supporting the War on Drugs, it seemed irrelevant whether this 18-person difference in heroin use truly reflected forthright reporting, sound methodology, or statistical significance. What was relevant were the 18 UH1H helicopters made available to Mexico alone in response to this survey and subsequent media coverage.[2]

More commonplace than the previous example is that many well-meaning prevention organizations, guided more by the passion behind their mission than by science, can misinterpret research results and arrive at conclusions that are overreaching and beyond what the study's authors intended. They may also focus on one finding and make claims about marijuana's potential harm based on that study alone; meanwhile, other studies may have not supported the hypothesis in question. One can see this play out in the literature exploring the relationship between marijuana and schizophrenia, which we will discuss in the next chapter. Unsupported messaging on the part of the prevention field serves to reinforce the beliefs of pro-marijuana college students (many of whom are knowledgeable in the sciences) that much of the alleged harm reported about weed is propaganda. Distorted information nullifies much of the firm research being disseminated. If we are to declare something bad about marijuana, we had better get it right.

Any organization or research group wanting to study the possible therapeutic properties of marijuana must run a gauntlet of administrative obstacles. First, they must obtain a Drug Enforcement Administration (DEA) license to handle a Schedule I substance. Second comes the undertaking of applying for and receiving funding through the National Institutes of Health (NIH) or an approved non-NIH entity registered with the Food and Drug Administration (FDA) as an Investigational New Drug (IND) study.[3] Finally, and perhaps most difficult, researchers must obtain scientific-grade marijuana to be used from the one source available to them, NIDA's cannabis farm at the University of Mississippi.[4] This is a major reason why much of the past research on the effects of cannabis utilized dronabinol—a synthetic THC—because it is easier to obtain, cleaner, and more consistent in dosage as it is one chemical versus a complex plant containing over 60 cannabinoids. Legalization proponents cite this as a research flaw, arguing that the effects of pure THC and those of smoking marijuana differ, though this has not been supported by the limited research.[56]

The problem seems to boil down to this: NIDA was instituted to study and combat *drug abuse*, not to investigate a drug's medicinal possibilities. Lyle Craker, professor and horticulturist at the University of Massachusetts Amherst, stated: "If you are going to run a trial to show this is going to have a positive effect, they are essentially not going to allow it."[7] This last issue is particularly problematic in arbitrating the debate about marijuana. The body of research on marijuana is clearly skewed because of its Schedule I status. The amount of studies showing the potential harmful effects of marijuana is massive. If this were a legal suit where a preponderance of evidence wins the judgment, the anti-legalization bloc would enjoy an overwhelming advantage while its opponent would be given little opportunity to even mount a case. But we are beginning to see a slight shift in this situation. Some articles submitted by researchers to respectable journals that are a departure from the marijuana-is-unhealthy norm are getting published; a few are even audacious enough to question the continued Schedule I status of marijuana as a continued obstacle to determining its medicinal properties.[8]

Accusations of Bias

The pro-marijuana messages students are exposed to offer a formidable challenge to those in the prevention and treatment fields, and they do not have to play by the same rigid rules. The anti-prohibition apparatus is now vast, adequately funded, and informed by research, and it uses various modes to disseminate its message. Pro-marijuana literature, internet resources, and social media are persuasive intellectually and emotionally. This is the place most students go to for information. In addition to offering credible arguments, they may be better at using language familiar to and more in tune with the culture of college-age readers. The pro-marijuana contingent is more social media savvy. Except for actual studies, many articles, tweets, blogs, and podcasts are unfettered by the rules of scientific rigor. However, some of the studies cited can appeal to the more sophisticated readers—educating them about such research principles as the difference between causality and correlation, or highlighting how selection bias can interfere with clear conclusions in government-sponsored studies. They expose issues such as null-set biases in marijuana research: only those studies that show a relationship between cannabis (or any other illicit drug) and a mental or medical problem get published, and those that do not never reach print.[9, 10] And they regularly decry the onerous task of obtaining federal funding for any study *not* designed to demonstrate undesirable medical, social, cognitive, or psychological effects of marijuana.

Many legalization advocates refer to a well-chronicled example of such a bias in cannabis research, found in the story of Melanie Dreher, Ph.D., and her work from the 1980s on marijuana prenatal exposure in Jamaica, finally published in 1994.[11] This study, initially funded by NIDA through the March of Dimes, looked at the long-term effects of regular maternal marijuana use during pregnancy among 24 infants compared to 20 non-exposed infants from the same working-class, Jamaican demographic. In the Jamaican culture, recreational use of *ganja* was commonplace, and it was also consumed for medicinal and spiritual purposes.[12] Dr. Dreher's research was motivated by previous studies in other cultures on neurobehavioral effects in cannabis-exposed neonates.[13] Based on prior research, a prevailing belief was that prenatal consumption of cannabis by the mother put the child at risk for birth defects.[14, 15]

In Dreher's study, infants measured at 3 days old and at 1 month old were compared with a control group of non-exposed children at the same chronological intervals.[16] What she and her fellow researchers found was that at 1 month, not only was there no difference between those in the exposed group versus the control group, but the exposed group actually did better on the Brazelton Neonatal Assessment Scale,[17] a measure of an infant's capabilities. The children had better organization and modulation of sleeping and waking, and they were less prone to stress-related anxiety. Dr. Dreher speculated neonatal environments of the exposed group had more single mothers with extended family available for help and less siblings in the home to compete for the mother's attention. Unlike the mothers in previous studies, Dreher noted less use of alcohol, tobacco, and other illicit substances by these cannabis-using mothers. She continued to follow this cohort for five years and reported that these children continued to show no developmental lags or neurobehavioral problems; they even seemed to excel.

Then, the funding was cut off. Dreher later stated in a YouTube video in 2007: "It was clear that NIDA was not interested in continuing to fund a study that didn't produce negative results. I was told not to resubmit. We missed an opportunity to follow the study through adolescence and through adulthood."[18] Nevertheless, she did follow this group of children for a total of ten years and continued to find that they were thriving. Whether NIDA discontinued the funding for the reasons Dreher claimed probably cannot be verified now, though it is doubtful there would be an official admission by the institute if it were true.

The heavily biased scientific inquiry about marijuana has actually lent power to arguments made by pro-legalization activists who say it is evidence of an intentional policy to oppose research on medical marijuana.[19] Lacking the sheer number of studies to offer as counterpoint, supporters of legalization must instead highlight how the system itself is a stacked deck—clear proof of the machinations of the War on Drugs. Pro-legalization articles can be artfully tinged with allusions to a greater anti-marijuana conspiracy, linking any research from universities and agencies to federal funding to dismiss them as pawns in the ongoing persecution of their maligned and misunderstood plant. This argument plays well with many college-aged adults; Americans seem to love a good conspiracy— the John F. Kennedy assassination, Area 51, and 9/11 theories standing as testimonies.

The Other Voices in Their Ears

Along with the National Organization for the Reform of Marijuana Laws (NORML), the Drug Policy Alliance (DPA) is an organization dedicated to changing drug policy in the United States. Its mission statement details that DPA "envisions a just society in which the use and regulation of drugs are grounded in science, compassion, health and human rights, in which people are no longer punished for what they put into their own bodies but only for crimes committed against others, and in which the fears, prejudices and punitive prohibitions of today are no more."[20] DPA's Honorary Board of Directors includes an interesting mélange of high-profile politicians, CEOs, entertainers, journalists, doctors, and fringe scientists—including former Chairman of the Federal Reserve Paul Volcker, former Secretary of State George Shultz, the late Walter Cronkite, Deepak Chopra, former Surgeon General Jocelyn Elders, and the late chemist and godfather of modern psychedelic drugs Alexander Shulgrin.

It was founded in 2000 by Ethan Nadelmann, who continues to serve as director. Mr. Nadelmann reaches college students on popular media outlets like TED Talks, where he can be viewed denouncing the present U.S. policy of prohibition. He was both popular and credible enough to be mentioned as a candidate for the Drug Czar position (Director of National Drug Control Policy) when Barack Obama was first elected, such was the optimism at the time. Prohibition reformers hoped that the new administration would overhaul and eventually dismantle the government policy on marijuana—a hope that remained unfulfilled.

The amount of all this compelling yet irreconcilable information available to students is mind-boggling. The result may be "investigation fatigue" where readers become so inundated with contrasting facts that out of exhaustion they gravitate toward those findings more aligned to previously held beliefs, accentuating a confirmation bias. Added to this, many college students may not be research-savvy enough to discern which competing studies are more methodologically sound than others.

A Shift in the Media Portrayal

Through history, media has usually portrayed the negative side of marijuana. However, that has changed in the past few years, coinciding with the movement toward legalization. The pendulum has begun to swing in the opposite direction. Increasingly, mainstream media outlets are choosing to feature reports that cast cannabis in a positive light, so much so that these are beginning to outnumber those in opposition. Online, cannabis activists have become a loud and powerful voice—launching advocacy blogs and sharing articles on Reddit and Twitter that support their case and lambast those that do not. NORML maintains an internal database of editorial boards nationwide that it considers anti-marijuana. In the late 1980s, the list encompassed more than 150 newspapers. Now it is down to just 30 or 40. Allen St. Pierre, recent past executive director of NORML, asserts that most of them are owned by a handful of corporate owners opposed to legalization.[21]

While anti-legalization coverage may be waning, the number of pro-legalization websites and blogs has skyrocketed in the past decade. In particular, social media has become the primary way students obtain and circulate information about marijuana among each other. It is in these arenas that the pro-legalization forces have a distinct advantage over their adversaries. This can be attributed, in part, to the younger generation of persons at the helm of the pro-legalization movement who are adept at broadcasting their message through such technological mediums. One probable cause—and result—is the growing trend toward public support for legalization over the last four to five decades. Supporters more than doubled in the 1970s, growing to 28%. Rates then plateaued during the 1980s and 1990s before inching steadily higher since 2000, reaching 50% in 2011. In 2013, 58% of Americans supported legalization, with the highest percentage (67%) between the ages of 18 and 29.[22] The only age group still not in favor were those 65 or older, and even this group had changed their minds by 14% since 2010.[23] More Americans favoring legalization grew up with smartphone technology and know how to use it more effectively.[24]

Those supporting repeal of marijuana prohibition have not entirely abandoned more grassroots activism. Starting your own campus-based chapter of NORML—the mother of marijuana advocacy lobbies—just requires mustering four other like-minded persons to establish a board.[25] NORML gives a caveat that warns readers that before following through with starting a chapter, they should carefully consider that they could henceforth be branded a marijuana user and that prospective employers and important others could Google their names and discover their pro-pot sympathies and activities. Provisional affiliation is granted after sending along a downloaded application with a $15 college membership fee and with copies of their student IDs and completing a Skype interview. The use of Skype is explained as a means of ensuring that prospective board members "look good"—an understandable requisite for a lobby organization. They are seeking marijuana consumers who do not look like more stereotypical marijuana consumers, at least not in the eyes of the congressional representatives they hope to influence. NORML wants affiliate board members who can put a fresh face on adult marijuana consumers in the mainstream media. They require representatives to have a basic understanding of the history and issues related to federal and state marijuana law, to possess leadership qualities for recruiting purposes, and to be able to fundraise. There are now about 30 college-based NORML chapters and an estimated 200 or so Students for Sensible Drug Policy groups across the higher-education landscape. They wield influence.

The sheer amount of pro-marijuana literature available to students is considerable and is focused locally in some instances. One example, *The Rooster*, is a magazine available online out of Boulder, Colorado,[26] that offers a variety of news reports, editorial pieces, humor, articles on travel and dining, and a sampler of decadent pursuits. Its mission statement declares: "Through our witty and thought-provoking content, we empower our readers to transform how they see the world."[27] Like *Playboy* (regardless of how highbrow it strove to be) was still essentially about sex, *The Rooster* remains at its core dedicated to all things cannabinoid. What is distinct about *The Rooster* is that it chronicles the views, norms, and mores of a geographic area that is built around college life—specifically the University of Colorado. So, it is a hometown favorite for the students who indulge in weed regularly. It brings marijuana and an expanded drug-use culture to the college mainstream, and it does so with an in-your-face attitude. On its homepage, a drop-down category labeled "Vices" offers a choice between weed and other means of intoxication. The articles therein tackle issues spanning from enthusiasts of psychedelic use, to organic MDMA alternatives, to political discourse on the pointlessness of increasing prison terms for heroin dealers. *The Rooster* is but a more recent and regional incarnation of pro-marijuana magazines that saw their nascence in the publication of *High Times* in 1974.[28] *High Times* has touted itself as the magazine of the marijuana counterculture, and it has over the years included contributions from renowned and provocative writers such as Hunter S. Thompson and Truman Capote. Students that have embraced cannabis society through the decades have always read literature like this, a sample declaration in their antiestablishment manifesto.

The internet, chock full of pro-marijuana sites, also includes social media networks such as *WeedLife*, *MassRoots*, *Duby*, and *Social High*, among others. They provide platforms, private messaging services, product reviews, relevant news, and the ability to download apps that allow students to connect with other marijuana users in their geographic area, a sort of *Tinder* for regular weed consumers. There is every reason to anticipate this arena growing exponentially as more states become legal for recreational use.

A recent and hopeful development is the emergence of organizations promoting a fair, unbiased view on issues like medical marijuana. They offer information through websites and social media to reach the millennial generation. For example, *ProCon.org* out of Santa Monica, California, states that their mission is "to provide resources for critical thinking and to educate without bias. [They] research issues that are controversial and important, and . . . present them in a balanced, comprehensive, straightforward, transparent, and primarily pro-con format at no charge."[29] Their purpose is to counter the "constant barrage of inaccurate, misleading, and biased news and information prevent[ing] many people from making informed decisions about important social issues." Regarding the central question—"should there be medical marijuana?"—consumers are provided a list of pros and cons along with corresponding opinions and statements of medical experts, relevant agencies, and policy makers on both sides of the debate. Also available is a complete list of medical conditions that marijuana may help treat, accompanied by studies that support therapeutic effectiveness, possibly refute them, or do neither with any certainty.[30]

One ironic development in the emergence of pro-marijuana websites is that some have begun to bridge the gap between those anchored to complete abstinence and those lauding marijuana's wonders by including harm-reduction information. For instance, sites like *Leafly*[31] will not only instruct readers about the use of high-THC products but also warn about how doing dabs can be problematic for consumers with low tolerances.

The tug-of-war being played out in the universe of information is but a click away for college students. The ease with which this material can be accessed may also contribute to a less than diligent exploration of the arguments on a given subject. To a generation inculcated with an expectation of instant results, searching the internet for some factoid is a reflexive, almost unconscious behavior, not a systematic inquiry. So, the first hits that come up on Google hold immense power in swaying the minds of a generation.

Notes

1 King, P. (1996, September 25). Dispatch from the drug war. *Los Angeles Times*. Retrieved from http://articles.latimes.com/1996-09-25/news/mn-47389_1_drug-war

2 Ibid.

3 National Institute on Drug Abuse. (2017, March). NIDA's role in providing marijuana for research. Retrieved from www.drugabuse.gov/drugs-abuse/marijuana/nidas-role-in-providing-marijuana-research

4 Ibid.

5 Musty, R. E., & Rossi, R. (2001). Effects of smoked cannabis and oral 9-tetrahydrocannabinol on nausea and emesis after cancer chemotherapy: A review of state clinical trials. *Journal of Cannabis Therapeutics*, *1*(1), 29–42. Retrieved from www.cannabis-med.org/data/pdf/2001-01-2.pdf

6 Wachtel, S. R., ElSohly, M. A., Ross, S. A., Ambre, J., & De Wit, H. (2002). Comparison of the subjective effects of Delta (9)-tetrahydrocannabinol and marijuana in humans. *Psychopharmacology*, *161*(4), 331–339. doi:10.1007/s00213-002-1033-2

7 Wachtel, S. R., ElSohly, M. A., Ross, S. A., Ambre, J., & De Wit, H. (2002). Comparison of the subjective effects of Delta (9)-tetrahydrocannabinol and marijuana in humans. *Psychopharmacology*, *161*(4), 331–339. doi:10.1007/s00213-002-1033-2

8 Wachtel, S. R., ElSohly, M. A., Ross, S. A., Ambre, J., & De Wit, H. (2002). Comparison of the subjective effects of Delta (9)-tetrahydrocannabinol and marijuana in humans. *Psychopharmacology*, *161*(4), 331–339. doi:10.1007/s00213-002-1033-2

9 Graham, K., & Einarson, T. (1989) Bias against the null hypothesis: The reproductive hazards of cocaine [Abstract]. *The Lancet*, *334*(8677), 1440–1442. http://dx.doi.org/10.1016/S0140-6736(89)92044-8

10 Peplow, M. (2014, August 28). Social sciences suffer from severe publication bias. *Nature*. Retrieved from www.nature.com/news/social-sciences-suffer-from-severe-publication-bias-1.15787

11 Dreher, M. C., Nugent, K., & Hudgins, R. (1994). Prenatal marijuana exposure and neonatal outcomes in Jamaica: An ethnographic study. *Pediatrics*, *93*(2), 254–260. Retrieved from www.bestdoulas.com/marijuana.pdf

12 Comitas, L. (1975). The social nexus of ganja in Jamaica. In V. Rubin (Ed.), *Cannabis and culture* (pp. 119–132). Chicago, IL: Mouton Publishers.

13 Ware, M. A., Adams, H., & Guy, G. W. (2005). The medicinal use of cannabis in the UK: Results of a nationwide survey. *International Journal of Clinical Practice*, 59(3), 291–295. doi:10.1111/j.1742-1241.2004.00271.x

14 Hingson, R., Alpert, J. J., Day, N., Dooling, E., Kayne, H., Morelock, S., . . . Zuckerman, B. (1982). Effects of maternal drinking and marijuana use on fetal growth and development [Abstract]. *Pediatrics*, 70(4), 539–546. Retrieved from www.ncbi.nlm.nih.gov/pubmed/6981792

15 Linn, S., Schoenbaum, R., Monson, R., Stubblefield P., & Ryan, K. (1983). The association of marijuana use with outcome of pregnancy [Abstract]. *American Journal of Public Health*, 73(10), 1161–1164. Retrieved from www.ncbi.nlm.nih.gov/pmc/articles/PMC1651077/

16 Peplow (2014).

17 Brazelton Institute, Boston Children's Hospital. Retrieved from www.childrens hospital.org/research-and-innovation/research/centers/brazelton-institute

18 Ruby Dunes Video (2007, July 19). *Marijuana cannabis use in pregnancy Dr. Dreher*. [Video file]. Retrieved from www.youtube.com/watch?v=K9WorI M0RhA

19 Hudack, J., & Wallack, G. (2015, October). *Ending the U.S. government's war on medical marijuana research*. Washington, DC: The Brookings Institution. Retrieved from www.brookings.edu/wp-content/uploads/2016/06/ Ending- the-US-governments-war-on-medical-marijuana-research.pdf

20 Drug Policy Alliance. (2017). *Mission and vision*. Retrieved from www.drug-policy.org/mission-and-vision

21 Warner, J. (2016, January 19). Marijuana has become a media darling, but are journalists too soft on pot? *International Business Times*. Retrieved from www.ibtimes.com/marijuana-has-become-media-darling-are-journalists-too-soft-pot-2268042

22 Swift, A. (2013, October 22). For first time, Americans favor legalizing marijuana. *Gallup*. Retrieved from www.gallup.com/poll/165539/first-time-americans-favor-legalizing-marijuana.aspx

23 Drug Policy Alliance (2017).

24 Swift (2013).

25 National NORML Offices. (2015, September 5). *Chapter starter packet*. Denver, CO. Retrieved from http://norml.org/pdf_files/NORML_Chapter-StarterPacket.pdf

26 *The Rooster*. Retrieved from www.therooster.com

27 Swift (2013).

28 *High Times Magazine*. Retrieved from www.hightimes.com

29 ProCon.org. (2017). Retrieved from www.procon.org

30 ProCon.org. (2017). *Should marijuana be a medical option?* Retrieved from http://medicalmarijuana.procon.org/

31 *Leafly*. (2017). Retrieved from www.leafly.com

Chapter 7

A Battleground of Facts

"What is truth?"
[Pontius Pilate to Jesus]
—John 18:38

More than at any other time in their lives, young adults in college are regularly barraged with conflicting information. The disparate messages they receive about the risks and hopes of cannabis are just one piece of an expanding universe of theories, laws, cultures, histories, social norms, and novel behaviors unfolding before them. It also comes at a time when they are individuating from the world of their parents and trying to forge their own, distinct identities. In the midst of this enormous task before them, what are some of the skirmish lines in this extensive debate about marijuana that our students must conclude for themselves?

Is Cannabis Addictive?

In April of 1994, Representative Henry Waxman, a Democrat from California, presided over congressional hearings focusing on the health risks posed by tobacco use.[1] The main event in these sessions was the testimonies of the heads of the country's largest tobacco companies: R. J. Reynolds, Phillip Morris, the Liggett Group, and American Tobacco, all of whom had been summoned to answer questions posed to them by members of the House Energy and Commerce Committee's Subcommittee on Health and the Environment. Representatives grilled these men for close to six hours on subjects, including reports that the companies were deliberately manipulating the nicotine content of their products to make smoking more habitual—charges they denied. At a momentous point in the hearing, when the seven executives were directly asked whether they believed that nicotine was addictive, all answered resolutely that they did not. One of the CEOs, James Johnston of R. J. Reynolds, added that he based his belief on the "fact" that nicotine did not meet the criteria for addiction as it did not create intoxication.[2] They were reminded that their opinions differed from most researchers in the field, including the surgeon general who had issued a report on the subject in 1988. The executives remained unmoved, though later did allow that cigarettes might cause lung cancer and heart disease, but that it was not yet conclusive. Mr. Johnston also stated that he would prefer that his daughter did not smoke.

It may seem unbelievable to anyone familiar with the ravages of tobacco addiction that such denial could be declared, let alone in such a public forum, under oath, and before members of Congress. Yet, before dismissing their testimonies as approaching depraved self-interest, we should examine their defense.

In that same year, the *Diagnostic and Statistical Manual, Fourth Edition* (DSM-IV)[3] had been released. The DSM is the primary guideline for physicians, nurses, psychologists, therapists, healthcare organizations, and insurance and pharmaceutical companies to identify and properly diagnose mental health disorders. Neither the term intoxication nor addiction is to be found in the criteria for the diagnosis "Nicotine Dependence" as outlined in the DSM-III-R[4] or DSM-IV.[5] Up to this day, with the publishing of the *Diagnostic and Statistical Manual, Fifth Edition*,[6] the term "addiction" has been problematic as there has been historically poor consensus as to what constitutes addiction among the experts in the field, some of whom contributed to the compilation of the DSM. Many also found the word pejorative, adding to the long-standing social stigma of the condition. However, as of DSM-5, all substance use diagnoses along with pathological gambling are now categorized under the heading of "Substance-Related and Addictive Disorders," officially associating them with that troublesome term. Further, the word "dependence" is no longer used as a diagnosis, a significant departure from the previous edition. In a historical prelude to this change, the decision whether to use the term "dependence" versus "addiction" back during the compilation of DSM-IV was so hotly debated within the committee that it came down to a vote and "dependence" won by just one ballot.[7]

Since that time, there has been enough agreement among experts that the term "dependence" should be reserved to describe only that process in which a person develops tolerance to a substance and experiences characteristic withdrawal symptoms upon ceasing use. This can happen in cases of medication use, for instance, where a patient is following physician orders, and is not characterized by other elements of addiction such as using more than intended, failed attempts to stop, or cravings. Another distinction in DSM-5 is the movement away from the previous splitting of the categories of substance abuse and substance dependence. Now, all disordered substance use is considered to be on a spectrum from mild to severe, based on the number of criteria met. For example, what was once "Cannabis Dependence" would probably now be coded as "Cannabis-Use Disorder, Severe." In short, the words "abuse" and "dependence" have all been removed from the diagnostic jargon, while "addiction" remains only in collective use.

In addition to the concept "addiction," the debate around terms like "dependence" and "abuse" has remained relevant for other commonly used substances, as in the case of nicotine and caffeine. These concepts remain salient as society considers the impact and role of cannabis use, particularly as they relate to addiction potential. Both nicotine and caffeine stood out in the DSM because while one could be diagnosed as dependent on them (as any avid coffee drinker who has tried to stop and experienced that headache can attest), neither substance could be abused in the same way as alcohol or cocaine. They did not create legal problems or markedly affect one's ability to drive. Had those Big Tobacco czars been posed the question, "Does nicotine develop dependence?" would they have answered differently? Were they smugly using a semantic loophole? This historic moment illustrates how the way we conceptualize dependence and abuse has important implications for how we define marijuana's addiction potential.

Some proponents of marijuana legalization have argued matter-of-factly that marijuana is not addictive, as it does not have a significant withdrawal syndrome. Indeed, until DSM-5 was unveiled, there was no diagnostic code for withdrawal from cannabis as there was for every other psychoactive substance, including nicotine and caffeine. The previous edition stated clearly the reasons for this: "Symptoms of possible cannabis withdrawal . . . have been described in association with the use of very high doses, but their clinical significance is uncertain."[8] In the current DSM however, the criteria include the following: irritability, anger, or increased aggression; nervousness or anxiety; sleep difficulty (insomnia); decreased appetite or weight loss; restlessness; depressed mood; stomach pain; tremors; sweating; fever; chills; or headache. It also notes reports of other symptoms that require more study, such as disturbing dreams (cannabis has been shown to inhibit REM—rapid eye movement—while prolonging deep state phases, so the cessation of its use could result in REM rebound),[9] fatigue, yawning, and difficulty concentrating.[10] Gender differences have also been found in the withdrawal syndrome with women experiencing more severe and numerous symptoms.[11]

Even in the absence of a characteristic withdrawal profile, the argument that cannabis only causes a psychological dependence is of limited persuasiveness. Up until 1987, there was no diagnosis for cocaine dependence, in part because that drug lacked a physical withdrawal profile. The epidemic of free-base and crack cocaine in the 1980s swiftly altered our narrow view of what comprised addiction, and a diagnosis of cocaine dependence was included by the time DSM-III-R was available in

1987.[12] It had become inarguable that the "psychological addiction" of crack cocaine or methamphetamine was no less powerful or destructive than that of alcohol or heroin. Just like diagnostic changes with its predecessors (nicotine, caffeine, cocaine), cannabis has entered a new stage of flux in the DSM with changes in how the medical world views this drug.

Perhaps the frequency of marijuana-use disorders can provide insight into the drug's addiction potential. Prevalence rates of marijuana use have increased from 4.1% in 2001 to 9.5% in 2013, with rates of marijuana use disorders doubling from 1.5% to 2.9% over that time period.[13] Hasin and colleagues (2015) found relative stability in marijuana-use disorders among roughly 30% of users, arguing that increased general use among the population will coincide with greater numbers experiencing problematic marijuana use.[14] Hasin commented, "Most Americans see marijuana, a natural substance as harmless, but it is not. Some can use without harm, but it's important . . . to be aware that users are at risk for addiction."[15] These statistics suggest that cannabis does have addiction potential when evaluated based on frequency of general population use and that which meets DSM criteria for a substance use disorder.

Consensus about addictiveness of marijuana even crosses "party lines" in the legalization debate. Many of the proponents for eliminating prohibition do acknowledge that cannabis is addictive. They maintain that while a percentage of all marijuana users do get hooked—about one in 11, or 9%[16, 17, 18]—this rate is significantly lower than the addiction potential of other substances, some of which are legal, like alcohol (15.4%).[19] However, some research has shown higher rates of cannabis dependence, one in six, when use is initiated in adolescence.[20, 21] Cannabis is certainly less addictive than other drugs such as heroin and cocaine (23.1% and 16.7%, respectively).[22] And the favorite of James Johnston of R. J. Reynolds? Tobacco weighed in at almost 32%.[23] Anti-prohibitionists further dispute the 9% estimation, stating that it is too high and that the government arrived at that statistic based on biased methodology. This finding was based on the 1994 National Comorbidity Survey that attempted to sample and apply standardized diagnostic assessments to determine prevalence of dependence on various psychoactive substances.[24] The critics argue that the researchers surveyed people employing the criteria for dependence as defined in DSM-III-R, skewing the responses toward pathology. Further, that percentage was partly influenced by the illegal status of marijuana, leading to higher rates of response to two of the criteria for cannabis dependence.[25] The National Survey on Drug Use and Health (2013) found that while 11.5% of marijuana-using adults who had started use by age 14 reported dependence, only 2.6% did so who started after age 18.[26]

There is another question often raised: is the addiction potential of cannabis related entirely to properties of the drug itself, or are some other factors at work, such as characteristics of individuals who become dependent? The action of a drug is but one of the factors involved in addiction. The primary psychoactive chemical in cannabis, delta-9-tetrahydrocannabinol (THC), has a pharmacology like that of other substances in that it binds to endogenous protein sites on neurons throughout the brain. In the case of marijuana, they are known as endocannabinoid receptors (C_1 and C_2 receptors).[27]

Partial activation of these receptors results in the psychoactive experience of cannabis use. Continued, constant use causes the brain to reduce such available receptor sites, in a process known as *downregulation*.[28] More of the substance is then needed to maintain the same level of effect—a phenomenon known as *tolerance*. In the aftermath of this neuro-adaptation, cessation of use leads to withdrawal symptoms that are typically opposite of the initial effects of the drug. This is the neurochemical origin of cannabis dependence in which continued use is required to maintain homeostasis since the brain has changed to accommodate a regular influx of cannabinoids. Increased use is very unlikely to lead to overdose given that there are no C_1 receptors found in the brain stem, which governs respiration. In contrast, alcohol and opioids can bind to such sites in the brain stem, slowing breathing and heart rate to the point of death in the event of overdose. It is estimated that the lethal dose of THC in its pharmaceutical form dronabinol as well as overdose by smoking would be highly improbable.[29] In fact, it was once estimated that a lethal dose would be the equivalent of smoking 800 joints consecutively and that death by that means would probably be due more to carbon monoxide poisoning than the action of the cannabinoids.[30]

Up until the mid-1990s, another reason for marijuana's questionable potential for addiction was due to an inability of researchers to identify if and how the cannabinoids interacted with the neurotransmitter dopamine. Experts believe that the stimulation of dopamine in the areas of the brain known as the *reward pathways*—the nucleus accumbens and ventral tegmentum—is one of the fundamental actions in the development of addiction. Drugs such as cocaine, heroin, and methamphetamine have been shown to increase dopamine action in these mesolimbic structures. Available research did not confirm this dopaminergic action for cannabis, casting doubt on its role in stimulating the reward pathways.[31] However, there have since been several studies over the past 20 years demonstrating that cannabinoids do, in fact, increase dopamine levels like other drugs and alcohol.[32, 33, 34] There is also evidence that the interaction between the primary cannabinoids, THC and cannabidiol (CBD), has a profound effect on the progression of an addicted brain. The role of CBD is interesting, in that it may block the action of THC on the C_1 receptor and attenuate the overall effects of marijuana in a pleasurable way.[35] Conversely, high THC content can create an experience marked by intense anxiety, especially in non-regular users.[36]

Among those who would keep marijuana illegal, there is also concern that the higher THC levels found in today's marijuana, and especially found in dabs or in edibles, may increase the potential for users to develop tolerance more rapidly over time. There remains an ongoing dispute between both sides of the issue as to whether the increased potency of plant marijuana is a problem. One side claims that the more potent cannabis tends to be self-limiting so that the smoker will not need to use as much to achieve the same effect. However, the other side remains concerned about the possibility of quicker tolerance developing among those who use this higher-THC cannabis. Even in states where recreational use is now legal, there has recently been movement to regulate the potency of the cannabis being sold by businesses. In 2015, a study by the state of Colorado found that the average potency of marijuana sold in Colorado stores had 17.1 percent THC, while concentrated forms had 62.1 percent.[37]

Despite increased concentrations of THC in available marijuana today, most users do not become addicted. Who does become addicted to marijuana, and why? There are several factors experts associate with increased risk of cannabis use disorders:

1   The age an individual starts using marijuana is linked to an increased likelihood of later addiction and even other drug use.[38, 39, 40] Introduction of marijuana use, especially before age 15, can cause lasting structural and functional connectivity changes in the developing brain,[41, 42, 43, 44] and these changes are seen in structures related to emotion, memory, and the reward pathways. Vulnerability in the teen brain may be related to its tremendous rate of growth and the "pruning" of weaker neural pathways to allow for growth of other, more trafficked connections.[45] Thus, regular substance use lays the groundwork for later addictive pathways to become hardwired. One can think of it this way: it is easier to add on to a house when it is being built than after the whole structure is already completed. To illustrate, there has been research suggesting that frequent marijuana use in college occurs among those who initiate use earlier in life.[46] Chronic marijuana use has also been associated with the worst functioning overall with more problems in functioning during escalation of use in adolescence,[47] and that early adolescent marijuana use was associated with lower levels of functioning in adulthood even when followed by discontinuation of use. In contrast, another study[48] did not find greater incidence of physical and mental health problems among men in their mid-thirties who had had early onset chronic

marijuana use compared to those with other patterns of lifetime use or no use.

2   An Australian twin study has suggested that shared genetic makeup plays an important role in the development of cannabis use disorders.[49] Those same researchers have also linked genetic predisposition with early onset of use to other comorbid disorders, like conduct disorder and depression.[50] The issue here is what confluence of genetic risk factors is coming into play. Heredity studies now attribute genetics to being responsible for between 50% and 60% of addiction.[51, 52]

3   Having a mental health disorder also increases one's risk for a cannabis-use disorder, although the direction of this relationship is unclear.[53] Research has found an association between cannabis use and other substance use disorders as well as mental health problems such as affective disorders, anxiety, post-traumatic stress, personality, and attention-deficit hyperactivity disorders.[54–61] Moreover, as cannabis use disorder severity increased (including frequency of use), virtually all associations became stronger.[62] In one survey, individuals diagnosed with mood disorders reported rates of marijuana use almost double that of all the respondents.[63] And it seems frequent use is not necessary in demonstrating marijuana's association with mental illness. To illustrate, an epidemiological study out of Canada examined a large representative sample of the Canadian general adult population and found that infrequent cannabis users who used less than monthly but at least once per year demonstrated increased likelihood of having an anxiety or mood disorder compared to abstainers.[64] They speculated this may reflect a possibility that there are those who may have a low threshold for the development of mood disorders with the use of cannabis or that, among the infrequent user group studied, there may be former heavy users who have restricted use.

In their review, Hyman and Sinha (2009) found that family dysfunction, negative life events, trauma, and maladaptive coping were all related to cannabis consumption.[65] It is possible that negative life events and mental health difficulties create deficits in one's ability to cope effectively with stress, thus increasing the risk for chronic cannabis use. Indeed, using cannabis for stress relief has the strongest link with chronic consumption, and that use of cannabis as a coping strategy was associated with young adults who had greater mental health problems with more distress than those who used cannabis for social reasons.[66] In their study, Beck and colleagues (2009) found that college students who tend to be depressed and have a cannabis use disorder were more likely to use marijuana to cope with emotional pain and to increase intimacy with others.[67]

That these symptoms and traits are common to various mental and substance use disorders highlights the conundrum of whether mental illness predisposes individuals to traits that drive drug-using behavior or whether substance use serves as a way to self-medicate mental health symptoms.[68] Or as Alan Leshner, the former head of NIDA, once suggested, there are two groups of people who use drugs: those who use to feel good and those who use to feel better.[69] And it is the latter group that is most at risk.

Rather than primary mental health difficulties, can changes in the brain resulting from drug use itself be a causal factor for increased or continued cannabis use? Alterations in the brain's stress and rewards systems resulting from chronic cannabis use[70] may break down an individual's ability to cope effectively with stress.[71] Could it be that chronic substance use itself may change brain chemistry, inducing symptoms of anxiety and depression as well?[72] Since alleviating symptoms of anxiety, depression, and stress was the most cited reason for medical usage among college-aged high-frequency cannabis users, is it possible they could have been smoking their way *back* into depression or anxiety?[73]

Recent studies have suggested a greater number of endocannabinoid receptors among persons *not* prone to anxiety disorders,[74] though others in field believe that this has not yet been clearly demonstrated.[75] If true, these genetically blessed individuals may have less attraction to heavy use of cannabis and other drugs because their robust number of cannabinoid receptors could attenuate a desire to use substances to maintain a sense of well-being. The co-occurrence between cannabis use disorder and social anxiety disorder can be as high as 29% as compared with a lifetime dependence rate within the general population.[76] The research above points to the powerful relationship marijuana has with anxiety, in particular.

4   Social and other environmental influences play a role in the development of problematic cannabis use. Parental attitudes and behaviors can have a positive and negative impact on the development of cannabis use disorders with a protective factor when there is perceived parental disapproval.[77] Pinchevsky and colleagues (2012) found that low levels of parental monitoring with rule-setting and communication during the last year of high school predicted exposure to and initiation of marijuana use in college.[78] Older sibling drug use—even more than parents—was shown in one study to play a role in younger teens beginning to use drugs.[79]

Individual and peer drug use (including cigarettes and alcohol) along with delinquency and school problems were found to be associated with cannabis use.[80, 81, 82, 83] This relationship was also found to predict various stages of marijuana involvement, including failure to discontinue experimental and regular use.[84] College students, in particular, may be prone to increased personal marijuana use based on how they perceive the frequency of others' use and whether their peers approve of the drug.[85] Once exposure to marijuana occurred in college, the decision whether to continue use was related to peer group influences more than earlier parental influences.[86] Other research suggests that peer influence on marijuana use is variable and can be influenced by relationship types, such as close friendships or connections motivated by perceived status.[87]

The complex interplay of these different risk factors determines whether someone eventually goes on to develop a cannabis use disorder. Even in the absence of meeting diagnostic criteria for a cannabis use disorder, a person's cannabis use may still be risky, compulsive, or problematic. Therefore, understanding cannabis-using behavior in the context of how it functions in a person's life is more useful in determining cannabis's addiction potential. Regardless of whether cannabis is labeled "addictive," it is more helpful to address the problematic and compulsive components of its use. Successful intervention in higher education will involve being able to identify those college students with problematic use and effectively communicating what factors put them at risk.

Does Cannabis Cause Cognitive and Learning Deficits?

In 2005, researchers at McLean Hospital in Massachusetts began to explore cognitive and brain differences in persons with chronic marijuana use versus non-marijuana users.[88] Compared with those who did not use marijuana, they found marijuana users scored much higher on an impulsivity scale and made more errors on something called the Stroop test, where the name of a color (e.g., "purple," "red," or "yellow") is printed in a color not indicated by the name (e.g., the word "purple" printed in yellow ink instead of purple ink). Via neuroimaging, they also found differences between the groups in organization of white matter (important in nerve signal conduction) in the frontal cortices, areas of the brain essential in coordinating neural communication for inhibition and decision-making. These findings are consistent with prior research that has found that onset of marijuana use, especially prior to age 16, is associated with deficits in inhibiting impulses.[89] Similarly, a link has been made between cannabis use and attention-deficit/hyperactivity disorder (ADHD), a neurodevelopmental disorder involving impulsive behavior, and those individuals whose ADHD symptoms persisted into adulthood had greater risks for cannabis dependence than those whose symptoms went into remission.[90] Along with differences in impulsivity and decision-making, research has also demonstrated an association between marijuana and decreased verbal learning.[91] Roebke and colleagues (2014) found that this decreased verbal memory was associated with an increase in the daily amount of marijuana smoked.[92] In other research, deficits in verbal memory were also found amongst young adults who reported early onset of marijuana use.[93] Despite this evidence, there is a limitation to such studies—they fail to measure baseline cognitive functioning before the onset of marijuana use. Consequently, one wonders to what degree these deficits were present prior to drug use.

The short-term effects of cannabis on memory and other cognitive functions is well-known, so much so that it has become a source of humor. Think of "The Dude" in *The Big Lebowski*. Studies clearly show that heavy marijuana users demonstrate short-term cognitive deficits in learning and memory.[94, 95] However, the acute effects on attention and concentration seem to be mediated by whether or not the subject was a heavy user or occasional one: the regular users actually performed better than the infrequent users under acute intoxication, suggesting that the heavy users were demonstrating aspects of neuroadaptation.[96] The duration of these effects is less clear as research findings differ. One study showed that impairments tend to dissipate in adults after a month following cessation of use,[97, 98, 99] while other research has demonstrated cognitive impairments persisting at six weeks and up to two years.[100] Yet another found that attention deficits persisted despite improvements in other cognitive functions up to four weeks after cessation in heavy chronic users.[101] The only clarity in this area is that the duration of effects is unknown.

To cloud the picture further, some research maintains that heavy long-term marijuana use does not permanently impair memory or other cognitive functions.[102] One factor contributing to these conflicting results is that other studies suggest that cannabidiol (CBD) may be protective against the deleterious effects of THC, implicating present-day cannabis's unfortunate combination of lower CBD and higher THC content in creating adverse cognitive effects.[103]

While many marijuana users claim that their use has no impact on their thinking and memory, this is one area where there is less controversy. Only a small minority of avid proponents tout that marijuana is a study-aid drug, and those that do may have such high tolerance that getting high is now needed to function at their usual level. There appears to be consensus that heavy cannabis use makes it difficult to think clearly, remember, and learn; stop smoking and your brain will eventually clear.

Maybe.

There may be indication otherwise arising from a NIDA-funded study out of New Zealand.[104] After assessing a group of 1,073 people born in 1972 and 1973 over a 25-year period, IQ was evaluated prior to age 13 and then again at age 38. In the interim, cannabis use was examined at 18, 21, 26, 32, and 38 years of age. They found that those who had used marijuana at least four times per week scored lower on their IQ tests and with greater decline associated with more persistent cannabis dependence. Of note, adolescent onset users diagnosed as dependent who had never reduced use showed the most dramatic decline in IQ, as high as eight points. Further, this cognitive decline was irreparable, even with stopping or reducing their use as adults. The deficits were global: "[A]ll kinds of functions were impaired, across the board. Virtually every kind of brain function was involved: memory, processing speed, executive functions, verbal skills, attention, and so forth," stated one of the researchers, Dr. Terrie Moffitt of Duke University.[105] After some initial criticism that the study failed to adequately control for socio-economic status, a follow-up analysis was done that controlled for variables such as socio-economic class: the findings held up.[106]

Cannabis use does not occur in a vacuum, and it is simplistic to assume that the drug just makes one less intelligent. There are undoubtedly more factors at play—such as socialization, emotional growth, brain development, comorbid mental health problems, avoidance behaviors, and school failure. The following proposed example can illustrate these dynamics:

A child is born with genetic risk factors for addiction, anxiety, and attention-deficit/hyperactivity disorder. He struggles academically and socially in elementary school, having difficulty maintaining attention and controlling his behavior. He has poor organization skills and often forgets his homework. His lowered academic functioning creates stress at school, and at home the environment is not supportive as his parents fail to adequately intervene. Problems may be further exacerbated by domestic conflict or parents acting in abusive or shaming ways due to his impulsive behaviors and poor school performance. This child has difficulty reading interpersonal cues from his classmates, and his impulsiveness is annoying to them; he is not well liked. In early adolescence, he gravitates toward other marginalized, older kids who may introduce him to cigarettes, alcohol, and marijuana. He tends to find this behavior exciting given he is predisposed to risk-taking and sensation-seeking behaviors. Marijuana helps him feel less socially anxious and reduces his stress related to school and home. He feels calmer and feels empowered by the thoughts he has while high, considering them special insights. For the first time, he feels accepted and is now part of a group, finding kinship and loyalty in the context of their mutual drug use and an anti-authority belief system. However, over time he needs to smoke more and more to feel "okay." Now his ability to focus in school and retain information is markedly impaired. He skips class because of the anxiety it creates for him and because the draw to hang out with his truant friends becomes increasing irresistible. His learning lags way behind those of his classmates, and, at a time when the adolescent brain is going through dramatic developmental changes, his is impoverished.

The above is a more stereotypical depiction of a "stoner's" development. But what about those early users who make it to college, some of whom deny that weed has any impact on their studies, even declaring that their focus and productivity improve with use? Limited research has looked at the effects of cannabis on the cognitive abilities of heavy-using college students, but, in one study, heavy users were compared with a control of those students who reported less-frequent, light use.[107] The heavy regular smokers (N=65) fared more poorly on standardized tests after at least 19 hours since their last use than the infrequent users (N=64) in attentional and executive functioning.[108] What is unclear was whether the differences in performance were due to more residual cannabinoids, withdrawal, or some other neurotoxic effects. While more and larger randomized studies would be welcome, there is evidence demonstrating that increased marijuana use over college enrollment is negatively associated with both GPA and class attendance.[109]

Does Marijuana Cause Schizophrenia?

It must have been a fascinating scene. Imagine being in a Parisian apartment sometime in the 1840s, witnessing some of the leading writers, poets, and artists of that time—possibly such luminaries as Théophile Gautier, Honoré de Balzac, Charles Baudelaire, and maybe even Alexandre Dumas and Eugène Delacroix—eating pieces of bread lathered with a sweet, nutty, greenish paste known as *majoun*. This Middle Eastern "confection" is made up of ground pistachios, spices, honey, and . . . hashish. The men then sit and wait for it to take effect. They are members of a group that came to be known as *Le Club Des Hashishins*, the Club of the Hashish Eaters.[110] Among them is Dr. Jacques-Joseph Moreau, a psychiatrist, known back then as an alienist. In 1845, he will publish the first scientific book about the effects of cannabis on the psyche, some of which was based on his own experimentations shared with this august group: *Du Hachisch et de l'aliénation mentale (Hashish and Insanity)*. Among Moreau's description of the psychotomimetic effects of hashish were as follows: "acute psychotic reactions, generally lasting but a few hours, but occasionally as long as a week." The reaction seemed dose-related, and its main features included paranoid ideation, "illusions, hallucinations, delusions, depersonalization, confusion, restlessness and excitement. There can be delirium, disorientation and marked clouding of consciousness."[111]

That marijuana can cause psychotic symptoms, an effect documented well over a century and a half ago, may have been forgotten throughout the latter part of the twentieth century. Most marijuana was of a lower

THC level and usually smoked, both limiting the psychoactive effects. Those in the field of substance abuse treatment, until recently, might talk about the mild perceptual effects of pot, referring primarily to the distortions in the sense of time, but would never liken it to the vivid experiences of using a psychedelic drug such as LSD, DMT, or mescaline. What is different is that in a couple of decades we are seeing an increase in the THC content of cannabis products (e.g., from 4% to 12%).[112] This high-THC marijuana of today may offset any antipsychotic properties that its sister cannabinoid, CBD, may have.[113] CBD, believed by some to mitigate the effects of THC, is too low in content in these new super-strains. This is no longer the kind of pot implied being smoked in the basement on *That '70s Show*. Even the primo strains—such as *Acapulco Gold, Maui Wowie*, and *Panama Red*—of that era had THC levels that would pale in comparison to what is readily available now.

Other than smoking cannabis, different routes of administration now seen more commonly these days can cause one to consume higher levels of THC. In edibles, the action of THC is distinct from smoking. High-potency oils and waxes, some containing THC levels of close to 90%, are eaten in either cookies, spreads, or drinks. When inhaled in "dabs," the wax is heated with a torch or electronically by a pen, and the THC is released in a concentrated vapor, similar to the process of freebasing cocaine. Both methods can lead to unanticipated powerful effects for consumers who may be familiar only with the high of the standard joint or pot brownie of the past. There is some belief that the THC in cannabis, if present in sufficient amounts, can hyper-stimulate the neurotransmitter dopamine in the prefrontal cortex of the brain, while diminishing dopaminergic activity in another part of the brain known as the striatum, evoking these psychotic symptoms.[114] These symptoms may include hallucinations—seeing, hearing, feeling, or smelling things that are not there, and/or delusions—fixed false beliefs. Indeed, emergency rooms, especially in those states such as Colorado and Washington where recreational use is legal, are now seeing sharp increases in patients complaining of severe anxiety and acute psychotic symptoms such as unpleasant hallucinations and extreme paranoia.[115]

Unlike psychosis, which is descriptive of symptoms characterizing a break from reality, schizophrenia is a progressive disorder that usually has an acute onset in early adulthood, around college age. In addition to hallucinations and delusions, known as positive symptoms, schizophrenia is often accompanied by negative symptoms: flat affect, interpersonal deficits, poor motivation, slowed movement, and cognitive decline.).[116] The association between marijuana use and schizophrenia first gained momentum in 1969, when over 50,000 male Swedish military conscripts, representing over 97% of the population between the ages of 18 and 20, were surveyed about their marijuana use.[117] These data were linked with psychiatric admissions for schizophrenia over the next 15 years, and the results showed a strong correlation between heavy marijuana use and the risk of developing schizophrenia.[118]

Subsequent studies[119] have also demonstrated this link finding that heavier marijuana use of high potency at earlier ages can negatively impact the trajectory of schizophrenia, such as advancing the age of the first psychotic episode. Those with persistent cannabis-use disorders were shown to have the worst treatment outcomes after first episode psychosis even when controlling for medication compliance.[120] There could be a physiological evidence of such a link. Among male participants with high genetic risk for schizophrenia, decreased cortical thickness was found in those with frequent, early onset of use compared with participants who had rare or no history of use.[121] It appears that heavy, regular use may impair brain maturation in young men at high risk for developing this serious thought disorder.

Even though an association between marijuana and schizophrenia has been found, this does not mean that a causal relationship has been proven. This distinction has been lost in service of sensationalism with press releases and headlines that marijuana causes schizophrenia. As a result, media has inadvertently given ammunition to the pro-legalization forces that promptly responded with their familiar counter-tactic of highlighting how federally funded marijuana research is distorted, its ulterior goal being the continued justification of the prohibition of cannabis. Paul Armentano, senior policy analyst of NORML, exemplifies this in a 2007 press release titled "NORML Responds to New Rash of Pot and Mental Health Claims."[122] In it, he answered a just-released study out of the United Kingdom demonstrating a link between use of "skunk weed" (marijuana with high THC content) and the risk of developing schizophrenia:[123]

> Despite the enormous popularity of cannabis in the 1960s and 1970s in numerous western cultures, rates of psychotic disorders haven't increased since then in any of these societies. Individuals suffering from mental illness such as schizophrenia tend to use all intoxicants—particularly alcohol and tobacco—at greater rates than the general population. Not surprisingly, many of these individuals also use cannabis.[124] Specifically with regards to schizophrenia, there does appear to be sharp decline in rates since the 1960s, probably for multiple reasons including shifts to alternative diagnoses.[125] This shift began even before marijuana use reached a peak in the 1970s. Frisher and colleagues (2009) highlight that rates of schizophrenia in the population remained stable despite increased rates of marijuana use.[126] Such evidence weakens the argument that marijuana increases prevalence of schizophrenia.

Associated with this debate, there has been conjecture that marijuana is an attractive drug for young persons in the prodromal stage of this illness. In the initial phase of the disorder, usually during the late teens or early twenties, subtle symptoms tend to mimic other mental health problems like anxiety and depression. It is possible that this early use could provide relief from prodromal symptoms like anxiety, encouraging tolerance to develop along with the need for increasing amounts of THC. The supporting evidence for this hypothesis now appears to be weak.[127] What may be a better explanation is that a combination of genetic predisposition, cannabis use, and other environmental factors place certain individuals at risk for developing schizophrenia. Proal and colleagues stated: "In summary, we conclude that cannabis does not cause psychosis by itself. In genetically vulnerable individuals, while cannabis may modify the illness onset, severity, and outcome, there is no evidence from this study that it can cause the psychosis."[128] What we can say with some confidence is that youth at risk for schizophrenia have been shown to smoke marijuana disproportionately more than other persons in that age group, and, when they do, full-blown psychotic episodes can come earlier and be more severe.

Does Medical Marijuana Really Work?

Prime Wellness, a medical marijuana dispensary near Hartford, Connecticut, is not much to look at from the outside. Located in a one-floor brick building adjacent a couple of other businesses, it is easily missed as there are but two small signs affixed on an entrance and an exit. There is a small anteroom as you enter with a security desk behind protective glass, the anticipated surveillance cameras overhead. Beyond the inner door of this vestibule, however, the place looks like the love child between a surgical group's office and a head shop. The waiting room is very professional and well-appointed with new contemporary furniture. On one wall is a large-screen television that displays alternating, vivid, and artistically shot photographs of their inventory. There is no actual marijuana to be seen, nothing contained in large glass apothecary jars on the counter as might be expected. The counter itself, behind which a customer service person is seated, does have an array of cannabis smoking, vaporizing, and atomizing devices.

The manager, Brett Sicklic, is an engaging young man who brought his experience working in the field from Colorado to this upstart company, the first such dispensary in Connecticut following the legalization of medical marijuana in the state. There are six such dispensaries in the state, and more are expected to petition for licensure in the future. In Connecticut, medical marijuana is administered through the state Department of Consumer Protection (DCP). Connecticut's law is more conservative than in other states and certainly more so than in Colorado where Brett learned the business; not only are there only six licensed dispensaries, but the marijuana they distribute can come from only four state-approved producers. Prior to cannabis being made legal for recreational use in Colorado, "caregivers," who acted as dispensaries, could cultivate their own marijuana for their clients, up to six total plants, with no more than three being mature at any time. When Amendment 20 was first passed in 2000, it lifted limits on the number of patients a caregiver could have.

Brett is enthusiastic about the potential for medical marijuana in his new home state: "Connecticut has an opportunity to spearhead research. Because the producers are so regulated, our marijuana is tested to a pharmaceutical standard." He opens a binder filled with pages of the types of cannabis each grower offers, including the breakdown of the primary cannabinoid ratios, THC and CBD. He explains, "There are standards to determine the cannabinoids and other *terpenoids*." Terpenoids are the aromatic chemicals found in marijuana as well as almost every other plant. The names of the products are unlike those jazzy, catchy marketing labels given strains where cannabis is legalized for recreational use. These read more like test pharmaceuticals, such as: "Theraplant Strain 14005, a hybrid strain 50/50 and Indica/Sativa.—19.6% THC."

When asked about what state-approved 13 illnesses they typically see most frequently, Brett answers that sickle-cell disease, amyotrophic lateral sclerosis, and multiple sclerosis are among the leaders. Post laminectomy patients also come to mind, as do those who suffer from post-traumatic stress disorder. "We try to do as much data-basing as possible. We hope to partner with Yale University to do some research on outcomes." Brett further explains that what they are really trying to do is to market to physicians, who are the initial step in Connecticut's referral process. Physicians must fill out an online registration through the DCP to recommend someone for medical marijuana, before that patient can go to a dispensary. "The problem is doctors don't want to refer their patients yet because the hard research isn't there yet," alluding to the problems getting funding in the United States to study the potential efficacy of medical marijuana. When asked if the dispensaries have concerns about Big Pharma rolling in and overtaking the industry, he points out studies showing that merely extracting THC or CBD from the plant does not necessarily lead to the expected results. Marijuana is a very complex thing. "There is something we call an entourage effect. It's not just the action of the THC or CBD, but all the chemicals within the plant in concert. We've even found that other chemicals in marijuana, terpenoids, can change the effect. If you take out one of them, even if all the others are the same, the action changes."

Once a patient is recommended for medical marijuana and goes to the dispensary, a consultation with the pharmacist is the next step. It is the pharmacist's role to educate consumers, evaluate the type of medical problem that needs treatment, and recommend what products might be best for each individual. The pharmacist at Prime Wellness defies any preconceptions of one working in a marijuana dispensary; instead of having long salt-and-pepper hair tied in a ponytail and wearing a Grateful Dead tee shirt, Al Domeika could pass for the chairman of the local Republican Town Committee. He is dressed in a conservative sports jacket and tie and is clean-shaven, pleasant, and soft-spoken. Asked how he became involved in a business that was still, on a federal level, unlawful, he explains in a matter-of-fact manner that he was working in a large retail pharmacy when he was approached by its owner Tom Nicholas to work for Connecticut's first medical marijuana dispensary. "I decided to do my own research, and after a while I determined that there was really something to this." He discusses the strains about which he counsels patients, describing how producers are at the point where they are now branding their products, like Coca-Cola or Budweiser. When asked about adverse reactions to marijuana, he states that the only one he typically sees is when a patient doses too high, and this is most frequently seen with edibles. He maintains that drug interactions are minimal with cannabis, and identifies only certain anti-fungal medications and, on rare occasions, fluoxetine (Prozac). The delivery system of medical marijuana is almost as important a discussion with the patients as the components within the drug itself. More patients prefer the experience they have with smoking versus ingesting the extracts. There is presently some buzz of an upcoming oral spray product, similar to the product Savitex, which is marketed in Europe.

It is early morning, and Prime Wellness has just opened for the day. The consumers who trickle into the waiting room vary in their appearances. Some are in business attire, probably picking up their marijuana before going off to their jobs, while others are clearly disheveled and seem to be struggling. It is hushed like in other medical offices, but not in a secretive sort of way. The transactions between customers and the service people behind the display case are relaxed and do not reveal any fear that what is transpiring between them was unimaginable a decade ago and still in violation of federal law.

Marijuana has been promoted to alleviate symptoms associated with a variety of medical ailments including cancer, HIV/AIDS, multiple sclerosis, Alzheimer's disease, PTSD, epilepsy, Crohn's disease, and glaucoma.[129] In June 2015, the *Journal of the American Medical Association* (JAMA) published a meta-analysis of 79 randomized clinical trials studying the medical effectiveness of cannabinoids for the treatment of an array of medical conditions, including nausea and vomiting due to chemotherapy, appetite stimulation in HIV/AIDS, chronic pain, spasticity due to multiple sclerosis or paraplegia, depression, anxiety disorder, sleep disorder, psychosis, glaucoma, and Tourette's syndrome.[130] Their conclusion was that while there was some evidence that cannabis demonstrated positive results, especially for chronic pain and spasticity, overall there was insufficient evidence that marijuana was significantly more effective than placebo.[131] The press releases that ensued were wildly variable in how these findings were interpreted and announced. Some, like the *Los Angeles Times*, highlighted the lack of clearly proven efficacy in medical marijuana, with headlines such as, "Most uses of medical marijuana wouldn't pass FDA review, study finds."[132] Other news agencies found that the journal findings supported medical marijuana use with some types of illnesses or conditions. Others were just as confused as before.

As swiftly as a boxer counterpunches, the ever-vigilant Paul Armentano of NORML went to the internet to publish a response of associated dysphoria because of difficulty controlling dose for proper therapeutic effect.[133] In it, he contended that the trials in the JAMA article did not focus on whole-marijuana effectiveness, but rather those studies used synthesized THC agents such as dronabinol that were administered orally. THC alone, he argued, lacks all the other important cannabinoids—especially CBD—and terpenoids found in the whole plant. He then promoted the importance of the entourage effect. Smoking or inhaling the entire plant may have allowed subjects in the study to obtain relief more quickly, while THC ingested gastro-intestinally could increase bioavailability and delay onset, leading to a greater chance of overdose.

Seizure disorders, amyotrophic lateral sclerosis, addictions, irritable bowel syndrome, multiple sclerosis spasticity, and Crohn's disease are among up to 45 or more presently identified as ailments that could be helped by CBD formulas. Like Armentano, proponents of CBD caution that isolating this cannabinoid is not the answer for healing. Martin A. Lee is the author of *Smoke Signals: A Social History of Marijuana*[134] and the director of Project CBD, a non-profit organization that promotes the research into the therapeutic uses of CBD. He argues that we have at least anecdotal evidence to suggest that cannabidiol works best in some sort of interplay with THC and other marijuana chemicals, a synergetic relationship not yet fully understood because of the lack of targeted research.[135] At present, research strongly suggests that CBD and THC interact in such a way as to potentiate anti-inflammatory properties in the treatment of colitis that surpass those of CBD alone.[136] In addition, research also points to an increased inhibition of certain cancer cells when THC is combined with CBD, including breast carcinoma.[137]

Stereotyping THC as the *bad gets-you-high cannabinoid* is a growing belief that Lee sees as both simplistic and detrimental to the full exploration of marijuana's capacity as medicine. He argues that the very mindset of isolating and using cannabinoids separately plays into the hands of

Big Pharma, which the drug companies need to develop synthetic and semi-synthetic cannabinoid formulas in order to gain FDA approval and secure the patents essential to making money. One cannot so easily patent whole plant extracts or license the term "entourage effect." According to Lee, THC by itself has proven to have medicinal use, as evidenced by its FDA-approval in drugs like dronabinol (Marinol), which have been available for over 20 years for the treatment of conditions like AIDS wasting syndrome or nausea caused by chemotherapy. Lee poses the following question: what if the potential euphoric effect that THC provides enhances the overall therapeutic quality? Perhaps the "high," which can be variable according to the strain, should not be seen as an adverse, unacceptable side-effect? After all, he adds, the word "euphoria" comes from the ancient Greek "having health," a sense of well-being.[138]

One glaring problem in the bulk of randomized studies on the medicinal use of cannabis is the lack of studies in the United States focusing on the potential of CBD versus the better-known THC, often used in a pure, synthetic form. Here again, the status of cannabis being a Schedule I substance prevents funding to either support or disprove the growing renown of this other cannabinoid as a non-psychoactive, safe treatment for a variety of medical and psychological conditions. An internet search reveals that most studies published on CBD and its medicinal potential are done in conjunction with foreign universities. However, there was a recent glimmer that the federal government is considering relaxing its grip on CBD and funding further marijuana research. NIDA is anticipating receiving a $68.7 million grant to expand its marijuana research capacities at the University of Mississippi, the only federally approved marijuana cultivation center.[139] This comes in concert with a mounting bipartisan push to pass the Compassionate Access, Research Expansion, and Respect States (CARERS) Act, that would reschedule marijuana from a Schedule I to a Schedule II substance, as well as remove CBD oil entirely from the Controlled Substances Act.[140] Additionally, it would dissolve any remaining banking restrictions linked to medical marijuana, so that such purchases would no longer be cash-only.

Until—or if—the CARERS Act passes into law, the restrictions on CBD remain convoluted. Even though imported CBD oil is legal in all 50 states, it must be derived from industrial hemp, must contain no more than 0.03% THC, and can be derived only from hemp's seeds or stalk, not the leaves or flowers. This is problematic in that CBD cannot be pressed or extracted from industrial hemp seeds and minimally from the stalk. People living in states that have passed medical marijuana laws have a clear advantage, but it would be a violation of those states' state and federal laws to transport CBD products to another state without such legalization.

Some critics do not deny the potential of medicinal marijuana but dislike how the system has evolved. Dr. Joseph Garbley, medical director of Caron Treatment programs, states in an interview for this book:

> Why are we bypassing the FDA instead of investing in more research to gauge whether marijuana is safe and effective? Why don't we have enough quality studies to look at the long-term side effects? We have this rigorous process for everything else, and it needs to apply to medicinal marijuana. A responsible way to deal with the ever-growing trend of marijuana legalization is to invest money in prevention, education, research, and treatment. The DEA recently decided not to reschedule marijuana, to have it remain as a Schedule I drug, but they did allocate resources for research. The DEA is looking for studies that may change their minds about the drug.

Then, in December of 2016, the DEA, suddenly, without warning, slammed the brakes on this momentum and made an announcement that shook the fledgling CBD extract industry. They stated effective January 13, 2017, all cannabinoids found in the marijuana plant were still Schedule I.[141]

Presently, the federal status of medical cannabis is uncertain, but, if marijuana with THC as treatment does become mainstream, the concern is whether it will be regulated sufficiently or whether the result will once again be an over-prescribed, diverted, illegally distributed medical substance that eventually ends up in the hands of even more minors. This is not unfounded or alarmist: our history is punctuated with examples of pharmaceuticals being over-sold to the medical establishment and to the public. As of the publishing of this book, we are in the midst of a heroin epidemic, which may largely be traced to the proliferate use of OxyContin from 1996 through the first decade of the new millennium.[142] The OxyContin epidemic was just the latest in a number of similar such crises resulting from unscrupulous or misguided drug companies duping the medical community and the citizenry. We need to remember that from 1969 through 1982, Valium was one of the most-prescribed drugs in the in the world—the Lipitor of its time. It was "Mother's little helper," immortalized in the 1966 song of that name by the Rolling Stones. And lest we also forget (although no one could possibly be old enough to remember), heroin itself was marketed as a wonderful anti-tussive by the Bayer company in 1898 to treat patients with pulmonary diseases like pneumonia and tuberculosis. It was hoped to be a less addictive alternative to morphine and more effective than codeine, but soon history proved to be otherwise.[143]

Is Marijuana a "Gateway Drug"?

It must truly be an absurd part of any job description: getting rats stoned. Yet, across the world, there are people for whom this is a regular part of their daily work. Many of our fellow mammals (e.g., rats, vervet monkeys, dogs, chimpanzees, cats, rabbits) are subjected to relentless cruelties in the name of science, but there seems to be something especially perverse about getting rats really baked, studying their behaviors, then euthanizing them and fractionating their brains. That we rely on these noble rodents to increase our knowledge of substance use and addiction should be self-evident: we could not ethically give drugs that we have already labeled as illicit to human subjects due to the potential for dependence, brain damage, or other undesirable results, except under extraordinary conditions and safeguards. And we certainly could not put them down to harvest their brains. Fortunately—for us, not the rats—the reward centers within their limbic systems are much like our own, albeit smaller. Therefore, a great deal of research on the effects of substances ends up involving these little rodents. One of the things we have learned from studies in rats is that introducing THC seems to increase their brains' sensitivity to future administrations of THC. Similarly, those rats sensitized to THC had increased reactions to morphine as well.[144] It seemed as though being given THC "primed" their brains to want more drugs. Pistis and colleagues (2004) found that adolescent rats exposed to cannabinoids demonstrated decreased reactivity of dopamine neurons.[145] Dopamine figures centrally in the brain's reward pathways, thus changing its response to drugs. These animal studies are just a snapshot of the vast literature suggesting marijuana's role as a "gateway drug."

In the 1970s, Columbia University researchers Denise and Eric Kandel began delving into the question of why addiction to illegal drugs is usually preceded by using legal ones. They found that mice that were first exposed to nicotine prior to cocaine use had a more protracted memory of cocaine than if cocaine preceded nicotine use or if either drug was used alone.[146] This gives us an insight into the molecular basis of the "gateway hypothesis." According to Eric Kandel, "We think that nicotine produces the perfect environment for cocaine to activate genes that turn on a long-term memory of the illegal drug. One of the reasons cocaine is so addicting is that most people are smokers when they try it.[147] They further postulated that nicotine somehow altered the brain in such a way that it turned on certain genes that created an environment more susceptible to other drug use, like cocaine.

How might marijuana fit into the gateway hypothesis? Cadoni and colleagues (2001) found that rats with prior exposure to THC more readily responded not only to more THC but to other drugs such as morphine, a behavior known as *cross-sensitization*.[148] NIDA acknowledges that the overwhelming majority of marijuana users do not go on to develop addiction to other substances and that other drugs such as nicotine and alcohol also create cross-sensitization, but that was not their emphasis.[149] In counterpoint, others have argued that many who use marijuana do not go on to use other drugs or develop other drug addictions, and marijuana may even help discontinue more harmful drug use by easing withdrawal symptoms.[150, 151]

The problem with the term "gateway drug" is that it can mean different things to different people. To some, it implies causality: not only does marijuana use start before other drugs, but no other explanation for the subsequent "harder" drug use is valid. Hall and Lynskey (2005) reminded us that although a randomized study on causality would provide the clearest evidence, it would be enormously problematic.[152] To illustrate, one would need to administer cannabis to a test group of human teenagers while withholding the drug from a control group. This protocol would be not only unethical but impractical from the standpoint of trying to keep the control group from using cannabis as well. Animal studies are not always applicable to a human population. Specifically, there are problems drawing comparisons to cannabis administered to laboratory rats, not only in terms of the obvious differences between the overall structures of their respective brains, but how cannabis is administered (usually orally with pure, high-potency THC to rats, while humans generally use marijuana via smoking in less-potent forms).

Hall and Lynskey also suggest that another possible way to interpret the term "gateway" is through the *social environment hypothesis*.[153] In this view, regular use of marijuana leads to other drug use because frequent marijuana-using adolescents are more likely to have increased opportunities for experimentation with other drugs like cocaine and heroin than non-marijuana-smoking youth. Wagner and Anthony (2002) found that those adolescents who reported using tobacco and alcohol were three times more likely to report an opportunity to use marijuana.[154] Furthermore, they found that youths who had used marijuana were four times as likely to report opportunity to use cocaine. Those who had used alcohol, tobacco, and marijuana reported exposure to cocaine almost six times more than non-using teens.

More importantly, the gateway theory leads us to consider how marijuana's illegal status impacts its use patterns. The theory itself can be spun to support either side of the legalization debate. The pro-legalization faction would say that legalizing marijuana could minimize youth exposure to persons who often sell other illicit substances. By the same token, youths who regularly get high on weed may find themselves becoming increasingly immersed in a culture where drugs like cocaine and heroin also lurk. Those against legalization say that making marijuana legal would only increase access to use and cause neurochemical changes leading to the use of other drugs.

Because of inconsistent and often discordant findings, the vast, overwhelming body of research on marijuana does not necessarily clarify the picture, and may contribute to confusion. Without a clear, unprejudiced lens through which students can examine the relative harm and therapeutic potential of marijuana, they will continue to fall back on and even become more firmly entrenched in their own previously held biases. This makes the job of helpful intervention with those at risk more difficult.

Notes

1 Hilts, P. J. (1994, April 15). Tobacco chiefs say cigarettes aren't addictive. *New York Times*. Retrieved from www.nytimes.com/1994/04/15/us/tobacco-chiefs-say-cigarettes-aren-t-addictive.html?pagewanted=all

2 Tobacco Free Florida. (2012, July 3). *1994—Tobacco company CEOs testify before congress*. [Video file]. Retrieved from www.youtube.com/watch?v=e_ZDQKq2F08

3 American Psychiatric Association. (1994). *Diagnostic and statistical manual of mental disorders* (4th ed.). Washington, DC: Author.

4 American Psychiatric Association. (1987). *Diagnostic and statistical manual of mental disorders* (3rd ed.). Washington, DC: Author.

5 American Psychiatric Association (1994).

6 American Psychiatric Association. (2013). *Diagnostic and statistical manual of mental disorders* (5th ed.). Washington, DC: Author.

7 O'Brien, C. P., Volkow, N., & Li, T-K. (2006). What's in a word? Addiction versus dependence in DSM-V. *The American Journal of Psychiatry*, 163(5), 764–765. doi:10.1176/ajp.2006.163.5.764

8 American Psychiatric Association. (2000). *Diagnostic and statistical manual of mental disorders* (4th ed., text rev.). Washington, DC: Author.

9 Feinberg, I., Jones, R., Walker, J., Cavness, C., & Floyd, T. (1976). Effects of marijuana extract and tetrahydrocannabinol on electroencephalographic sleep patterns. *Clinical Pharmacological Therapy*, 19(6), 782–794. Retrieved from www.ncbi.nlm.nih.gov/pubmed/178475

10 Budney, A. (2011, April 28). Marijuana withdrawal syndrome: Should cannabis withdrawal disorder be included in DSM-5? *Psychiatric Times*. Retrieved from www.psychiatrictimes.com/substance-use-disorder/marijuana-withdrawal-syndrome-should-cannabis-withdrawal-disorder-be-included-dsm-5#sthash.yTwtnaUe.dpuf

11 Herrmann, E. S., Weerts, E. M., & Vandrey, R. (2015). Sex differences in cannabis withdrawal symptoms among treatment-seeking cannabis users. *Experimental and Clinical Psychopharmacology*, 23(6), 415–421. http://dx.doi.org/10.1037/pha0000053

12 American Psychiatric Association (1987).

13 Hasin, D. S., Saha, T. D., Kerridge, B. T., Goldstein, R. B., Chou, S. P., Zhang, H. . . . Grant, B. F. (2015). Prevalence of marijuana use disorders in the United States between 2001–2002 and 2012–2013. *JAMA Psychiatry*, 72(12), 1235–1242. doi:10.1001/jamapsychiatry.2015.1858

14 Ibid., 1235–1242.

15 Davis, M. (2015, October 23). Marijuana use, disorders double in US adults. *Medscape*. Retrieved from www.medscape.com/viewarticle/853145

16 Haberstick, B. C., Young, S. E., Zeiger, J. S., Lessem, J. M., Hewitt, J. K., & Hopfer, C. J. (2014, March 1). Prevalence and correlates of alcohol and cannabis use disorders in the United States: Results from the national longitudinal study of adolescent health. *Drug and Alcohol Dependence*, 136, 158–161. doi: 10.1016/j.drugalcdep.2013.11.022

17 Lopez-Quintero, C., Perez de los Cobos, J., Hasin, D. S., Okuda, M., Wang, S., Grant, B. F., & Blanco, C. (2011). Probability and predictors of transition from first use to dependence on nicotine, alcohol, cannabis, and cocaine: Results of the national epidemiologic survey on alcohol and related conditions (NESARC). *Drug and Alcohol Dependence*, *115*(1–2), 120–130. doi:10.1016/j.drugalcdep.2010.11.004

18 Walton, A. G. (2014, October 7). What 20 years of research has taught us about the chronic effects of marijuana. *Forbes*. Retrieved from http://onforb.es/1tvEdvJ

19 Joy, J. E., Watson, S. J., & Benson, J. A. (1999). *Marijuana and medicine: Assessing the science base*. Washington, DC: Institute of Medicine, National Academies Press.

20 Hall, W., & Degenhardt, L. (2009). Adverse health effects of non-medical cannabis use. *The Lancet*, *374*(9698), 1383–1391. http://dx.doi.org/10.1016/S0140-6736(09)61037-0

21 Walton (2014).

22 Nutt, D., King, L. A., Saulsbury, W., & Blakemore, C. (2007). Development of a rational scale to assess the harm of drugs of potential misuse. *Lancet*, *369*(9566), 1047. doi:10.1016/S0140–6736(07)60464-4

23 Anthony, J. C., Warner, L. A., & Kessler, R. C. (1994). Comparative epidemiology of dependence on tobacco, alcohol, controlled substances, and inhalants: Basic findings from the national comorbidity survey. *Experimental and Clinical Psychopharmacology*, *2*(3), 244–268. Retrieved from https://pdfs.semanticscholar.org/60cd/d49b5ed6a84423762a366727ae4880c6f255.pdf

24 Ibid., 244–268.

25 Richards, K. (2015, April 13). Is marijuana addictive? A look at the scientific research. *The Stranger*. Retrieved from www.thestranger.com/pullout/Green-Guide-Spring-2015/2015/04/13/22033669/is-marijuana-addictive

26 Substance Abuse and Mental Health Services Administration. (2014). *Results from the 2013 national survey on drug use and health: Summary of national findings* (NSDUH Series H-48, HHS Publication No. (SMA) 14–4863). Rockville, MD: Author.

27 Mackie, K. (2008). Cannabinoid receptors: Where they are and what they do. *Journal of Neuroendocrinology*, *1*, 10–4. doi:10.1111/j.1365-2826.2008.01671.x

28 Hirvonen, J., Goodwin, R. S., Li, C-T., Terry, G. E., Zoghbi, S. S., Morse, C., . . . Innis R. B. (2012). Reversible and regionally selective down-regulation of brain cannabinoid CB1 receptors in chronic daily cannabis smokers. *Molecular Psychiatry*, *17*(6), 642–649. doi:10.1038/mp.2011.82

29 Aggarwal, S. K., Kyashna-Tocha, M., & Carter, G. T. (2007). Dosing medical marijuana: Rational guidelines on trial in Washington state. *Medscape General Medicine*, *9*(3), 52.

30 Booth, M. (2004). *Cannabis: A history*. New York, NY: St. Martin's Press.

31 Castaneda, E., Moss, D. E., Oddie, S. D., & Whishaw, I. Q. (1991). THC does not affect striatal dopamine release: Microdialysis in freely moving rats. *Pharmacology Biochemistry and Behavior*, *40*, 587–591. doi:10.1016/0091-3057(91)90367-B

32 Cheer, J. F., Wassum, K. M., Heien, M. L., Phillips, P. E., & Wightman, M. (2004). Cannabinoids enhance subsecond dopamine release in the nucleus accumbens of awake rats. *The Journal of Neuroscience*, *24*(18), 4393–4400. doi:10.1523/JNEUROSCI.0529–04.2004

33 Oleson, E. B., & Cheer, J. F. (2012). A brain on cannabinoids: The role of dopamine release in reward seeking. *Cold Spring Harbor Perspectives in Medicine*, *2*(8), a012229. http://doi.org/10.1101/cshperspect.a012229

34 Wickelgren, I. (1997, June 27). Marijuana: Harder than thought? *Science*, 276(5321), 1967–1968. doi:10.1126/science.276.5321.1967

35 Zuardi, A. W., Shirakawa, I., Finkelfarb, E., & Karniol, I. G. (1982). Action of cannabidiol on the anxiety and other effects produced by delta 9-THC in normal subjects. *Psychopharmacology*, 76(3), 245–50. Retrieved from www.ncbi.nlm.nih.gov/pubmed/6285406

36 Giddenson, J. (2013, November 20). Cannabidiol: The side of marijuana you don't know. *Chicago Tribune*. Retrieved from www.chicagonow.com/chicago-medical-marijuana/2013/11/cannabidiol-the-side-of-marijuana-you-dont-know/

37 Ingold, J. (2016, April 8). One of the attempts to limit Colorado's THC potency fails, for now. *The Denver Post*. Retrieved from www.denverpost.com/2016/04/08/one-attempt-at-colorado-marijuana-potency-limit-fails/

38 Chen, C-Y., Storr, C. L., & Anthony, J. C. (2009). Early-onset drug use and risk for drug dependence problems. *Addictive Behaviors*, 34(3), 319–322. doi:10.1016/j.addbeh.2008.10.021

39 Hall, W., & Degenhardt, L. (2007). Prevalence and correlates of cannabis use in developed and developing countries. *Current Opinion in Psychiatry*, 20(4), 393–397. doi:10.1097/YCO.0b013e32812144cc

40 Pinchevsky, G. M., Arria, A. M., Caldeira, K. M., Garnier-Dykstra, L. M., Vincent, K. B., & O'Grady, K. E. (2012). Marijuana exposure opportunity and initiation during college: Parent and peer influences. *Prevention Science*, 13(1), 43–54. doi:10.1007/s11121-011-0243-4

41 Batalla, A., Bhattacharyya, S., Yücel, M., Fusar-Poli, P., Crippa, J. A., Nogué, S., . . . Martin-Santos, R. (2013). Structural and functional imaging studies in chronic cannabis users: A systematic review of adolescent and adult findings. *PLOS ONE*, 8(2), e55821. doi:10.1371/journal.pone.0055821

42 Filbey, F., & Yezhuvath, U. (2013). Functional connectivity in inhibitory control networks and severity of cannabis use disorder. *The American Journal of Drug and Alcohol Abuse*, 39(6), 382–391. doi:10.3109/00952990.2013.841710

43 Zalesky, A., Solowizj, N., Yücel, M., Lubman, D. I., Takagi, M., Harding, I. H., . . . Seal, M. (2012). Effect of long-term cannabis use on axonal fibre connectivity. *Brain*, 135(7), 2245–2255. doi:10.1093/brain/aws136

44 Grant, B. F., and Dawson, D. A. (1998). Age at onset of drug use and its association with DSM—IV drug abuse and dependence: Results from the National Longitudinal Alcohol Epidemiologic Survey. *Journal of Substance Abuse*, 10(2), 163–173. Retrieved from www.ncbi.nlm.nih.gov/pubmed/9854701

45 Restak, R. (2001). *The secret life of the brain: Adult guide*. The Dana Press and Joseph Henry Press, Educational Broadcasting Corporation. Retrieved from https://www-tc.pbs.org/wnet/brain/pdf/brainadultguide.pdf

46 Pinchevsky, Arria, Caldeira, Garnier-Dykstra, Vincent, & O'Grady 43–54.

47 Epstein, M., Hill, K. G., Nevell, A. M., Guttmannova, K., Bailey, J. A., Abbott, R. D., . . . Hawkins, J. D. (2015). Trajectories of marijuana use from adolescence into adulthood: Environmental and individual correlates. *Developmental Psychology*, 51(11), 1650–1663. doi:10.1037/dev0000054

48 Bechtold, J., Simpson, T., White, H. R., & Pardini, D. (2015). Chronic adolescent marijuana use as a risk factor for physical and mental health problems in young adult men. *Psychology of Addictive Behaviors*, 29(3), 552–563. http://dx.doi.org/10.1037/adb0000103

49 Lynskey, M. T., Agrawal, A., Henders, A., Nelson, E. C., Madden, P. A. F., & Martin, N. G. (2012). An Australian twin study of cannabis and other illicit drug use and misuse, and other psychopathology. *Twin Research and Human Genetics*, 15(5), 631–641. doi:10.1017/thg.2012.41

50 Prescott, & Kendler (1999).
51 Prescott, C. A., & Kendler, K. S. (1999). Genetic and environmental contributions to alcohol abuse and dependence in a population-based sample of male twins. *American Journal of Psychiatry*, *156*(1), 34–40. doi:10.1176/ajp.156.1.34
52 Enoch, M. A., & Goldman, D. (2001). The genetics of alcoholism and alcohol abuse. *Current Psychiatry Reports*, *3*(2), 144–51. Retrieved from www.ncbi.nlm.nih.gov/pubmed/11276410
53 Blanco, C., Hasin, D. S., Wall, M. M., Florez-Salamanca, L., Hoertel, N., Wang, S., . . . Olfson, M. (2016). Cannabis use and risk of psychiatric disorders: Prospective evidence from a US national longitudinal study. *JAMA Psychiatry*, *73*(4), 388–395. doi:10.1001/jamapsychiatry.2015.3229
54 Breyer, J. L., Lee, S., Winters, K. C., August, G. J., & Realmuto, G. M. (2014). A longitudinal study of childhood ADHD and substance dependence disorders in early adulthood. *Psychology of Addictive Behaviors*, *28*(1), 238–246. doi:10.1037/a0035664
55 Cheung, J. T. W., Mann, R. E., Ialomiteanu, A., Stoduto, G., Chan, V., Ala-Leppilampi, K., & Rehm, J. (2010). Anxiety and mood disorders and cannabis use. *The American Journal of Drug and Alcohol Abuse*, *36*, 118–122. doi:10.3109/00952991003713784
56 Copeland, J., Rooke, S., & Swift, W. (2013). Changes in cannabis use among young people: Impact on mental health. *Current Opinion in Psychiatry*, *26*(4), 325–329. doi:10.1097/YCO.0b013e328361eae5
57 Di Forti, M., Sallis, H., Allegri, F., Trotta, A., Ferraro L., Stilo, S. A., . . . Murray, R. M. (2014). Daily use, especially of high-potency cannabis, drives the earlier onset of psychosis in cannabis users. *Schizophrenia Bulletin*, *40*(6), 1509–1517. doi:10.1093/schbul/sbt181
58 Hasin, D. S., Kerridge, B. T., Saha, T. D., Huang, B., Pickering, R., Smith, S. M., . . . Grant, B. F. (2016). Prevalence and correlates of DSM-5 cannabis use disorder, 2012–2013: Findings from the national epidemiologic survey on alcohol and related conditions—III. *American Journal of Psychiatry*, *173*(6), 588–599. http://dx.doi.org/10.1176/appi.ajp.2015.15070907
59 Kevorkian, S., Bonn-Miller, M. O., Belendiuk, K., Carney, D. M., Roberson-Nay, R., & Berenz, E. C. (2015). Associations among trauma, posttraumatic stress disorder, cannabis use, and cannabis use disorder in a nationally representative epidemiologic sample. *Psychology of Addictive Behaviors*, *29*(3), 633–638. doi:10.1037/adb0000110
60 Patton, G. C., Coffey, C., Carlin, J. B., Degenhardt, L., Lynskey, M., & Hall, W. (2002). Cannabis use and mental health in young people: Cohort study. *British Medical Journal*, *325*(7374), 1195–1198. Retrieved from www.ncbi.nlm.nih.gov/pmc/articles/PMC135489/
61 Weinberger, A. H., Platt, J., & Goodwin, R. D. (2016). Is cannabis use associated with an increased risk of onset and persistence of alcohol use disorders? A three-year prospective study among adults in the United States. *Drug and Alcohol Dependence*, *161*, 363–367. doi:10.1016/j.drugalcdep.2016.01.014
62 Copeland, Rooke, & Swift 633–638.
63 Conway, K. P., Compton, W., Stinson, F. S., & Grant, B. F. (2006). Lifetime comorbidity of DSM-IV mood and anxiety disorders and specific drug use disorders: Results from the national epidemiologic survey on alcohol and related conditions. *Journal of Clinical Psychiatry*, *67*(2):247–257. Retrieved from www.ncbi.nlm.nih.gov/pubmed/16566620
64 Copeland, Rooke, & Swift 325–329.

65 Hyman, S. M., & Sinha, R. (2009). Stress-related factors in cannabis use and misuse: Implications for prevention and treatment. *Journal of Substance Abuse Treatment*, 36(4), 400–413. doi:10.1016/j.jsat.2008.08.005

66 Brodbeck, J., Matter, M., Page, J., & Moggi, F. (2007). Motives for cannabis use as a moderator variable of distress among young adults. *Addictive Behaviors*, 32(8), 1537–1545. doi:10.1016/j.addbeh.2006.11.012

67 Beck, K. H., Caldeira, K. M., Vincent, K. B., O'Grady, K. E., Wish, E. D., & Arria, A. M. (2009). The social context of cannabis use: Relationship to cannabis use disorders and depressive symptoms among college students. *Addictive Behaviors*, 34(9), 764–768. doi:10.1016/j.addbeh.2009.05.001

68 Gage, S. H., Zammit, S., & Hickman, M. (2013). Stronger evidence is needed before accepting that cannabis plays an important role in the aetiology of schizophrenia in the population. *F1000 Medicine Reports*, 5(2). doi:10.3410/M5-2

69 Leshner, A. (n.d.). Why do sally and johnny use drugs? *National Institute of Drug Abuse Archives, National Institute of Health*. Retrieved from https://archives.drugabuse.gov/Published_Articles/Sally.html

70 Eldreth, D. A., Matochik, J. A., Cadet, J. L., & Bolla, K. I. (2004). Abnormal brain activity in prefrontal brain regions in abstinent marijuana users. *Neuroimage*, 23(3), 914–920. doi:10.1016/j.neuroimage.2004.07.032

71 Brodbeck, Matter, Page, & Moggi 1537–1545.

72 Malone, D. T., Hill, M. N., & Rubino, T. (2010). Adolescent cannabis use and psychosis: Epidemiology and neurodevelopmental models. *British Journal of Pharmacology*, 160(3), 511–522. doi:10.1111/j.1476-5381.2010.00721.x

73 Fischer, B., Dawe, M., Mcguire, F., Shuper, P. A., Jones, W., Rudzinski, K., & Rehm, J. (2012). Characteristics and predictors of health problems from use among high-frequency cannabis users in a Canadian university student population. *Drugs: Education, Prevention, and Policy*, 19(1), 49–58. doi:10.3109/09687637.2011.614970

74 Dincheva, I., Drysdale, A. T., Hartley, C. A., Johnson, D. C., Jing, D., King, E. C., . . . Lee, F. S. (2015). FAAH genetic variation enhances fronto-amygdala function in mouse and human. *Nature Communications*, 6(6395). doi:10.1038/ncomms7395

75 Horgan, J. (2015, March 13). The feel-good gene leaves me feeling bad. *Scientific American*. Retrieved from https://blogs.scientificamerican.com/cross-check/n-y-times-hype-of-8220-feel-good-gene-8221-makes-me-feel-bad/

76 Agosti, V., Nunes, E., & Levin, F. (2002). Rates of psychiatric comorbidity among U.S. residents with lifetime cannabis dependence. *American Journal of Drug and Alcohol* Abuse, 28(4), 643–652. Retrieved from www.ncbi.nlm.nih.gov/pubmed/12492261

77 Boyle, M. H., Sanford, M., Szatmari P., Merikangas, K., & Offord, D. R. (2001). Familial influences on substance use by adolescents and young adults. *Canadian Journal of Public Health*, 92, 206–209. Retrieved from www.ncbi.nlm.nih.gov/pubmed/11496632

78 Pinchevsky, Arria, Caldeira, Garnier-Dykstra, Vincent, & O'Grady 43–54.

79 Boyle, Sanford, Szatmari. Merikangas, & Offord 206–209.

80 Creemers, H. E., Dijkstra, J. K., Vollebergh, W. A. M., Ormel, J., Verhulst, F. C., & Huizink, A. C. (2010). Predicting life-time and regular cannabis use during adolescence; the roles of temperament and peer substance use: The TRAILS study. *Addiction*, 105, 699–708. doi:10.1111/j.1360-0443.2009.02819.x

81 Kristjansson, A. L., Sigfusdottir, I. D., & Allegrante, J. P. (2013). Adolescent substance use and peer use: A multilevel analysis of cross-sectional

population data. *Substance Abuse Treatment, Prevention, and Policy*, 8(27). doi:10.1186/1747-597X-8-27

82 Riou França, L., Dautzenberg, B., Falissard, B., & Reynaud, M. (2009). Are social norms associated with smoking in French university students? A survey report on smoking correlates. *Substance Abuse, Treatment, Prevention, and Policy*, 4(4). doi:10.1186/1747-597X-4-4

83 Silins, E., Hutchinson, D., Swift, W., Slade, T., Toson, B., & Rodgers, B. (2013). Factors associated with variability and stability of cannabis use in young adulthood. *Drug and Alcohol Dependence*, 133, 452–458. http://dx.doi.org/10.1016/j.drugalcdep.2013.07.003

84 Van den Bree, M. B. M., & Pickworth, W. B. (2005). Risk factors predicting changes in marijuana involvement in teenagers. *Archives of General Psychiatry*, 62(3), 311–319. doi:10.1001/archpsyc.62.3.311

85 Neighbors, C., Geisner, I., & Lee, C. M. (2008). Perceived marijuana norms and social expectancies among entering college student marijuana users. *Psychology of Addictive Behaviors*, 22(3), 433–438. doi:10.1037/0893-164X.22.3.433

86 Pinchevsky, Arria, Caldeira, Garnier-Dykstra, Vincent, & O'Grady 43–54.

87 Tucker, J. S., de la Haye, K., Kennedy, D. P., Green Jr., H. D., & Pollard, M. S. (2014). Peer influence on marijuana use in different types of friendships. *Journal of Adolescent Health*, 54(1), 67–73. doi:http://dx.doi.org/10.1016/j.jadohealth.2013.07.025

88 Gruber, S. A., & Yurgelun-Todd, D. A. (2005). Neuroimaging of marijuana smokers during inhibitory processing: a pilot investigation. *Science Direct*, 23(1), 107–118. doi:10.1016/j.cogbrainres.2005.02.016

89 Gruber, S. A., Silveri, M. M., Dahlgren, M. K., & Yurgelun-Todd, D. (2011). Why so impulsive? White matter alterations are associated with impulsivity in chronic marijuana smokers. *Experimental and Clinical Psychopharmacology*, 19(3), 231–242. http://doi.org/10.1037/a0023034

90 Breyer, Lee, Winters, August, & Realmuto 238–246.

91 Roebke, P. V., Vadhan, N. P., Brooks, D. J., & Levin, F. R. (2014). Verbal learning in marijuana users seeking treatment: A comparison between depressed and non-depressed samples. *The American Journal of Drug and Alcohol Abuse*, 40(4), 274–279. doi:10.3109/00952990.2013.875551

92 Roebke, Vadhan, Brooks, & Levin 274–279.

93 Schuster, R. M., Hoeppner, S. S., Evins, A. E., & Gilman, J. M. (2016). Early onset marijuana use is associated with learning inefficiencies. *Neuropsychology*, 30(4), 405–415. http://dx.doi.org/10.1037/neu0000281

94 Crean, R. D., Crane, N. A., & Mason, B. J. (2011). An evidence based review of acute and long-term effects of cannabis use on executive cognitive functions. *Journal of Addiction Medicine*, 5, 1–8. doi:10.1097/ADM.0b013e31820c23fa

95 Ferraro, D. P. (1980). Acute effects of marijuana on human memory and cognition. *NIDA Research Monograph*, 31, 98–119. Retrieved from www.ncbi.nlm.nih.gov/pubmed/ 6775234

96 Haney, M., Ward, A. S., Comer, S. D., Foltin, R. W., & Fischman M. W. (1999). Abstinence symptoms following smoked marijuana in humans. *Psychopharmacology*, 141(4), 395–404. Retrieved from www.ncbi.nlm.nih.gov/pubmed/10090647

97 Pope, H. G., Jr., Gruber, A. J., Hudson, J. I., Huestis, M. A., & Yurgelun-Todd, D. (2001). Neuropsychological performance in long-term cannabis users. *Archives of General Psychiatry*, 58(10), 909–915. doi:10.1001/archpsyc.58.10.909

98 Pope, H. G. Jr., Gruber, A. J., Hudson, J. I., Huestis, M. A., & Yurgelun-Todd, D. (2002). Cognitive measures in long-term cannabis users. *Journal of Clinical Pharmacology*, *42*(11 Suppl), 41S–47S. Retrieved from www.ncbi.nlm.nih.gov/pubmed/12412835

99 Jager, G., Kahn, R. S., Van den Brink, W., Van Ree, J. M., & Ramsey, N. F. (2006). Long-term effects of frequent cannabis use on working memory and attention: An fMRI study. *Psychopharmacology*, *185*(3), 358–368. doi:10.1007/s00213-005-0298-7

100 Solowij, N., Michie, P. T., & Fox, A. M. (1995). Differential impairments of selective attention due to frequency and duration of cannabis use. *Biological Psychiatry*, *37*(10), 731–739. doi:10.1016/0006-3223(94)00178-6

101 Bolla K. I., Brown, K., Eldreth, D., Tate, K., & Cadet, J. L. (2002). Dose-related neurocognitive effects of marijuana use. *Neurology*, *59*(9), 1337–1343. Retrieved from www.ncbi.nlm.nih.gov/pubmed/12427880

102 Jacobus, J., Squeglia, L. M., Infante, M. A., Castro, N., Brumback, T., Meruelo, A. D., & Tapert, S. F. (2015). Neuropsychological performance in adolescent marijuana users with co-occurring alcohol use: A three-year longitudinal study. *Neuropsychology*, *29*(6), 829–843. http://dx.doi.org/10.1037/neu0000203

103 Niesink, R. J. M., & van Laar, M. W. (2013). Does cannabidiol protect against adverse psychological effects of THC? *Frontiers in Psychiatry*, *16*(4), 130. doi:10.3389/fpsyt.2013.00130

104 Meier, M. H., Caspi, A., Ambler, A., Harrington, H., Houts, R., Keefe, R. S. E., . . . Moffitt, T. E. (2012). Persistent cannabis users show neuropsychological decline from childhood to mid-life. *Proceedings of the National Academy of Sciences of the United States of America*, *109*(40), E2657–E2664. doi:10.1073/pnas.1206820109

105 Calkins, K. (2013). Early-onset, regular cannabis use is linked to IQ decline. *NIDA Notes*. Retrieved from www.drugabuse.gov/news-events/nida-notes/2013/08/early-onset-regular-cannabis-use-linked-to-iq-decline

106 Moffitt, M. H., Meier, M. H., Caspi, A., & Poulton, R. (2013). Reply to Rogeberg and Daly: No evidence that socioeconomic status or personality differences confound the association between cannabis use and IQ decline. *Proceedings of the National Academy of Sciences of the U S A*, *110*(11), E980–E982. doi:10.1073/pnas.1300618110

107 Pope, H. G., & Yurgelun-Todd, D. (1996). The residual cognitive effects of heavy marijuana use in college students. *Journal of the American Medical Association*, *275*(7), 521–527. doi:10.1001/jama.275.7.521

108 Moffitt, Meier, Caspi, & Poulton E980–E982.

109 Arria, A. M., Caldeira, K. M., Bugbee, B. A., Vincent, K. B., & O'Grady, K. E. (2015). The academic consequences of marijuana use during college. *Psychology of Addictive Behaviors: Journal of the Society of Psychologists in Addictive Behaviors*, *29*(3), 564–575. http://doi.org/10.1037/adb0000108

110 Booth (2004).

111 Radhakrishnan, R., Wilkinson, S. T., & D'Souza, D. C. (2014). Gone to pot—a review of the association between cannabis and psychosis. *Frontiers in Psychiatry*, *5*, 54. http://doi.org/10.3389/fpsyt.2014.00054

112 Blaszczak-Boxe, A. (2016, February 8). Potent pot: Marijuana is stronger now than it was 20 years ago. *Live Science*. Retrieved from www.livescience.com/53644-marijuana-is-stronger-now-than-20-years-ago.html

113 Zuardi, Shirakawa, Finkelfarb, & Karniol 245–250.

114 How marijuana may drive the brain into psychosis. (2012 January 3). *Live Science*. Retrieved from www.livescience.com/17707-marijuana-thc-brain-psychosis.html

115 Dukakis, A. (2014, April 29). Denver emergency room doctor seeing more patients for marijuana edibles. *Colorado Public Radio*. Retrieved from www.cpr.org/news/story/denver-emergency-room-doctor-seeing-more-patients-marijuana-edibles

116 American Psychiatric Association (2013)

117 Andréasson, S., Engström, A., & Allebeck, P. (1987). Cannabis and schizophrenia: A longitudinal study of Swedish conscripts. *Lancet*, *1*(2), 1483–1486. http://dx.doi.org/10.1016/S0140-6736(87)92620-1

118 Ibid., 1483–1486.

119 Di Forti, Sallis, Allegri, Trotta, Ferraro L. Stilo, . . . Murray 1509–1517.

120 Schimmelmann, B. G., Conus, P., Cotton, S., Kupferschmid, S., McGorry, P. D., & Lambert, M. (2012). Prevalence and impact of cannabis use disorders in adolescents with early onset first episode psychosis. *European Psychiatry*, *27*, 463–469. doi:10.1016/j.eurpsy.2011.03.001

121 French, L., Gray, C., Leonard, G., Perron, M., Pike, B., Richer, L., . . . Paus, T. (2015). Early cannabis use, polygenic risk score for schizophrenia, and brain maturation in adolescence. *JAMA Psychiatry*, *72*(10), 1002–1011. doi:10.1001/jamapsychiatry.2015.1131

122 Armentano, P. (2007, August 7). NORML responds to new rash of pot and mental health claims. *National Organization for the Normalization of Marijuana Laws*. Retrieved from http://medicalmarijuana.procon.org/view.answers.php?questionID=000220

123 Moore, T. H., Zammit, S., Lingford-Hughes, A., Barnes, T. R., Jones, P. B., Burke, M., & Lewis, G. (2007). Cannabis use and risk of psychotic or affective mental health outcomes: A systematic review. *Lancet*, *370*(9584), 319–328. doi:http://dx.doi.org/10.1016/S0140-6736(07)61162-3

124 Warner, R. (1995). Time trends in schizophrenia: Changes in obstetric risk factors with industrialization. *Schizophrenia Bulletin*, *21*(3), 483–500. Retrieved from www.mentalhealth.com/mag1/scz/sb-time.html

125 Rodrigo, C., & Rajapakse, S. (2009). Cannabis and schizophrenia spectrum disorders: A review of clinical studies. *Indian Journal of Psychological Medicine*, *31*(2), 62–70. http://doi.org/10.4103/0253-7176.63575

126 Frisher, M., Crome, I., Martino, O., & Croft, P. (2009). Assessing the impact of cannabis use on trends in diagnosed schizophrenia in the United Kingdom from 1996 to 2005. *Schizophrenia Research*, *113*(2–3), 123–228. doi:10.1016/j.schres.2009.05.031

127 Proal, A. C., Fleming, J. A., Galvez-Buccollini, J., & DeLisi, L. E. (2014). A controlled family study of cannabis users with and without psychosis. *Schizophrenic Research*, *152*(1), 283–288. doi:10.1016/j.schres.2013.11.014

128 Ibid., 9.

129 Volkow, N. D., Baler, R. D., Compton, W. M., & Weiss, S. R. B. (2014). Adverse health effects of marijuana use. *The New England Journal of Medicine*, *370*(23), 2219–2227. http://doi.org/10.1056/NEJMra1402309

130 Whiting, P. F., Wolff, R. F., Deshpande, S., Di Nisio, M., Steven, D., Hernandez, A. V., . . . Kleijnen, J. (2015). Cannabinoids for medical use: A systematic review and meta-analysis, *Journal of the American Medical Association*, *313*(24), 2456–2473. doi:10.1001/jama.2015.6358

131 Ibid., 2456–2473.

132 Kaplan, K. (2015, June 23). Most uses of medical marijuana wouldn't pass FDA review, study finds. *LA Times*. Retrieved from www.latimes.com/

science/sciencenow/la-sci-sn-medical-marijuana-review-20150623-story.
html

133 Armentano, P. (2015, June 28). Why the media can't get its story straight about the amazing medical potential of cannabis. *AlterNet*. Retrieved from www.alternet.org/drugs/why-media-all-over-place-when-it-comes-talking-about-scientific-discoveries-tied-medical

134 Lee, M. A. (2012). *Smoke signals: A social history of marijuana—medical, recreational, and scientific*. New York, NY: Scribner.

135 Lee, M. A. (2015, February 18). CBD misconceptions. *Project CBD*. Retrieved from www.projectcbd.org/guidance/cbd-misconceptions

136 Marcu, J. P., Christian, R. T., Lau, D., Zielinski, A. J., Horowitz, M. P., Lee, J., . . . McAllister, S. D. (2010). Cannabidiol enhances the inhibitory effects of Δ9-tetrahydrocannabinol on human glioblastoma cell proliferation and survival. *Molecular Cancer Therapeutics*, 9(1), 180–189. http://doi.org/10.1158/1535-7163.MCT-09-0407

137 Ligresti, A., Moriello, A. S., Starowicz, K., Matias, I., Pisanti, S., De Petrocellis, L., . . . Di Marzo, V. (2006). Antitumor activity of plant cannabinoids with emphasis on the effect of cannabidiol on human breast carcinoma. *Journal of Pharmacology and Experimental Therapeutics*, 318(3), 1375–1387. doi:https://doi.org/10.1124/jpet.106.105247

138 Lee (2015).

139 Ferner, M. (2015, March 26). Feds may spend nearly $70 million on marijuana for research. *Huffington Post*. Retrieved from www.huffingtonpost.com/2015/03/26/federal-marijuana-research_n_6947876.html

140 The Compassionate Access, Research and Respect States Act of 2015, *S.683*. Retrieved from www.congress.gov/114/bills/s683/BILLS-114s683is.pdf

141 Establishment of a new drug code for marihuana extract—81 Fed. Reg. 90194. (2016). Retrieved from www.gpo.gov/fdsys/pkg/FR-2016-12-14/pdf/2016-29941.pdf

142 Mariani, M. (2015, March 4). How the American opiate epidemic was started by one pharmaceutical company. *The Week*. Retrieved from http://theweek.com/articles/541564/how-american-opiate-epidemic-started-by-pharmaceutical-company

143 Scott, I. (1998). Heroin: A hundred-year habit. *History Today*, 48(6). Retrieved from www.historytoday.com/ian-scott/heroin-hundred-year-habit

144 Cadoni, C., Pisanu, A., Solinas, M., Aquas, E., & Di Chiara, G. (2001). Behavioural sensitization after repeated exposure to Δ9-tetrahydrocannabinol and cross-sensitization with morphine. *Psychopharmacology*, 158, 259–266. doi:10.1007/s002130100875

145 Pistis, M., Perra, S., Pillolla, G., Melis, M., Muntoni, A. L., & Gessa, G. L. (2004). Adolescent exposure to cannabinoids induces long-lasting changes in the response to drugs of abuse of rat midbrain dopamine neurons. *Biological Psychiatry*, 56(2), 86–94. doi:10.1016/j.biopsych.2004.05.006

146 Kandel & Kandel—a marriage of science: In their first scientific collaboration, Denise and Eric Kandel are investigating the neurobiological underpinnings of the "gateway" hypothesis of drug addiction. (2011, October 3). *Columbia University College of Physicians and Surgeons News*. Retrieved from http://ps.columbia.edu/news/kandel-kandel

147 Ibid.

148 Cadoni, Pisanu, Solinas, Aquas, & Di Chiara 259–266.

149 The National Institute on Drug Abuse. (2017, April 28). *Marijuana*. Retrieved from www.drugabuse.gov/publications/research-reports/marijuana

150 Hall, W. D., & Lynskey, M. (2005). Is cannabis a gateway drug? Testing hypotheses about the relationship between cannabis use and the use of other illicit drugs. *Drug and Alcohol Review*, 24, 39–48. doi:10.1080/09595230500126698

151 Wagner, F. A., & Anthony, J. C. (2002). From first drug use to drug dependence: Developmental periods of risk for dependence upon marijuana, cocaine, and alcohol. *Neuropsychopharmacology*, 26, 479–488. doi:10.1016/S0893-133X(01)00367–0

152 Hall & Lynskey 39–48.

153 Ibid., 39–48.

154 Wagner & Anthony 479–488.

Chapter 8

Nate

Nate seems jittery as we sit down alone on the patio. It is unclear whether he is anxious about being interviewed or merely reacting to the steady drop in temperature as the spring sun gets lower in the evening sky. He is asked to talk openly about his experience, his relationship with marijuana. "Currently, weed and I have a love/hate relationship. I'm not gonna lie, I love being high. But, there are times when I don't want to get carried away with this, I don't want to be smoking forever. But I don't want to be labeled as a stoner. But at the same time when I was going through that time with my brother dying, or stuff with my girlfriend, if I smoke, I'll cover it up. But I don't want to go through life just covering stuff up, I'm going to have to face it. I think about my health. Thank God I've never been pulled over by a cop or ever had experiences like that. I think, 'what if I get tested for a job one day?'" Nate is graduating soon, and this realization continues to pop up as he talks about his marijuana use.

"All my friends are for marijuana, except my girlfriend; she is against it. She doesn't smoke or drink or anything like that." When asked why she is against it, what he hears her say, Nate quickly lists the following, counting on his fingers in apparent exasperation: "She doesn't like the feel of it. She doesn't want me to get carried away with it. She gets worried about me. She doesn't like the smell of it." When asked further if his cannabis use has created conflict in his relationship, he is quick to admit it. "It hasn't until recently. We've been fighting a lot because of it. She'll give me an attitude about being high, but then it goes back on her, it's like if you knew I was going to do that, why are you hanging out with me? She knows what to expect, and I tell her that she doesn't have to hang out with me that day if she doesn't want to. There are days when we hang out and I don't smoke." When their relationship began four years ago, he had already been regularly smoking marijuana with his two older brothers. "The first time I started smoking weed was, my brother who died and my other brother, we would have people over when my mother was out."

When asked again if it was his very first time, he corrected himself. "The very first time was with this girl Gina and this kid Anthony. When my brothers found out they were cool with it." He was age 15. When asked what his very first time was like with Gina and Anthony, he described them taking the tobacco out of a cigarette, filling it with marijuana, and smoking it. "I was laughing a lot. I was acting like somebody the first time they smoked, silly and stuff. I didn't smoke again, like only once every blue moon. From 15 to 16 to 18, I would just smoke every now and then. I rarely smoked."

Nate's use increased when he came to college. "The summer after my freshman year I started to smoke more because I loved the feeling." Then, without even a pause: "But, then around that time when my brother had died, I started to use it because I didn't want to think about it. I didn't want to deal with anything. I'm still dealing with it, honestly. I still try not to think about it." Nate states that his brother died in 2014 but that "it still feels like it was a couple of months ago." He becomes silent. He is asked more about this time, if he is willing to share it. Was he at school when he heard about his brother? "My dad called me and told me to come home. He had texted his girlfriend and said 'goodbye, I love you.' My father found him the next morning."

This is clearly still very raw and painful, and, by unstated agreement, there is a shift in the interview back to safer content, his relationship with marijuana. In the parlance of psychotherapy, this is known as a parallel process. "Whenever I didn't want to feel something, I'd smoke. It is the only thing that gets in my way." When asked how he prefers to use, he replies that he usually smokes out of a pipe, though his friend has a bong. He denies ever doing dabs. "I've tried to stop, did so for weeks. Then I'll smoke and say to myself, 'oh, this is what I'm missing.' That's what I'll do. I'll smoke for a while and stop for a while, then, start up again."

When Nate is asked what he likes about marijuana, other than being able to change how he is feeling, he can add little else; he just likes being high. When asked about what he likes less about it, he repeats that he does not want it to be the rest of his life. He is asked if he worries that he will reach a point when he can no longer stop. He dismisses this but adds that he is worried about it. "I worry about if I have kids. I don't want them to think smoking is okay." He is asked why he would not want his children to smoke. "I wouldn't want them to get in trouble with it. Like, I have this one friend whose family—her mother doesn't smoke, but her family is okay with it. Her boyfriend buys her an ounce every time and he also buys her bongs and bubblers and all that stuff. Her dad smokes a lot too, every day, I think. They're not bad people or anything. If that's something they want to do, that's fine. They have a house, a couple houses actually." Nate wants to work in social services. He would like to work in a children's home with those kids who come from troubled families and are placed there by the state. "I plan on being a social worker, so I may have to stop smoking."

Nate sums up the interview with this statement: "I don't advocate for it. I don't care if you smoke, but I'm not going to be wearing a pot shirt." With that, he declared it was time for him to leave. Besides, it was now getting much colder.

Chapter 9

From Prohibition to
Prevention and Intervention

> *Parents must not only have certain ways of guiding by prohibition and permission, they must also be able to represent to the child a deep, almost somatic conviction that there is meaning in what they are doing.*
>
> —Erik Erickson[1]

Prohibition is one of society's original public health prevention strategies. *Merriam Webster Dictionary* defines prohibition as "the act of not allowing something to be used or done" and prevention as "the act or practice of stopping something bad from happening: the act of preventing something."[2] The history of society attempting to prohibit intoxication by its citizenry may well be as old as the use of substances themselves.

In our distant past, religious canon served as the earliest basis for prohibition. Over 4,000 years ago in Western Siberia, mushrooms such as fly agaric (*Amanita muscaria*), which produces dissociation and hallucination, may have been restricted to ceremonies by shamans.[3] The Bible serves as another example of religious proscription, denouncing drunkenness numerous times. Alcohol was not forbidden entirely, but there were circumstances where consumption was prohibited—such as Aaron being warned by God not to drink anything alcoholic before going to the tent to worship (Leviticus 10:8–10).

Islam provides another example of edicts against intoxication. There is evidence that cannabis may have been treated as an acceptable alternative to alcohol since the Quran specifically warned against alcohol, known as *khamr*, while hashish was not mentioned.[4] As the Quran was compiled, the net seemed to widen over agents and associated behaviors deemed *haram* (forbidden). The later versions of the Quran interpreted *khamr* as a broader category of inebriants seen as sinful, as well as "gambling, idolatry, and games of chance."[5] Partaking of hashish was not without controversy, with some attempts at interdiction. In the late fourteenth century, the emir of Cairo tried to stamp out cannabis use, even resorting to pulling out the teeth of those unfortunates found using the plant. There is no record evaluating the effectiveness of this early War on Drugs.[6]

In addition to solely religion-based prohibition, public education has driven prevention strategy as a way of affecting public abstention. Before the passing of alcohol prohibition under the Volstead Act in 1920, the forces of prohibition, most prominently the Women's Christian Temperance Union (WCTU) and the Anti-Saloon League (ASL), had already made significant inroads into the American education system. The WCTU managed to pressure public schools to teach a curriculum on the evils of demon rum. The ASL had even developed and sponsored a youth peer movement known as the Lincoln League after Abraham Lincoln, who had warned about the dangers of alcohol in several speeches decades before.[7] Young people, in joining, were given a certificate that included a pledge to abstain from the use of intoxicating liquors as a beverage.[8] This pledge foreshadowed the strategies and tone of the "Just Say No" campaign that would surface 80 years later.

Public education as a form of prevention could take on a hysterical, over-the-top character as seen in the 1936 movie *Reefer Madness*.[9] Despite its absurd, laughable depiction, the film was originally a serious attempt to educate parents about the seductive perils of reefer, a substance virtually unknown to the majority of the public at the time. This period, under the shadow cast by Harry Anslinger and the Federal Bureau of Narcotics, also saw the publishing of numerous anti-marijuana books and magazines. Many of these depicted lurid accounts of youths and women whose use of the drug led to death, prison, insanity, or irredeemable moral collapse. Forgotten for decades, *Reefer Madness* was rediscovered in the 1970s by a then firmly established marijuana-using youth culture and was viewed as a vivid example of how clueless their parents' generation was about the drug.

Earlier efforts like these to inhibit substance-using behavior in the populace inevitably influenced later substance-abuse prevention strategies. The thesis that fear alone could sway a person's choice about seeking intoxication was a cornerstone in this philosophy. Moreover, it perpetuated the belief that a substance had the power to pervert and destroy even the best, the strongest, and the most pious of men and women through its fundamental action alone. This was the same abiding concept that had existed for over a century, guiding our nation's first prohibitions. The belief of the drug as the enemy persists today, imbued in the core of American substance abuse prevention philosophy.

The Science of Prevention

The evolution of prevention as a science has had several markers throughout history, with origins in the prevention of medical disease. In the 1940s, the concept of *primary prevention* was first described: that diseases could be averted through policies and programs such as health promotion, improved diet, proper sanitation, and immunizations. Later, the models of *secondary* and *tertiary prevention* were introduced.[10] Secondary prevention involves detecting and treating symptoms when they first arise. Tertiary prevention entails rehabilitation or impeding the spread of a pathogen and curtailing larger public health risks. *Interventions* are those actions taken to improve a condition or interrupt a situation from worsening. The concept of *risk factors* is attributed to Dr. William B. Kannel, who first described the major determinants in the development of cardiovascular disease.[11] Kannel was referring to those antecedent conditions such as high blood pressure, obesity, and smoking. *Protective factors* refer to those conditions that contribute to resilience in individuals against potential harmful conditions, like substance abuse.[12] The terms *risk factors* along with *protective factors* remain firmly imbedded in the primary prevention lexicon today. The language of risk and protective factors did not find its way into the realm of substance abuse prevention until much later.[13] In the early 1990s, Drs. Hawkins and Catalano as well as others from the University of Washington developed a theoretical framework for substance abuse prevention for at-risk youth.[14] In their work, they identified elements such as community, family, school, and individual/peer risk factors as targets for prevention efforts. Also described were four protective factors for substance abuse including gender, a resilient temperament, a positive social orientation, and intelligence.

Until that time, while the science of prevention in the health field was evolving, substance abuse prevention remained mired in its own Dark Ages. The lag in the development of substance abuse prevention as a field was partly due to the continued stranglehold of the Federal Bureau of Narcotics under the Anslinger administration, which continued its doctrine of scare tactics. For a period of several decades, fact-based information about cannabis use and attitudes was unavailable. Meanwhile, marijuana use grew in the 1960s, and there were limited data to serve as guidance.

In 1974, three researchers from the University of Michigan—Lloyd Johnston, Jerald Bachman, and Robert Kahn—embarked on an ambitious project to survey the attitudes of high school seniors on a wide range of subjects, such as race relations, gender roles, politics, and the environment. Their goal was to follow such trends over time to see if they saw any changes in those beliefs and behaviors. But, first they had to pitch their idea to someone who could fund such a costly undertaking. Robert DuPont, who was soon to become the head of the new National Institute on Drug Abuse (NIDA), had been reading Johnston's research on substance use by high school students in his book titled *Drugs and American Youth*.[15] DuPont was so impressed that he invited Johnston to meet with him in Washington to discuss his findings. To state that the conversation was fruitful would be an understatement. The research team became the beneficiary of a five-year $3 million grant from NIDA to survey and measure the substance use behaviors and attitudes of eighth- to twelfth-grade students. By 1976, the initiative *Monitoring the Future* published its first findings, and it continues to be a primary assessment of high school age substance use to this day. Since its inception, *Monitoring the Future* has expanded its survey to include 60,000 respondents and is following some of them after graduation.[16] Among the early contributions of *Monitoring the Future* was demonstrating that an increase in the perceived risk of a drug would cause its use to fall.[17] This finding remains a key concept in prevention strategies to this day.

Monitoring the Future was an early attempt to provide data for further prevention research efforts. As the field of substance abuse prevention began to unfold, several distinct approaches sprang forth: *information dissemination, affective education,* and *social influence*.[18] The first was *information dissemination,* predicated on the long-believed concept that if youth were educated about the negative effects and adverse consequences of substance use, it would result in decreased use because students would make more rational decisions. This information was usually coupled with fear-arousal or scare tactics—not a complete break from the previous methodology employed by the FBN. Unfortunately, studies eventually proved that while information dissemination increases the knowledge base of subjects, it is ineffective at meeting its primary objective of reducing use.[19]

One possible reason for the inefficacy of information dissemination lies in how the potential for risk is communicated. Straightforward messaging may not be the most effective way and can even be counterproductive. In their proposed *The Law of Indirect Effect*, Hansen and McNeal state that direct effects of a program on behavior are not possible, as "the expression or suppression of a behavior is controlled by neural and situational processes over which the interventionist has no direct control."[20] Instead, programs need to modify their processes to achieve a more indirect outcome. Prevention programs should not attempt direct behavioral change but must focus on altering indirect supporting variables. For example, programs can aim to change cognitions like perceived social context of the behavior and teach specific skills to engage in different behavior. According to this concept, the essence of health education is changing predisposing and enabling factors that lead to behavior, not the behavior itself.

Another possible explanation could be the *boomerang effect* or *psychological reactance*.[21] Defined as the reaction to a perceived threat to a firmly held ideal or position, it results in the opposite response to the intended message, a reassertion of a threatened freedom. We can see this in many arenas, including political discourse, where both sides of the debate seem not only impervious to information contradictory to their chosen beliefs but instead filled with a greater resolve. Challenging a belief directly, aggressively, can cause the recipients to become even more entrenched in their held position.

In conclusion, attempting to influence college students to use less marijuana may be less effective than modifying what and how they think about marijuana. Although this sounds straightforward enough, substance abuse prevention has historically been predicated upon a very direct mission: stopping substance use. This could be attributed to the zeal of an older generation of public health professionals (who may also have been frightened parents!) and funding by a results-oriented government. The overarching goal has always been to sway young adults from substance use, not to educate them. In this direct approach, education has always been a means to an end, not the end in and of itself.

The second school-based prevention approach, *affective education*, focuses on teaching adolescents skills to better introspect, communicate, and assert themselves. This approach assumes that if students have better self-understanding, then they will be able to make better decisions. This too has proved ineffective at reducing substance use.[22]

The last school-based prevention approach, *social influence*, focuses on building social skills and appears to be effective with young adolescents.[23] This approach utilizes life-skills training and improves abilities to mediate social influences. Life-skills training is designed to teach students various self-management competencies to improve decision-making, problem-solving, self-control, coping with stress, properly understanding media influences, and anger/impulse control. Bolstering social and drug-information/resistance skills are additional components in the curriculum. The program also encourages students to develop their own personal improvement project and record their struggles, discoveries, and successes along the process.

Improving abilities to mediate social influences includes helping students better refuse drugs, engage in peer leadership, and correct normative expectations.[24] Changing social normative expectations is a mainstay approach of college prevention programs to this day. The skills taught in the social influence approach are associated with earlier theories from the 1960s and 1970s of *social inoculation*—the concept of strengthening an individual's position (in this case, saying "no" to drug use) in the face of persuasion by influential peers or others.[25] Social inoculation provided the theoretical underpinning for prevention campaigns, like "Just Say No" in the 1980s, spurring the growth of the present-day prevention industry. "Just Say No" was probably the most high-profile substance abuse prevention movement since the years preceding Prohibition under the Volstead Act. Large amounts of federal money were allocated to staunch the eruption of the cocaine epidemic that was plaguing the United States at that time. This funding targeted the demand market of our nation's youth, while interdicting the supply side through beefed-up law enforcement. Born of an impromptu remark by the first lady, Nancy Reagan, "Just Say No" evolved into a global social messaging initiative once the media and political strategists joined the fray. Although the campaign was criticized as being simplistic, there was actually a significant reduction in illicit drug use—marijuana predominantly—by youth during this era.[26] Given the complexity of the problem, any causal role the campaign may have had in this outcome remains beyond proof after over 25 years. What is inarguable is its profound influence on later prevention programming.

Even though his national campaign of anti-drug law enforcement had not yielded desired results, Ronald Reagan salvaged some encouraging statistics and credited his wife Nancy's "Just Say No" campaign in his last State of the Union Address:

> Cocaine use is declining, and marijuana use was the lowest since surveying began. We can be proud that our students are just saying no to drugs. But let us remember what this menace requires: commitment from every part of America and every single American, a commitment to a drug-free America. The war against drugs is a war of individual battles, a crusade with many heroes, including America's young people and also someone very special to me. She has helped so many of our young people to say no to drugs. Nancy, much credit belongs to you, and I want to express to you your husband's pride and your country's thanks.[27]

This excerpt of Reagan's address captures the essence of a problem essential to the thesis of this book. It highlights a watershed moment in time that altered the trajectory of the field, when prevention of substance use—previously a health policy strategy—was spliced into law enforcement. For in the late 1980s, the War on Drugs and the field of substance abuse prevention were—quite literally—married.

Other popular government-endorsed prevention programs then took the stage. "Just Say No" gave way to similar promotions such as "Winners Don't Use Drugs," which employed messaging to youth via the growing video game industry.[28] However, the most widespread and enduring prevention program to arise from this era was Drug Abuse Resistance Education (D.A.R.E.), conceived by Los Angeles police officer Daryl Gates (who once stated before a Senate Judiciary Committee that casual drug users "ought to be taken out and shot").[29] The mission of D.A.R.E was to reduce drug use and gang violence by establishing a cooperative relationship early on between youth and law enforcement. Specially trained community police officers collaborated with middle school teachers trained in the D.A.R.E. curriculum to teach students life skills and how to resist peer pressure to use drugs or become involved in violence. Substance use education explored and sought to challenge normative beliefs youths may have had about illicit intoxicants. D.A.R.E. became so prominent, bolstered by funding from practically all the federal law enforcement and justice agencies, that it was implemented in the United Kingdom by the mid-1990s. Disappointingly, a decade of studies on the D.A.R.E. program showed little evidence in the way of reducing youth substance use.[30] In fact, a couple of studies demonstrated that it might have had the opposite impact, a boomerang effect, associated with a later increase in use of certain illicit substances like hallucinogens.[31]

In response to the growing criticism, D.A.R.E. shifted its tactics in 2009 by adopting the evidence-based "Keepin' it REAL" curriculum developed by Penn State University.[32] REAL is an acronym for *Refuse*, or resisting offers to use, *Explain* the reasons for refusal, *Avoid* situations that might potentially be risky, and *Leave* any such scenario. The "Keepin' it REAL" curriculum incorporates awareness of multi-cultural differences in social and communication patterns when training students to make healthier decisions given the opportunity to use drugs.[33] "Keepin' it REAL" is among a list of evidence-based prevention practices that is listed in the National Registry of Evidence-Based Programs and Practices (NREPP), sponsored by the Substance Abuse and Mental Health Services Administration (SAMHSA)—the primary federal agency that oversees drug and alcohol policy.

Prevention programs, like "Keepin' it REAL" along with research funded by the National Institute on Drug Abuse (NIDA) and other federal research organizations, tend to target youth and adolescents. Despite this younger focus, prevention research provides scaffolding for working with students in higher education and is worth mentioning. For example, NIDA outlines a prevention research program focusing on risks for drug abuse and other problem behaviors that occur throughout a child's development, from pregnancy through young adulthood. Sixteen principles have been listed to serve as guidelines for organizations, and among them several stand out.[34] At the top of the list is the principle that earlier prevention is more effective than later efforts and that it should enhance protective factors as well as reduce risk factors. While early prevention may be mostly pertinent in work with children and young teens, it could be helpful to some incoming freshman that have not shown other risk factors or previously used cannabis. Another principle emphasizes the importance of interventions being culturally sensitive. Colleges are far behind in this area despite enormous opportunities to fine-tune prevention messaging to diverse groups that have already self-identified and coalesced (e.g., campus LGBTQ organizations and ethnic groups). Of the principles recommended, one that could prove most valuable to include in the higher education arena is to create prevention programs that are long-term with repeated interventions (i.e., booster programs) to reinforce the original prevention goals.

College Substance Abuse Prevention

While primary and secondary substance abuse focused on teenage use of tobacco, marijuana, gangs, and alcohol, college prevention studies began with a focus solely on alcohol—the most high-profile substance contributing to student problems despite the widespread use of tobacco. These efforts to curb alcohol misuse in college constructed the template for later marijuana prevention models. Probably the first published research on college substance use was the work of Robert Straus and Selden Daskam Bacon of the Yale Center of Alcohol Studies in 1953, which described a milieu where excessive drinking was commonplace.[35]

With the passing of the Comprehensive Alcohol Abuse and Alcoholism Prevention, Treatment, and Rehabilitation Act of 1970, and the subsequent forming of the National Institute of Alcohol Abuse and Alcoholism (NIAAA), one of the early acts of the prevention division was funding a grant known as the University Demonstration Alcohol Education Project (DAEP).[36] Eventually piloted by University of Massachusetts and four schools, DAEP was an education-based prevention program that focused on changing attitudes and values associated with alcohol use, including trying to reframe alcohol as a drug that could be misused rather than as a harmless beverage. Another assumption of the model was that the more severe consequences of heavy alcohol use were usually preceded by clear warning signs of an eventual calamitous event. DAEP also proposed identifying and intervening with at-risk students earlier in their ill-fated trajectory. This prevention paradigm remains within the basic models of college alcohol and other drugs (AOD) programs. In fact, the acronym AOD exists primarily in higher-education institutions, adopted to communicate that alcohol is, indeed, a drug.

The name G. Alan Marlatt is not well known to the majority of people, but to those who work in substance abuse prevention and treatment, he is among the most influential researchers and innovators in the history of the field. Marlatt defined and led a shift in the way we conceptualize and intervene with substance use behaviors. His work loosened the bonds that limited options available to those struggling with chemical-use problems and the professionals helping them.

Marlatt played a prominent role in bringing the still-controversial concept of *harm reduction* into the chemical-dependency treatment discussion. This model was first conceived in the early 1980s in Amsterdam and discovered by Marlatt while there on sabbatical.[37] The Dutch had chosen to deviate from the prevailing American modalities of treatment, predicated on the standard that all addicted persons must embrace total, sustained abstinence for treatment to be effective. Such treatments embraced the Medical Model, which defined addiction as an incurable, chronic, and progressive disease where any attempts to consume the drug would lead to a complete relapse.[38] Marlatt was heavily criticized, and some in the 12-step community accused him of endangering recovering alcoholics by giving them false hope of returning to controlled, safe drinking (which a small percentage do). Marlatt was never in disagreement that most individuals who are dependent on alcohol should refrain from drinking. Where he differed was in the expectation that they must first achieve abstinence before further treatment was offered. He saw this as excluding many people who might otherwise be engaged in a process of substance abuse therapy, with abstinence optimistically being the goal, not the prerequisite. Marlatt's book with Judith Gordon, *Relapse Prevention: Maintenance Strategies in the Treatment of Addictive Behaviors* (1985), was the culmination of the harm-reduction model he had been developing.[39] It proposes a framework of cognitive-behavioral strategies to help individuals preserve established cessation of addictive behaviors. *Relapse Prevention* also introduced terms such as *lapse, relapse, triggers,* and *high-risk situations* into the lexicon of intervention and treatment providers.

While at the University of Washington, the tragic death of a student who fell off a balcony during a party deeply affected Marlatt. It was found post-mortem that the student had a blood-alcohol level of .26—three times the legal limit and at a point when most people have difficulty walking and talking. What additionally caught Marlatt's attention was information from the student's family and friends that he was not much of a partier in high school. This extreme level of drinking was acquired in college. From this terrible event, he—along with Linda Dimeff, John Baer, and Daniel Kivlahan—developed a program they named the Brief Alcohol Screening and Intervention for College Students (BASICS).[40] BASICS provides a foundational model for how institutions of higher education tackle the problem of substance use prevention. A harm-reduction intervention, it does not just try to lower alcohol use but focuses on reducing risky behaviors and harmful effects associated with college students' alcohol consumption. BASICS is comprised of two interviews. The first interview follows a self-report questionnaire about a student's drinking patterns, amounts, behaviors, and beliefs about his or her alcohol use. The second interview occurs a week later, where the interviewer provides the student with feedback about his or her use; this includes a comparison with actual data on prevalence of student use, associated health consequences, and ways to decrease these risks. Since its inception, BASICS has become the gold standard for collegiate alcohol prevention and intervention programming. Many higher-education institutions, from large state universities to small liberal arts schools, employ this tool in their work with students presenting at risk for alcohol-use problems. It is adaptable, relatively user friendly, and evidence-based; the latter quality being essential—even a buzzword—to the culture of higher education.

With the coming of the new millennium, alcohol continued to be the targeted drug for prevention efforts on college campuses partly in response to the release of the critical publication *A Call to Action: Changing the Culture of Drinking at U.S. Colleges.*[41] This publication was the product of a task force established by the National Institute on Alcohol Abuse and Alcoholism (NIAAA) and served as a clarion sound, rallying universities to improve their prevention and intervention efforts to decrease rampant alcohol use by college students. It highlighted how dismally universities had been performing in meeting federal funding requirements. The data in *A Call to Action* demonstrated that alcohol use by college students, especially episodes of binge drinking, had reached near epidemic proportions. National surveys showed 40% of students had engaged in this behavior.[42]

In response, university prevention and intervention programs proliferated. Between 1998 and 2008, those deemed "model programs" were awarded $3.5 million by the federal government.[43] These programs employ an array of methods and demonstrate effective assessment procedures illustrating outcomes. Data collection via surveys such as those developed by the CORE Institute[44] and National College Health Assessment (NCHA)[45] are used, as are screening and intervention tools such as BASICS[46] and Alcohol EDU,[47] the latter serving as a primary prevention instrument usually given to incoming freshman. Other standard campus programs include alcohol-free, alternative social activities; other types of "social norm" media campaigns; targeting high-risk populations such as fraternities, sororities, and athletes; community-focused efforts such as server guidelines, alcohol promotional bans on campus, and safe driver programs.

Sadly, while the aforementioned prevention initiatives have shown promise of effectiveness, recent surveys show no evidence that prevention efforts have resulted in an overall decrease of drinking on campus.[48] The binge-drinking rate among college students has hovered around 40% for over a decade now and with few signs in the future of any dramatic shifts. Some universities have even begun to move on from financing their prevention programs, as the cost-to-benefit analyses show that sustaining such efforts are no longer feasible.[49] In doing so, these institutions dare the Department of Education to enforce the Drug-Free School and Communities mandate, wagering their eligibility for federal funding. Whether this trend continues and universities sufficiently fund their prevention programs, cut them, or allow them to wither slowly on the vines remains to be seen.

College Cannabis Use Prevention

College-based research on prevention specifically targeting cannabis use has been emerging since the start of the new millennium.[50] Program components vary by university, but most campuses utilize the following methods: distributing flyers, brochures, and other educational materials; peer education; curriculum inclusion; policy review; drug-free activities and administrative interventions; and a variety of substance abuse awareness events. As with alcohol, a dominant focus of educational components in collegiate cannabis prevention has become changing perceived social norms. This strategy involves altering students' misconceptions of the prevalence, frequency, and intensity of other students' marijuana use. The viability for this was highlighted in 2005, when Jason Kilmer, Christine Lee, et al. at Evergreen State University surveyed student marijuana use and their perceptions of use by other students.[51] What they discovered was that over two-thirds (67.4%) of those surveyed denied using cannabis. Despite this rate of use, a remarkable 98% of those polled believed that college "students in general" use marijuana at least once per year. This misperception is attributed to an erroneous generalization of perceived peer drug use to that of the larger population.

Screening and assessment tools for substance use have become big business. At prevention-themed conferences, the gauntlet of tables manned by industry representatives will assuredly include a couple advertising their screening product. Screening is an initial identification that a person is at risk. Assessment tools evaluate the level of risk and severity of the problem and may even provide information recommending treatment options. There are a variety of instruments for cannabis available to prevention specialists, with a smaller number appropriate for college students. This subgroup would include, but is not limited to, the Cannabis Use Disorder Identification Test (CUDIT-R);[52] the Cannabis Use Problems Identification Test (CUPIT);[53] the Cannabis Abuse Screening Test (CAST);[54] the Marijuana eCHECKUP TO GO (formerly e-TOKE);[55] and the Severity of Dependence Scale: Cannabis (SDS).[56] The CUDIT, an evidenced-based screening tool, was adapted from the Alcohol Use Disorder Identification Test (AUDIT) and revised in 2010.[57] It contains eight items, such as questioning how often the student has used in the past six months, how often there has been an inability to stop use once started, perceived consequences following use such as diminished concentration or memory, and impaired role performance. Although similar, the CUPIT has twice as many items and focuses more on a respondent's subjective experiences of the use. A major downside for use within university clinics is that since it is more comprehensive, it is less quick and easy to administer.

Among the screening instruments listed above, only the eCHECKUP TO GO provides an online intervention component coupled with personalized feedback that attempts to reshape students' drug use perceptions and attitudes.[58] This feedback is based on "social norming" by comparing students' personal responses with a large database of responses from students throughout the country. It also includes some educational items about potential risks of marijuana based on how students responded to certain questions. Marijuana e-CHECKUP TO GO acknowledges that education about cannabis alone is insufficient to change behavior, and therefore also incorporates motivational enhancement strategies. It guides participants to identify their own personal motivators and tailors feedback to these motivations. It can be used in conjunction with other programs that have also been developed to address collegiate cannabis violations. The use of online tools has increased with the recognition of how much time college students spend on the internet and social media. According to one study, college students spend 60% of the day or 14.4 hours daily interacting with technology.[59]

Researchers at the University of Washington, including Jason Kilmer, have further studied the potential of employing a web-based brief intervention model with high-risk college students.[60] This is just another example of the growing emphasis on developing online capabilities and using social media to communicate prevention education and implement intervention programs targeting students acculturated to this technology. Dr. Kilmer had previously worked with Alan Marlatt focusing primarily on alcohol studies. Dr. Kilmer along with Dr. Christine Lee and their colleagues have been at the forefront of research on marijuana prevention and intervention strategies for college students. In 2010, they developed a brief web-based motivational enhancement intervention that showed promise with those students considering change in their marijuana use or who came from families with reported drug-use histories. Kilmer, Lee, and colleagues were sufficiently encouraged by the results to try again—this time including a test group with an in-person, individualized intervention. At a three-month follow-up, they saw significant reductions—not in the number of days that marijuana was used, but in the amounts used. Unfortunately, at a six-month follow-up, these effects had waned.[61] In an interview for this book, Dr. Kilmer proposed that future research could include extended multi-session interventions, although single-session interventions had shown more success. He also noted that the academic calendar itself was an unavoidable reality in evaluating the effects of any college-based intervention since schools may be going into summer break at six-month follow-up, reflecting an interruption of patterns of use by students during the previous academic terms.

Other variables related to the structure of collegiate life along with unpredictable student characteristics make research and intervention with this population challenging. We can also see how any tool is only as effective as the person wielding it. Most intervention instruments for marijuana used in universities involve a prevention specialist or trained graduate student initially meeting with the student to take personal information and a history of substance use and to provide an orientation to the procedure. Next comes the actual screening, later followed by a personalized feedback session with the student to review the results of the screening. Another important component, not extractable from any toolkit, is the establishment of rapport—the cultivation of a sense of trust between the student and the staff person. However, rapport can be difficult to achieve due to the circumstances of the meeting itself. Few students voluntarily seek screening to discover whether they have a dependency on marijuana. Those who believe they do generally seek counseling directly, yet this could change with the increased availability of convenient, anonymous online screening tools. In general, the majority of these encounters are the result of some sort of violation of student conduct; the initial meeting is set up as adversarial from the start. The prevention person is faced with the difficult task of trying to achieve some buy-in to the screening from mandated clients who may consider the entire process noxious, pointless, and further evidence of unjust laws intruding into their lives. And there are usually only one or two sessions to accomplish this kind of investment from the student. Such a scenario highlights only some of the problems prevention personnel at colleges encounter with this student population.

There can be a very real distinction between those students presenting with marijuana violations and those referred for alcohol-related infractions. Apart from underage drinking tickets, those students charged with violations to student conduct codes are there because of behaviors associated with their drunkenness. These situations could be emergency room transports, disturbing the peace, destruction of university property, or physical altercations. Many students feel embarrassed based on their own values—they know they messed up and may bring to the meetings a level of humility, even remorse. They may already be contemplating changes in their drinking and can be open to new information. This is less so in the case with students charged with violations due to marijuana use. Their behaviors under the influence (except for DUIs) are usually not at issue. They may have been caught by a residence hall assistant who spied the bong in their rooms. Perhaps someone complained to campus police because of the smell of marijuana wafting down the hall. Some are nabbed by officers, who come to the floor due to complaints of raucous behavior by others in the dormitory, only to notice the unmistakable aroma of burning weed. These students may not see themselves as doing wrong; they see themselves as victims.

Those who work in university alcohol and other drug prevention must cultivate methods to engage these students to have any hope of affecting positive results. Elizabeth M. (real name kept confidential) provided marijuana screenings and interventions at a state university and claims she honed her skills primarily through sheer experience. A believer in the *Transtheoretical Model of Change*,[62] she explains that she would spend her first session with referred students getting to know them and taking a history of their relationship with marijuana, all the while assessing their present stage of change. Using this model as a framework, students might come to her in the *precontemplative* stage and not yet be considering modification to their marijuana use.[63] Students in the *contemplative* stage are already thinking about altering their use. In some cases, those students may have already progressed to the point where they enacted a significant change prior to the initial meeting. Knowing what stage each student is in guides Elizabeth in how to proceed with the interview. Elizabeth describes spending time trying to defuse any pre-existing fears or biases about the meeting: "I like to ask them questions about their relationship with marijuana. I will ask them what they like about it, for instance." She finds that those students who use marijuana the most are usually the most defensive. "Students already know most of the information we are trying to share with them," adding that some of the research available to prevention specialists seems out-of-date. She admits that this can make the intervention difficult: "I feel like I'm trying to sell it." Instead, she reframes what she does as encouraging students to be "informed consumers." She recommends that they read *all* sides of the marijuana debate. "I want them to challenge what they read."

Darrel Kirby, an alcohol and other drug specialist at the University of Iowa, sees it similarly: "I have found that acknowledging the benefits of marijuana use and avoiding discussion of marijuana as 'good or bad' allows students to open up to considering or acknowledging the problems created by use." Kirby encourages students to recognize when use is helpful and when it is not. "Students respond very well to the discussion of using to avoid the natural pain and discomfort of life. Most students have awareness that the benefits of smoking to avoid pain is temporary and they are faced with the same discomfort once the high is over." Kirby also believes it is helpful to know how to approach the student who insists marijuana is not addictive. "I like to have the conversation about social versus psychological dependence, or emotional versus physiological dependence, and not get caught up in the debate of whether it is or is not addictive. This allows for a discussion of how far would one go to acquire marijuana and how much would one be willing to give up to continue using. Another approach I find helpful is to review what matters to students, what they hope to achieve and whether marijuana use is helping them get there or not. We find few examples in pop culture where marijuana use is presented as the key to goal achievement." According to Kirby, the majority of students he sees will recognize that marijuana use serves as a barrier to goal achievement, either in decreasing motivation or in creating conflict with parents, significant others, school, or the law. With all this said, some students report trying marijuana and having no desire to use ever again. Some students will smoke on occasion if it is made available, and other students use it to wake up and go to bed, insisting is solves many of life's problems.

Jason Kilmer also acknowledges the importance of engaging students by inquiring what they like about marijuana. But he emphasizes the importance of thoroughly asking students what they like *less* about it, which is an essential part of making the intervention effective. Another colleague in the field observed that at times interviewers would abbreviate this "not-so-good" list, often by asking questions in a way that ended discussion prematurely (e.g., "anything else?"). To remedy this, student responses need to be followed by directive inquiry (e.g., "what else?") resulting in students identifying and acknowledging more negative associations, heightening their ambivalence about drug use.

Not everyone doing prevention work with college students has found the work to be adversarial. Dr. Chris Edwards at the University of Puget Sound has been pleasantly surprised with how positive their screening and interventions have been.

> We do pre and post questionnaires for our Decrease Your Risk program, and students have an overwhelmingly positive experience. They report that going through student conduct maybe wasn't so great, and feel [the intervention] is punitive, rather than educational, but after meeting with myself or one of the interns, after going through the 90-minute workshop and the class, they left with a greater understanding of their relationship to marijuana, of those motivations and positive expectancies . . . that was very much in opposition to my assumptions going into this role that it would be very adversarial, that I would get a lot of push back and defensiveness. Over the last four years there has been openness to having the conversation or opening the dialogue . . . over that period of an hour, those students shifting their perspective and recognizing that harm reduction doesn't necessarily mean we're trying to manipulate them into not using. Maybe that's the goal of Res Life or Student Conduct, because they are in violation of school policy. But my role and the person who is meeting with them is to really have them, with a critical lens, look at these patterns of behavior and understand that marijuana is much bigger than smoking a joint, talking about concentrates and dabbing, and integrate up-to-date research and they see that as credible.

Dr. Edwards states that they can find a delicate balance—maintaining a positive discourse while providing a consistent message that marijuana can be addictive and harmful.

> We have the 'Hashing Out the Truth' campaign to help articulate that. And at the same time, we . . . address that, yes, there is evolving research to support use of medical marijuana for certain individuals for certain conditions. We don't sweep that under the rug or

downplay that. We highlight those students who abstain and use data from the Core Survey[64] and we'll be doing the Healthy Minds study [collegiate web-based survey examining mental health and related issues][65] this coming year to look at any changes in perception. But at least from a student perspective . . . it's refreshing. I don't know if it's because it's unique to their contacts with our counseling center or medical providers or if that is starting to expand across campus. If they have questions like, 'my roommate said it is helpful for anxiety and sleep'; [we are] able to correct those misperceptions.

In efforts at cannabis harm reduction, educational interventions such as "Hashing Out the Truth" still convey the potential for unhealthy consequences and can include information on different THC levels of various cannabis products and results based on method of use. Dr. Edwards often refers students to local resources or to "learnaboutmarijuanawa.org,"[66] a website facilitated by the Alcohol and Drug Abuse Institute at the University of Washington. There, students who are thinking he is emphasizing only the downsides of marijuana can get additional research-based information. The website itself is comprehensive in its inclusion of marijuana and other drug-related topics, and, although the overall tenor lists toward abstinence, it attempts balance by including information about the medicinal possibilities of cannabis.

––––––

While substance abuse prevention has roots in medicine and public health, it was later grafted to a government policy that sought to criminalize away drug use. In this relatively new field, prevention practitioners have largely had to create many of their own science and methods. Although they borrowed appropriate principles and methods from the medical and scientific fields, not all this groundwork has been proven applicable and effective. Overall, primary and secondary substance use prevention works best with children and adolescents—the goal being to reduce environmental, behavioral, and social risk factors to later use and intervening with those children and youth who start exhibiting related signs. Collegiate prevention and intervention is beginning to reap results, some promising, but has not yet found the main artery of its effectiveness.

Notes

1 Erikson, E. (1968). *Identity: Youth and crisis*. New York, NY: W. W. Norton & Company.
2 *Merriam-Webster's collegiate dictionary*(10th ed.). (1999). Springfield, MA: Merriam-Webster Incorporated.
3 Nyberg, H. (1992). Religious use of hallucinogenic fungi: A comparison between Siberian and Mesoamerican cultures. *Karstenia*, 32, 71–80. Retrieved from www. samorini.it/doc1/alt_aut/lr/nyberg-religious-use-of-hallucinogenic-fungi.pdf

4 Nahas, G. G. (1982). Hashish in Islam 9th to 18th century. *Bulletin of the New York Academy of Medicine, 58*(9), 814–831. Retrieved from www.ncbi. nlm.nih.gov/pmc/articles/PMC1805385/?page=11

5 Tahir, M. A. (2009). Surah Al Baqarah (2:219). *The miraculous Quran.* Retrieved from http://miraculousquran.blogspot.com/2009/08/surah-al-baqarah-2219-wisdom-behind.html

6 Booth, M. (2003). *Cannabis: A history.* New York, NY: St. Martin's Press.

7 Behr, E. (1996). *Prohibition: Thirteen years that changed America.* New York, NY: Arcade Publishing, Inc.

8 Sayre, J. (1997, February). Temperance movement had roots in Shelby County, Ohio. *Shelby County Historical Society.* Retrieved from www.shelby countyhistory.org/schs/archives/women/cnationwomena.htm

9 Hirliman, G. (Producer), & Gasnier, L. J. (Director). (1936). *Reefer madness.* [Motion picture]. United States: National CineMedia/Fathom. Retrieved from http://publicdomainreview.org/collections/reefer-madness-1938/

10 Lindsey, V. V. (2003). Primary, secondary and tertiary youth prevention programs. *Journal of Addictive Disorders.* Retrieved from http://m.breining.edu/jad03vl.pdf

11 Kannel, W. B., Dawber, T. R., Kagan, A., Revotskie, N., & Stokes, J. (1961). Factors of risk in the development of coronary heart disease—six year follow-up experience. The Framingham Study. *Annals of Internal Medicine, 55,* 33–50. doi:10.7326/0003-4819-55-1-33

12 Cowen, E. L., & Work, W. C. (1988). Resilient children, psychological wellness and primary prevention. *American Journal of Community Psychology, 16*(4), 591–607. doi:10.1007/BF00922773

13 Hawkins, J. D., Catalano, R. F., & Miller, J. Y. (1992). Risk and protective factors for alcohol and other drug problems in adolescence and early adulthood: Implications for substance abuse prevention. *Psychological Bulletin, 112*(1), 64–105. Retrieved from https://cre8tiveyouthink.files.wordpress. com/2011/12/social-developmental-prevention-and-yd.pdf

14 Cowen & Work 591–607.

15 Johnston, L. (1971). *Drugs and American youth.* Ann Arbor, MI: Institute for Social Research, University of Michigan. Retrieved from http://doi.apa.org/record/1973-31126-000

16 Rosegrant, S. (2013, May 14). The origins of monitoring the future. *Institute for Social Research*, University of Michigan. Retrieved from http://home.isr. umich.edu/sampler/the-origins-of-monitoring-the-future/

17 National Institute of Drug Abuse. (2013, May 14). *NIDA info facts: High school and youth trends.* Retrieved from www.drugabuse.gov/sites/default/files/drugfactsmtf.pdf

18 Botvin, G. J. (1996). Substance abuse prevention through life skills training. In R. D. Peters & R. J. McMahon (Eds.), *Preventing childhood disorders, substance abuse, and delinquency* (pp. 215–240). Thousand Oaks, CA: Sage Publications. doi:http://dx.doi.org/10.4135/9781483327679.n10

19 Swisher, J. D., & Hoffman, A. (1975). Information: The irrelevant variable in drug education. In B. W. Corder, R. A. Smith & J. D. Swisher (Eds.), *Drug abuse prevention: Perspectives and approaches for educators* (pp. 49–62). Dubuque, IA: Brown.

20 Hansen, W. B., & McNeal, R. B. (1996). The law of maximum expected potential effect: Constraints placed on program effectiveness by mediator relationships. *Health Education Research, 11*(4), 501–507. Retrieved from https://academic.oup.com/her/article-pdf/11/4/501/1693716/11-4-501.pdf

21 Bensley, L. S., & Wu, R. (1991). The role of psychological reactance in drinking following alcohol prevention messages [Abstract]. *Journal of Applied Social Psychology, 21*(13), 1111–1124. doi:10.1111/j.1559-1816.1991.tb00461.x/abstract

22 Botvin, G. J. (n.d.). *Preventing drug abuse through the schools: Intervention programs that work.* National Conference on Drug Abuse Prevention Research, NIDA Archives. Retrieved from https://archives.drugabuse.gov/meetings/CODA/Schools.html

23 Botvin, G., & Griffin, K. (2004). Empirical findings and future directions. *The Journal of Primary Prevention, 25*(2), 216–217. Retrieved from www.researchgate.net/profile/Gilbert_Botvin/publication/226086316_Life_Skills_Training_ Empirical-Findings-and-Future-Directions.pdf

24 Griffin, K. W., & Botvin, G. J. (2010). Evidence-based interventions for preventing substance use disorders in adolescents. *Child and Adolescent Psychiatric Clinics of North America, 19*(3), 505–526. http://doi.org/10.1016/j.chc.2010.03.005

25 Compton, J., Jackson, B., & Dimmock, J. A. (2016). Persuading others to avoid persuasion: Inoculation theory and resistant health attitudes. *Frontiers in Psychology, 7*, 122. http://doi.org/10.3389/fpsyg.2016.00122

26 Blake, B. (2016, March 11). Nancy Reagan's 'Just say no' campaign helped halve number of teens on drugs. *Hudson Institute.* Retrieved from www.hudson.org/research/12306-nancy-reagan-s-just-say-no-campaign-helped-halve-number-of-teens-on-drugs

27 Wooley, J., & Peters, G. (2017). Ronald Reagan: Address before a joint session of congress on the State of the Union, January 25, 1988. *The American Presidency Project.* Retrieved from www.presidency.ucsb.edu/ws/?pid=36035

28 Hutchinson, S. (2015, August 19). How the F.B.I. made 'winners don't use drugs' the arcade motto of the '90s. *Inverse.* Retrieved from www.inverse.com/article/5193-how-the-f-b-i-made-winners-don-t-use-drugs-the-arcade-motto-of-the-90s

29 Ostrow, R. J. (1990, September 6). Casual drug users should be shot, Gates says. *Los Angeles Times.* Retrieved from http://articles.latimes.com/1990-09-06/news/mn-983_1_casual-drug-users

30 Berman, G. (2009). Lessons from the battle over D.A.R.E.: The complicated relationship between research and practice. *Center for Court Innovation.* Retrieved from www.courtinnovation.org/sites/default/files/DARE.pdf

31 Nordrum, A. (2014, September 10). The new D.A.R.E program—this one works. *Scientific American.* Retrieved from www.scientificamerican.com/article/the-new-d-a-r-e-program-this-one-works/

32 National registry of evidence-based programs and practices. (2016, January 7). *Substance Abuse and Mental Health Services Administration.* Retrieved from www.samhsa.gov/nrepp

33 Pennsylvania State University. (n.d.). *"Keepin' it REAL" curriculum.* Retrieved from www.kir.psu.edu/about.shtml

34 Drug facts: Lessons from prevention research. (2014). *NIDA Notes.* Retrieved from www.drugabuse.gov/publications/drugfacts/lessons-prevention-research

35 Straus, R., & Bacon, S. D. (1953). *Drinking in college.* New Haven, CT: Yale University Press.

36 Kraft, D. P. (1984). A comprehensive prevention program for college students. In P. M. Miller & T. D. Nirenberg (Eds.), *Prevention of alcohol abuse* (pp. 327–369). New York, NY: Plenum Press. Retrieved from https://link.springer.com/chapter/10.1007%2F978-1-4613-2657-1_17#page-1

37 Yalom, V., & Aponte, R. (Interviewers), & Marlatt, A. (Interviewee). (2011). *Alan Marlatt on harm reduction therapy.* [Interview transcript]. Retrieved from Psychotherapy.net. Web site: www.psychotherapy.net/interview/marlatt-harm-reduction

38 Kraft 327–369.

39 Marlatt, G., & Gordon, J. R. (Eds.). (1985). *Relapse prevention: Maintenance strategies in the treatment of addictive behaviors.* New York, NY: Guilford Press.

40 Dimeff, L. A., Baer, J. S., Kivlahan, D. R., & Marlatt, G. (1999). *Brief alcohol screening and intervention for college students (BASICS): A harm reduction approach.* New York, NY: Guilford Press.

41 National Institute on Alcohol Abuse and Alcoholism (NIAAA). (2002). *A call to action: Changing the culture of drinking at U.S. colleges* (NIH Pub. No. 02–5010). Bethesda, MD: Author. Retrieved from https://pubs.niaaa.nih.gov/publications/aa58.htm

42 Faden, V. B., Corey, K., & Baskin, M. (2009). An evaluation of college online alcohol-policy information: 2007 compared with 2002. *Journal of Studies on Alcohol and Drugs* (Supplement, 16), 28–33. Retrieved from www.ncbi.nlm.nih.gov/pmc/articles/PMC2701094/

43 Office of Safe and Drug-Free Schools. (2008). *Alcohol and other drug prevention on college campuses: Model programs.* Washington, DC: Department of Education. Retrieved from www.alcoholeducationproject.org/DOEModel Programs2008.pdf

44 *Core Institute* (2017, August 25). Southern Illinois University. Retrieved from http://core.siu.edu

45 American College Health Association. (2014). *National College Health assessment.* Retrieved from www.acha-ncha.org/overview.html

46 Marlatt & Gordon (1985)

47 Everfi. (2017). Retrieved from https://everfi.com/higher-education-old/alcoholedu/

48 Substance Abuse and Mental Health Services Administration. (2014). *Results from the 2013 national survey on drug use and health: Summary of national findings* (NSDUH Series H-48, HHS Publication No. (SMA) 14–4863). Rockville, MD: Author. Retrieved from www.samhsa.gov/data/sites/default/files/NSDUHresultsPDFWHTML2013/Web/NSDUHresults2013.pdf

49 McMurtrie, B. (2014, December 14). Why colleges haven't stopped binge drinking. *The Chronicle of Higher Education.* Retrieved from www.nytimes.com/2014/12/15/us/why-colleges-havent-stopped-binge-drinking.html

50 Larimer, M. E., Kilmer, J. R., & Lee, C. M. (2005). College student drug prevention: A review of individually-oriented prevention strategies. *Journal of Drug Issues, 35*(2), 431–456. doi:https://doi.org/10.1177/002204260503500210

51 Kilmer, J. R., Walker, D. D., Lee, C. M., Palmer, R. S., Mallett, K. A., Fabiano, P., & Larimer, M. E. (2006). Misperceptions of college student marijuana use: Implications for prevention [Abstract]. *Journal of Studies on Alcohol, 67*(2), 277–281. Retrieved from www.ncbi.nlm.nih.gov/pubmed/16562410

52 Adamson S. J., Kay-Lambkin F. J., Baker A. L., Lewin T. J., Thornton L., Kelly B. J., & Sellman, J. D. (2010). An improved brief measure of cannabis misuse: The Cannabis Use Disorders Identification Test—Revised (CUDIT-R). *Drug and Alcohol Dependence, 110*(1–2), 137–143. doi:10.1016/j.drugalcdep.2010.02.017

53 Bashford, J., Flett, R., & Copeland, J. (2010), The Cannabis Use Problems Identification Test (CUPIT): Development, reliability, concurrent and

predictive validity among adolescents and adults [Abstract]. *Addiction*, *105*(4), 615–625. doi:10.1111/j.1360-0443.2009.02859.x

54 Legleye, S., Guignard, R., Richard, J-B., Kraus, L., Pabst, A., & Beck, F. (2015). Properties of the Cannabis Abuse Screening Test (CAST) in the general population [Abstract]. *International Journal of Methods in Psychiatric Research*, *24*(2), 170–183. doi:10.1002/mpr.1465

55 San Diego State University, Research Foundation (N.D.). *Marijuana eCHECK UP TO GO research*. Retrieved from www.echeckuptogo.com/research/research-mj

56 Ferri, C. P., Marsden, J., De Araujo, M., Laranjeira, R. R., & Gossop, M. (2000). Validity and reliability of the Severity of Dependence Scale (SDS) in a Brazilian sample of drug users [Abstract]. *Drug and Alcohol Review*, *19*(4), 451–455. doi:10.1080/713659418

57 Kilmer, Walker, Lee, Palmer, Mallett, Fabiano, & Larimer 277–281.

58 Legleye, Guignard, Richard, Kraus, Pabst, & Beck 170–183.

59 Fiala, A. (2013, June 28). How much time do college students spend with technology? *Research That Drives Results*. Retrieved from https://researchresults.wordpress.com/2013/06/28/how-much-time-do-college-students-spend-with-technology/

60 Lee, C. M., Neighbors, C., Kilmer, J. R., & Larimer, M. E. (2010). A brief, web-based personalized feedback selective intervention for college student marijuana use: A randomized clinical trial. *Psychology of Addictive Behaviors*, *24*(2), 265–273. http://doi.org/10.1037/a0018859

61 Lee, C. M., Kilmer, J. R., Neighbors, C., Atkins, D. C., Zheng, C., Walker, D. D., & Larimer, M. E. (2013). Indicated prevention for college student marijuana use: A randomized controlled trial. *Journal of Consulting and Clinical Psychology*, *81*(4), 702–709. http://doi.org/10.1037/a0033285

62 Prochaska, J., & DiClemente, C. (1983). Stages and processes of self-change of smoking: Toward an integrative model of change. *Journal of Consulting and Clinical Psychology*, *51*(3), 390–395. Retrieved from http://old.sfu.ac.at/data//Skripten_Batthyany/Stages%20and%20Processes%20of%20self%20change%20of%20Smoking.pdf

63 Lee, Kilmer, Neighbors, Atkins, Zheng, Walker, & Larimer 702–709.

64 Office of Safe and Drug-Free Schools (2008).

65 Healthy Minds Network. (2017). Retrieved from http://healthymindsnetwork.org/research/hms

66 Alcohol and Drug Abuse Institute, The University of Washington. (2016). *Learn about marijuana: Science-based information for the public*. Retrieved from http://learnaboutmarijuanawa.org/

Chapter 10

Cannabis Use Treatment

In a 2014 NBC interview about the opioid epidemic ravaging this country, Thomas McLellan, Ph.D., founder of the Treatment Research Institute who developed the popular Addiction Severity Index (ASI), momentarily shared a glimpse of his personal pain as father of a child lost to addiction.[1] Over seven years before that interview, he was already embroiled in his oldest son's battle with cocaine addiction, when he received the call that is many parents' nightmare: his youngest son had just died from an overdose of alcohol and sedative medication. During this tragic chapter in his family's life, he, a world-renowned expert in addictions, learned what many other parents already knew—that finding good treatment for drug abuse is not only difficult but seemingly impossible. "If I don't know," he states in the interview, "nobody else knows. Where does a teacher turn? How about a truck driver? A cop?"

Despite a vast amount of research suggesting what does and does not work in the treatment of substance use disorders, the available treatment options appear limited. Many of these are 28-day or less programs steeped in a 75-year-old philosophy born of Prohibition-era alcoholism. And that is if someone can afford it, as insurance plans usually will not fully cover that level of care, resulting in out-of-pocket costs totaling thousands of dollars. Additionally, the threshold for what insurance plans deem as a "medical necessity" requires patients to be extremely sick to qualify. This severity of illness precipitates high relapse rates within a year of discharge and to overall poor outcomes, further hiking up treatment costs long-term.

A Rapidly Growing Demand

Only recently has it become a necessity for universities to provide resources for treatment, as the increased demand for substance abuse and mental health services have college counseling centers pushed to the edge of their resources. In a 2010 survey, the American College Counseling

Association found that 44% of the students presenting at counseling centers had severe psychiatric problems, almost three times that in 2000.[2] Several reasons for this are possible. One is simply that more students are attending college; overall enrollment increased 32% from 2001 to 2011, according to the National Center for Education Statistics.[3] Another explanation is that more students are on psychotropic medications such as antidepressants, mood stabilizers, and even antipsychotics; some of them are coming in as freshman taking these medications. From 1994 to 2006, the percentage of students treated at college counseling centers who were using antidepressants nearly tripled, from 9% to over 23%.[4] In previous generations, these students may not have been able to attend college due to the disabling nature of their conditions.

What has become apparent is that marijuana use by treatment-seeking students is associated with other psychiatric problems, academic performance, frequency of use, age, and employment issues.[5] Most universities refer students needing substance abuse programming to outside agencies and licensed counselors, if they are accessible. Urban-based colleges have a larger pool of referrals for students requiring substance abuse outpatient therapy or more intensive levels-of-care. Schools in less populous areas have a more difficult challenge, as do extremely under-funded community colleges.

Some schools have developed partnerships with chemical dependency programs as a way of ensuring that their students have access to such care. Close working relationships between schools and treatment facilities allow students to receive needed services and return to school without suffering major interruption in their studies. Intensive outpatient programs offer many of the same services as inpatient rehabilitation facilities (e.g., individual, group and family counseling, medication management) but do it on an outpatient basis for three to four hours per session, three to five days/evenings per week. There are programs willing to accommodate college students' class schedules, but staffing and other problems make that difficult. Due to many factors like these, college students are far less likely to seek help than non-college attending young adults.[6] Even more problematically, there is evidence that students with marijuana use disorders may be particularly at risk for not seeking help.[7]

The inpatient-residential programs, or "rehab" that Amy Winehouse—poignantly, in retrospect—sang about, tend to be longer-term and involve the student having to withdraw from school to complete. They can offer an array of different treatments, but, like outpatient programs, most of what they provide is done in a group format. Making groups the primary modality is more cost-effective. Historically, substance abuse treatment pioneered groups earlier than the rest of the mental health field. Possible reasons for this include fewer trained staff and roots in Alcoholics

Anonymous (AA), Narcotics Anonymous (NA), and therapeutic community programs such as Synanon, Daytop, and Marathon House. In the more remote past, many residential programs employed counselors who were treatment graduates with no formal training, relying solely on their personal recovery journey.

The emphasis on the group as the *sine qua non* of programming can alienate college students because they find themselves in groups with older patients with addictions progressed to levels unimaginable to them. Plopping an 18-year-old who abuses alcohol and marijuana into a group with 40- and 50-year-old lifelong heroin addicts may be an eye-opener, but not necessarily a recipe for successful treatment. All effective group interventions require some degree of identification among its members. Additionally, such blending issues are often an obstruction to college students connecting well to AA or NA meetings. Seeking support from these groups is made even more challenging for students with primary cannabis use problems, as they do not fit neatly into either AA or NA culture.

Peer Support Groups

Bill Wilson—better known by his anonymous moniker Bill W.—did not bring down the 12-Steps of Alcoholics Anonymous etched in stone tablets from some mountaintop. The failed stockbroker and alcoholic drafted them after much input from others who were in the fledgling organization back in 1939. Bill W. along with Dr. Bob Smith, a proctologist who also suffered "under the cruel lash of John Barleycorn,"[89] are associated with the birth and growth of this now international establishment. In the treatment of substance use disorders, there may be nothing more universally prescribed or as perplexing to mental health professionals than the 80-year-old worldwide organization Alcoholics Anonymous. Many treatment providers still refer their substance-abusing clients to AA meetings despite knowing very little about the organization and even holding it with certain derision.

The reasons for this ambivalence are varied, but two stand out. First, insufficient consistency across AA meetings fails to instill confidence in providers, making it difficult for them to adequately prepare clients for what to expect. Meetings are comprised of aggregates of people from a wide socio-economic cross section, coming together, often irregularly, to listen and share about each other's problems with alcohol. There is no regularly assigned group leader or clinician, only rotating chairpersons. The only connective fibers between meetings are the 12 Steps of AA, along with the 12 Traditions—the latter outlining AA's lack of hierarchal structure and underscoring the program's foundations of anonymity and political non-affiliation.[10] Then there are all the different types of meetings: speaker meetings, Big Book meetings, step-discussion meetings, open and closed meetings, women's and men's meetings, gay and lesbian meetings . . . and a meeting can suddenly disappear as quickly as it materialized.

Somehow, despite its amorphous composition, AA has managed to grow to over 118,000 meetings worldwide, with an estimated membership of over two million people.[11] Vacationing in Kuala Lumpur and in recovery? No problem. One can choose from nine meetings, at least one every day—although two are Tamil-speaking groups. A recovering person does not even need to be on terra firma, as many cruise ships offer AA meetings onboard as respite from the alcohol-infused activities found throughout the vessel. Due to the sheer plurality and variations between meetings, mental health providers who are not part of the 12-step *cognoscenti* do not know what kind of group they are referring patients to or whether they might find a therapeutic connection to the group.

Second, the other major component of AA that remains problematic to mental health professionals is its spiritual core. In 12-step philosophy, the goal is to achieve a spiritual awakening where serenity can be achieved by removing the impediments of alcohol or drug use. This key feature is spelled out in the second and third steps:

> "Came to believe that a Power greater than ourselves could restore us to sanity."
>
> "Made a decision to turn our will and our lives over to the care of God as we understood Him."[12]

For the 12-step program to be effective, the alcohol user must develop a belief and a trust in a stronger and wiser force, then allow this other power to direct a large amount of life decisions. Members of AA explain that the steps are not commandments to be followed fundamentally; rather, it is the process of "doing" the steps that lends personal meaning to each of them. The concept of a higher power is not limited to believing in some patriarchal deity; for example, a higher power could be the collective wisdom of a group's members. While this may sound reasonable enough, many young adults who hold no firm religious beliefs or who have non-Christian backgrounds may find themselves standing in a circle hand-in-hand with others reciting the Lord's Prayer at the conclusion of the meeting.

When Bill W. was first constructing the 12 steps, he tried to make them as universal and palatable to as many people striving for sobriety as possible.[13] Despite his efforts to make AA applicable to a diverse population, its origins remain inescapable: it is the product of Christian, upper-middle-class, white males. Minority group participation in AA is mixed in terms of the regularity of attendance and level of involvement.[14] African Americans may attend only those meetings found in areas with a large black population, and more than with other ethnic groups, are less likely to believe that addiction is a disease, a basic tenant of 12-step philosophy.[15] Although Hispanics are less likely to attend AA meetings than their Caucasian counterparts, they demonstrate the same or even more involvement than whites when they do and gain the same benefits, such as sustained abstinence.[16] Regarding LGBTQ individuals, there is little to no research on how helpful 12-step groups are with this population, yet gay and lesbian meetings are not only available but listed as such in the meeting schedules.[17]

AA reports that about a third of the meeting attendees are women. Some critics claim that women who attend meetings are often subjected to being hit on by the male members.[18] Critics propose the first step's admission of powerlessness may run counter to the needs of recovering women—many of whom have low self-esteem, have experienced abuse and exploitation, and know all too well what it means to be powerless.[19] Contrary to this speculation, research suggests women who attend AA realize more benefits—such as longer, more stable periods of sobriety than male participants.[20]

Research has shown that regular attendance in 12-step support groups is associated with improvement in both substance abuse and mental illness symptoms.[21] This is important to consider given elevated comorbidity of psychiatric disorders with substance-use disorders—as many as six out of ten illicit drug users have co-occurring psychiatric problems, especially bipolar disorder and panic disorder with agoraphobia.[22] If support groups help with abstinence from destabilizing chemicals, then it would make sense that they would also improve psychiatric conditions. However, the difficulty lies in how often individuals with comorbid addiction and mental illness are actually referred to meetings. Those substance abuse patients with other psychiatric problems are less likely to be referred to 12-step meetings by their providers.[23] In addition to more consistent referral, professionals should have knowledge of local meetings cultures since a few groups embrace fundamentalist ideologies espousing "a drug is a drug is a drug" dogma and discourage participants from taking prescribed psychiatric medications.[24] One wonders what Bill W., who experimented with LSD as a treatment for alcoholism, might think about such an inflexible ethos.[25]

There have been numerous attempts to measure the effectiveness of 12-step based programs in controlled studies, but the results have been mixed. In project MATCH, a study funded by the National Institute of Alcohol Abuse and Alcoholism (NIAAA) in the mid-1990s, Twelve-Step Facilitated (TSF) treatment was studied along with Cognitive-Behavioral Therapy and Motivational Enhancement Therapy (a form of Motivational Interviewing, modified for the MATCH study) in the treatment of alcohol-use disorder, not to compare the relative effectiveness between them, but to match which therapy worked best for certain subgroup populations. The Twelve-Step Facilitation Approach included an initial 12-session program that incorporated much of the spiritual and medical model inherent in Alcoholics Anonymous, with a specific focus on the first five steps and meeting attendance outside of the programming.[26] Measurements, done at three-month intervals following treatment, showed that frequent AA meeting attendance was associated with higher reported abstinence.[27] One problem: participants in all three treatments attended AA meetings, and there was an even greater rate of attendance by those who participated in the CBT and MET groups. This may have been influenced by the fact that these other groups also attended inpatient programs prior to the study aftercare treatments and that these inpatient programs were heavily based in 12-step philosophy.[28] In another study on the long-term effects of 12-step groups, higher attendance—especially in the first year after seeking help—was associated with less alcohol problems at the one-year, eight-year, and 16-year intervals.[29]

In stark contrast, other meta-analyses fail to demonstrate the effectiveness of AA attendance or even show that AA has worse outcomes than receiving no treatment at all.[30] The inconsistency of these findings, especially when science cannot narrow down the mechanisms of change, continues to keep 12-step groups a confounding, yet useful component of substance use treatment. It seems to help when people attend (one of the slogans in AA is "it works if you work it!"), but we still do not know why.

It should come as no surprise that there is Marijuana Anonymous (MA), as there are 12-step based programs for a myriad of addictions, dependencies, and impulse-control problems. MA is based on AA architecture, and meetings began to pop up in several states (mostly in California) in 1986 to 1987. Many of the early members reported having difficulty identifying with others who attended AA and NA meetings, and they felt that theirs was seen as a "high-bottom" drug.[31] Marijuana Anonymous attendance is hampered by a lack of meetings available in many geographic areas. For example, there is only one MA meeting within a 100-mile radius from Boston, according to the website meeting finder.[32] However, MA seems to be making an effort to promote online meetings as a means of reaching more people.

There are other self-help support groups out there as an alternative to those 12-step based, some without a spiritual framework. However, none of them have proliferated to the point where they can be readily accessible to substance users at that often-fleeting moment when they become motivated to seek help. These include, but are not limited to:[33, 34]

- Self-Management and Recovery Training (SMART) Recovery
- Women for Sobriety

- Secular Organizations for Sobriety (SOS)
- LifeRing Secular Recovery
- Moderation Management
- Refuge Recovery
- Rational Recovery
- Celebrate Recovery

Motivational Interviewing: A Paradigm Shift

When it comes to counseling methods, there has been little research into those that work best with college students. Narrow that further to include those that work best with students with cannabis-use disorders, and that number is very small. Brief individual interventions utilizing Motivational Interviewing (MI) methods have yielded some encouraging initial results in reducing cannabis use in college students, following other studies that showed promising findings in older adults and adolescents.[35] Seemingly ubiquitous as of late, and applied in so many diverse areas of behavioral health, one might think MI was some brand new, cutting-edge therapy, when in fact it was developed by William Miller over 30 years ago.[36]

MI is a directive, client-centered counseling style for eliciting behavior change by helping clients to explore and resolve ambivalence. At its foundation is the premise that clients are responsible for change, not the counselor, whose role is to direct the clients to explore their *ambivalence* about their behavior, thus eventually finding their own motivation to change. Unlike Carl Rogers's client-centered approach, exploration is not the goal. Instead, MI counselors are directive through partnership in moving the client toward resolving ambivalence and thus motivating change.[37]

Miller began to formulate his theory while training at a veteran's hospital in Milwaukee, where he was first exposed to the problem of alcohol use disorders.[38] He described taking part in a study in which an experimental group of people with alcohol use disorder were given counseling compared to a self-help control group who was only given literature on staying sober. They found that the experimental group showed improvement in the amount and frequency of their alcohol use.[39] What he found fascinating, however, was that the control group did so as well and, in some cases, even better. Further explorations into this phenomenon eventually revealed that people who abuse alcohol respond positively when properly encouraged: "People have an impressive capacity to change when they think that they can."[40] This concept may not seem novel, but back in the 1970s substance abuse counseling was, as described by Miller, "pretty much in your face."[41] Treatment techniques were highly directive and even confrontational, while the goal was complete abstinence with a very limited number of pathways to achieve it. Dismissive platitudes such as "our way or the highway" or "you've tried it your way, now you need to do it our way," or the even more chilling "maybe you just need to go back out there and do some more research," could be commonly heard echoed by substance abuse program counselors of the time. To suggest that effective counseling would involve anything but a complete dismantling of the patient's "denial system" represented a major paradigm shift bordering on malpractice. MI was, at the time, revolutionary.

Miller and his co-investigators went even further. They next looked at differences between the effectiveness of different counselors. They viewed counselors who employed different styles, rating them on characteristics such as empathy and confrontation. The results clearly showed that the more confrontational a counselor was, the more the patient drank.[42] The greater the degree of expressed empathy and allowing patients to find their own reasons for change, the less drinking occurred. Miller explained empathy was not being able to completely identify with a patient's the emotional experience; this would imply that counselors had to be in recovery themselves. Rather, he described empathy similar to the therapy skill in Rogerian psychotherapy, "the ability to listen well to people, understand what they mean, and reflect it back to them in a way that helps them keep exploring."[43]

In Miller's experience, people with alcohol use disorders were not *resistant* to getting help. They did not like the consequences of their drinking either. Rather, they were highly *ambivalent* about what they thought, felt, and wanted to do about it. Prior to MI, aggressive, confrontational therapists would inadvertently replace the side of the patient arguing against substance use, leaving only the other side of the internal debate available—why they *did not* want to quit. This, in turn, was interpreted as resistance and denial by the counselor, leading to increased polarization and use of the therapeutic jackhammer. In that style of counseling, the method was the mechanism of change; in MI, the agent of change is the patient.

As Motivational Interviewing evolved, Miller, along with Stephen Rollnick and others, identified some of the mechanics of this therapy. They described an essential component for success they termed "change talk": verbal evidence that a patient was moving toward modifying unhealthy behaviors.[44] These are key phrases that indicate elements such as wanting to change, having confidence in ability, citing reasons, needs, and commitment. Cultivating "change talk" within session led to patients moving beyond ambivalence about substance use and into an action phase of change of their own choosing.[45]

The concept of helping patients move toward a goal other than complete, sustained abstinence was difficult for many counselors of that era to swallow. Many treatment centers at the time were steeped in what was and still is known as the "Disease Model" of alcoholism (or addiction). This model had a binary conceptualization of addiction as a distinct, chronic, and abnormal disease that you either had or not. It was genetically and biologically based: all other symptoms of the problem were projections of that physiologic essence. It was defined as a constitutional inability to stop drug use once it was initiated. It was progressive if left untreated and incurable. One could arrest the progression, but, like any other chronic condition, relapses could occur.[46]

As treatment programs emerged in the 1960s and 1970s, the disease model became synonymous with 12-step philosophy. While the Disease Model had some roots in Alcoholics Anonymous literature, these programs eventually adopted a hardline ideology over time and diverged from the more spiritual, inclusive core found in AA. On the other hand, Motivational Interviewing was falsely seen as antithetical to 12-step belief.[47] In fact, MI counselors should not be invested in whether or not their clients go to AA: the pathway to change is their client's choice alone.

This shift in the role of the counselor from being the prime agent of change leads to a question: does MI free professionals from the pitfalls of the "Is marijuana good or bad debate?" Further, is the absence of an abstinence-based outcome also advantageous in the therapeutic discussion? Let's take a look at Motivational Interviewing for cannabis use in action.

Bryce Crapser, a clinician at Eastern Connecticut State University, recalls his prevention work as a graduate assistant. They used a system modeled after BASICS that pulled from another program out of the United Kingdom named "Cutting Down on Marijuana." He took part in program evaluation, and what they found was that the students were being more intentional about marijuana, no longer passive users, and less prone to giving into cues from their peers. He adds that what students reported as being most helpful was the "honest, candid conversation" about cannabis.

In his present clinical role at the counseling center, Bryce finds that taking a MI approach is best with students whose cannabis use is problematic. He now sees an increasing number of students who are self-medicating mental illness (notably anxiety disorders) with marijuana, which is ultimately compounding the problem. Bryce states that among the biggest challenges he faces in working with marijuana-using students is the myth that it is not addictive. Another major challenge is that students are not forthcoming about how much and how often they use cannabis. He describes one such case where a student came to him complaining of panic attacks, reporting using marijuana once a week when he was really smoking daily. When he finally admitted to the extent of his use, he explained that he smoked to manage panic episodes. Postulating that his marijuana smoking use had become counterproductive, Bryce asked the student to try an experiment where he would not smoke for two weeks until their next session. The student returned as scheduled, reporting that it had "worked like a miracle," although the first week was tough. The student's panic attacks, previously experienced as seeming to come out of nowhere, became less frequent. Further, the student noticed the triggers of those he did have. Despite the robust benefits of abstaining from use, the client eventually returned to smoking on weekends, pointing to difficulty with abstinence-only approaches and the persistent nature of problems with cannabis.

According to Darrel Kirby at the University of Iowa, students who use marijuana regularly may have difficulty sitting with discomfort or pain. "Students often describe the benefit of using marijuana as taking the edge off. One student stated it well in describing marijuana use as 'dulling all the sharp edges of life.' Students who make the decision to quit will often have a period of general edginess as they adapt to feeling some of the normal discomfort of emotions, and possibly withdraw as THC slowly leaves their body. I see that students who started smoking early in their teens appear to have more difficulty accepting emotional distress."

In addition to anecdotal reports by professionals, do we know how people who stop or greatly reduce their marijuana use manage such success? Do we know the reasons that motivate them? In 2015, 119 Canadian adults with at least one year sustained remission of their cannabis use disorder were interviewed to find out their reasons and methods for change.[48] Multiple factors were assessed, including what percentage of participants embraced abstinence versus moderate use, and whether they sought professional treatment, self-help groups, or no treatment (a phenomenon more recently referred to as "natural recovery"). Within the sample, 68 reported abstaining entirely from marijuana, while 51 now only used moderately. Abstainers were older with more severe symptoms, had engaged in treatment more, and had endorsed using to help cope or for mind-expansion more than moderators. The reasons indicated for change were the same for both abstainers and moderators. The top three were that marijuana use was no longer compatible to them socially or individually (i.e., inconsistent with values and personal goals), or they had concerns about the impact it was having on their mental health. Moderators were more likely than abstainers to employ cognitive strategies such as weighing consequences and benefits, decrease time spent with using friends, pursue distracting behaviors, and avoid situations that might trigger use. The group that continued to use moderately reported having more cannabis-using friends in their social network. They were less likely to see marijuana as harmful than those who had stopped completely. Importantly, this study gave an initial glimpse into how professionals can more effectively match clients with compatible treatment strategies based on the severity of their problem. However, more research is needed to determine if these results are generalizable to women and diverse populations.

Toward Integrated Treatment

The treatment of students with cannabis use disorders largely takes place at the university counseling center. There is now a growing industry of substance abuse treatment centers that are competing with each other to create liaisons with universities for referrals. Such relationships enable the programs to coordinate transfers back to partner universities and their counseling centers to facilitate a seamless continuum of care. As a result, there is more programming at these substance abuse treatment centers specifically tailored to the needs of college students and young adults. Given high rates of comorbidity between substance use disorders and other psychiatric diagnoses, treatment programs are also increasingly offering full mental health evaluations and psychotropic medication management. This was not always the case, since many such programs were steeped in orthodox philosophies of chemical dependency treatment of years ago. They used to view the majority of psychiatric symptoms as caused by the addiction to the substance, not as an underlying disorder. A patient who became floridly psychotic would undoubtedly be referred to appropriate psychiatric care, but one with an anxiety disorder premorbid to the onset of substance use might be more likely be labeled as suffering from post-acute withdrawal syndrome. It takes a clinician experienced in both substance abuse and other mental health disorders to be able to tease out chemically induced symptoms from a pre-existing mental health condition.

Over the last decade, there has been more education around treatment for co-occurring disorders. A reason for the delay in this new, integrated approach to care can be attributed to the historical, philosophical, and financial divide between the fields of mental health and chemical dependency treatment. The mental health system in the United States is over a century old, emerging from a psychiatric hospital system that eventually transformed into a more community-based model.[49] On the other hand, chemical dependency treatment began to flourish in the early 1970s as a result of federal monies available through the establishment of the Special Action Office for Drug Abuse Prevention (SAODAP) under President Nixon.[50] Unfortunately, different streams of funding led to separate systems and a "siloing" of services. Research data on the considerable rates of co-occurrence between addictions and other mental health diagnoses were not available until the 1980s.[51, 52] By then, mental health treatment and substance abuse programs were almost cultures alien to each other. To further fracture the picture, in some states (e.g., Connecticut), there was even licensure for alcohol treatment separate from that of drug treatment programs through the 1980s.

The existence of separate public mental health and substance abuse treatment systems has created sizable barriers to providing appropriate treatment services for people who have both addictive disorders and other mental health problems. Treatment is still often available only in sequence, or at best, parallel, and not offered within an integrated entity. One diagnosis is identified as primary, designated as the initial focus of treatment while co-occurring disorders are put on the back burner and, at the very least, minimally stabilized pending resolution of the "main" problem.[53] For instance, someone with severe depression may not have treatment initiated until the co-occurring drug dependence is resolved. Or, treatment for a serious addiction to painkillers may be delayed while a manic episode is addressed. What studies show is that failure to treat these kinds of problems at the same time leads to poorer outcomes for either condition.[54, 55] Integrated, concomitant treatment of depression, psychosis, and cannabis use disorders has been shown to reduce marijuana use in those patients, provided on-going treatment and support were provided.[56]

Substance abuse treatment arose from several places, many of them community-based and involving member peer support. Its history began with organizations such as AA and NA, the Minnesota Model (also referred to as the medical model in that it combined professional with trained non-professional, recovering staff), and other grass-roots therapeutic communities such as Synanon, Daytop Village, and Marathon House. Public substance abuse treatment models emerged from community recovery movements, which embraced the notion of rehabilitation with a supportive, self-policing community of peers (such as Alcoholics Anonymous and therapeutic communities). The substance abuse treatment workforce thus includes many counseling staff with experience-based rather than formal training. This contrasts with a professional tradition of formal training and credentialing of mental health service providers in academic departments of psychiatry, psychology, and social work.

These distinctive origins have been associated with divergent treatment philosophies and ideologies that, earlier in their respective histories, created distrust of mental health treatments by substance abuse providers and vice versa. Moreover, relatively few substance abuse organizations had budgets that would afford psychiatric intervention more comprehensive than contracting a psychiatrist for periodic medication visits. This has clearly been changing over the last 25 years. In addition to more vigorous attention to mental health services, some substance abuse programs now offer specialized tracks sensitive to the needs of females or the LGBTQ population.

Caron Treatment Centers is a well-known example of substance abuse programming available to students who need this higher level of care. In addition to detoxification units, they offer residential and intensive outpatient programs in several locations in the eastern United States. In 2016, they received a lot of publicity when Elizabeth Vargas, former co-anchor of ABC news, revealed in an episode of *20/20* that she had sought treatment there during her struggle with alcoholism.[57] Additionally, people with cannabis use disorders have been well-represented among those seeking treatment there, especially adolescents and college-aged young adults. According to Gina Riggs (Caron Corporate Director of Admissions) and Joseph Garbely (Caron Medical Director and Vice President of Medical Services), marijuana is a pervasive factor to be reckoned with based on what they are seeing. Riggs indicates that among the 2,544 adolescents admitted to Caron between 2006 and 2012, marijuana use at admission has shown a slow, steady increase from 75% to 84%. "We recently obtained new data for January 2015 through June 2016. Within this period, 252 patients under the age of 18 were admitted and 92.1% reported cannabis as their drug of choice. And of the 714 patients between the ages of 18–25, 73.9% had cannabis as their drug of choice." The recent trend toward legalization of marijuana has not yet created an overall influx of cannabis-abusing patients seeking admission: "Currently at our Pennsylvania facility, we have not seen a significant increase. However, if you look at the states that have legalized recreational use of cannabis, it may be possible to see a different trend in admissions."

One problem all individuals have getting access to affordable care is what their healthcare insurer is willing to pay for. Typically, insurance companies are loathe to pay for inpatient levels of care unless there exists what is known as "medical necessity." Detoxification can meet that threshold, for example, but often only in cases of alcohol or benzodiazepine withdrawal, both of which can result in serious, even life-threatening conditions. Residential treatment is usually not covered, making that level-of-care only available to those with the financial resources. And what about intensive outpatient programming?

Can those seeking treatment at places like Caron for cannabis addiction get the help they need without paying for the bulk of it out-of-pocket? Or does a problem with a "harder" drug need to be highlighted for any chance of insurance reimbursement? Riggs admits that persons coming into treatment primarily for cannabis problems rarely meet the medical necessity for any inpatient/residential treatment. "Substance use disorders are defined by level of severity. By the time most individuals seek inpatient treatment, they have escalated to polysubstance use and have much more than solely a cannabis use disorder. Additionally, patients often have other mental health issues and may have started using cannabis as a way to self-medicate and cope." Fortunately, insurance carriers normally are willing to authorize intensive outpatient treatment. Dr. Garbely adds: "Nationally, marijuana is one of the most common substances for which young adults and adolescents seek treatment; it is also a common substance among adults who seek treatment. This is reflected at Caron, as well, where a majority of patients have cannabis as one of their drugs of choice. Marijuana may not have been the drug that necessitated treatment, however, it is an ever-present problem on our campus."

"Caron makes a great effort to provide financial assistance to those who need it," Riggs reassures. "It's critical to Caron's mission to provide treatment scholarships to those who are financially eligible. Last fiscal year, we provided $16 million in scholarship funds."

Both Gina Riggs and Dr. Garbely note a relationship between cannabis use and other mental health disorders. She expands further that "patients often have other mental health issues and may have started using cannabis as a way to self-medicate and cope. As tolerance develops, drug usage increases and often times other drugs are sought for relief from these co-occurring disorders. It should be noted, however, that substance use disorders may be misdiagnosed as mental health issues prior to addiction treatment. This is why patients at Caron are assigned multidisciplinary treatment teams."

"Anxiety and depression are certainly exacerbated by cannabis use," adds Dr. Garbely. "During treatment, we try to look at premorbid factors: Are there any underlying mental health disorders (anxiety, depression, bipolar illness, etc.) that may exist? Do the patients have a history with psychotic disorders (schizophrenia, schizoaffective disorder, etc.)? Attention issues like ADHD? Do the patients' families have a history with other issues? Knowing a patient's history would allow us to predict whether marijuana will worsen these issues. Regarding self-medication, this goes back to the idea that marijuana is medicinal—without any substantial studies. So, allowing people to go to a dispensary to get the drug for whatever ails them makes the drug seem like a panacea. Again, it's the lack of understanding of potential risks associated with marijuana, medicinal marijuana, as well."

What are some of the specific problems in treating the younger marijuana-primary patients? Dr. Garbely: "Young adults have the mistaken belief that marijuana is harmless, so it can be difficult to make them understand that the drug is causing problems in their lives." He goes on to include the increased difficulties they have had treating younger patients since the emergence of synthetic marijuana—K2 or Spice. "While K2 is not marijuana, the chemical structure bears a mild resemblance. K2 causes mental health issues and triggers a psychotic, dissociative experience. Patients lose touch with reality. This is very difficult to manage, even on our campus. In some instances, Caron enlists the help of local acute psychiatric units to stabilize these patients. It's important to talk about K2 and Spice when talking about cannabis because a lot people switch over thinking they are the same thing. They also make the switch to avoid detection. It's hard to monitor for these drugs, simply, because they won't show up in drug testing the same way marijuana does." Drug testing is a very important issue in the treatment of cannabis use disorders, as a significant percentage of those adolescents and young adults admitted have legal pressures and may be monitored by juvenile or adult probation. The long period for marijuana to be eliminated from the body would make K2 an attractive way to circumvent the legal system to an unrepentant 17-year-old cannabis user.

Do the older patients at Caron, those who are abusing substances such as heroin, cocaine, alcohol, and methamphetamine, find it difficult to be in treatment with marijuana-primary patients? Do they often invalidate the severity of marijuana addiction? Yes, Dr. Garbely admits: "Patients in treatment for heroin, crack, etc. often see themselves at the other end of the bell curve compared to patients in treatment for marijuana. However, we standardize that curve at Caron to accurately reflect the seriousness of substance use disorders. We treat marijuana and heroin patients the same—a drug is a drug. That's the first lecture patients attend here; we do a good job at leveling that out." He expands on this further. "We find that marijuana is often a drug (along with alcohol) that many patients who are now addicted to cocaine and heroin begin with. Marijuana and alcohol are the two drugs that are experimented with early on in life. Because many of these patients began their use with marijuana, it's important for them to look upstream—to pinpoint where their use began. This allows them to understand that when they started smoking marijuana (or drinking alcohol), it changed the circuitry in their brains. The patients who are addicted to heroin/cocaine tell the younger patients who smoke marijuana to stop now because they know and they have lived the consequences. They are very helpful to our younger patients."

Caron embraces abstinence as a treatment philosophy. Is abstinence-based recovery a harder sell for these young adult patients? Or are they more invested in just taking a prolonged break from use, stabilizing other domains of their lives, with the intention of eventually attempting a return to controlled recreational use in the future? Dr. Garbely acknowledges this reality. "This is true when it comes to our younger patients—it's difficult for them to adopt an abstinence-based recovery philosophy. It's hard for them to envision tomorrow, let alone 30 years from now. The word 'never' is definitely a tough sell in their vernacular. It's hard for them to say, 'I'm never going to use again.' It's often better to ask them to just 'give it a shot'—to give the abstinent lifestyle and recovery a chance. If it improves your life, keep going! We don't engage in a dogmatic argument. We encourage our adolescent and young adult patients to access recovery on their own terms because if they do, their lives get better and the likelihood is that they'll continue down that road. Through the Caron approach, many young people find their lives really do improve, so they keep maintaining their recovery. The logic is, why should I stop? And many of them find others in 12-Step programs to whom they become really close; they form strong bonds around recovery. For example, Caron works closely with organizations dedicated to creating fun events and productive opportunities for young people in a sober environment, such as the New York City-based non-for-profit Big Vision."

Regarding 12-step recovery: Caron uses 12-step meeting attendance as an outcome measure. Is this more difficult with their marijuana-using patients, especially those that are younger? Does Caron see them fitting into the AA and NA communities? "Patients should choose a recovery community in which they feel most comfortable and connected. Marijuana Anonymous (MA) communities are not common, but they can go to AA or NA. It's better for patients to learn what fits best for them. AA meetings typically normalize the experience so that it applies to any mood-altering substance, but I do not want to generalize. MA meetings are more difficult to find. They are not as plentiful in the community because the infrastructure is nowhere near the AA/NA infrastructure. You can search for AA/NA meetings online according to where you are located, but MA is newer so they don't seem to have as many online resources for those individuals addicted to marijuana to locate groups. There may not be a good representation of all the MA meetings online."

It is clear to see how creating an interconnected web of resources is vital for students in recovery. Programs may focus differently on harm-reduction versus abstinence, and the worlds of substance abuse and mental health treatment continue to merge. An area where this also plays out is in the pharmacological treatment of physical and psychological symptoms of cannabis use disorders.

The Era of Psychopharmacology

We are deeply nestled, for better or worse, in the era of modern psychopharmacology. Discovering an essential medication, a chemical magic bullet, to treat specific disorders is an enduring quest for researchers and drug companies alike. To find such an agent to treat cannabis use disorder is no exception.

The first major hurdle to clear for a college student trying to quit a serious cannabis habit can be managing some initial withdrawal symptoms. As the potency of marijuana has increased, so has the severity of the withdrawal. Cannabis abstinence syndrome can be serious enough to require some medical attention in treatment programs, a condition Dr. Garbely of Caron expounds on: "Withdrawal is best defined as the opposite of the intoxication effect. There are various types of marijuana that produce different effects. Occasionally, antidepressants can be used to stabilize mood changes associated with the early stages of cessation and treatment. We will also use non-addictive drugs to treat other symptoms of withdrawal." These symptoms can include loss of appetite, anxiety, irritability, and, more infrequently, night sweats. "It's not a 'one size fits all' approach. We are very interested in treating withdrawal symptoms with the understanding that withdrawal is a time-limited issue. Withdrawal is a 'now' issue. We use these medications to address symptoms only on an as-needed basis. If patients don't have the symptoms, they are not prescribed the medications. In time, the symptoms will decrease."

The most common complaint with cannabis use disorders is insomnia. With the progression of cannabis dependence, individuals often find themselves using it at night to help themselves fall asleep. Over time, the system begins to rely more and more on cannabinoids to induce sleep. Insomnia is one of the symptoms inpatient and outpatient programs address most often. In treating this problem, physicians or nurse practitioners employed by the programs typically use medications with very low potential for abuse, such as trazodone (Desyrel, Oleptro) and mirtazapine (Remeron), two antidepressants prescribed for their respective side-effects in sub-therapeutic low dosage—they induce sleep. But there are a few problems with these drugs. As discussed in a previous chapter, marijuana tends to shorten dream state or rapid eye movement (REM) sleep, while elongating deep-state or slow-wave sleep.[58] Once use has stopped, marijuana users often experience a REM-state rebound, typified by vivid, even disturbing dreams. Both trazodone and mirtazapine can increase REM-state density, amplifying already dream-hyperactive brains in withdrawal. This results in patients being able to fall asleep, but they find their slumber fitful, interrupted, and not restful. Other agents, such as zolpidem (Ambien) and zaleplon (Sonata), have a capacity for developing dependency and are generally avoided in substance abuse programs, as are any drugs of the benzodiazepine family like temazepam or lorazepam. Prescribers often treat cannabis withdrawal based on the presenting symptoms. This is unlike protocols for opioid or alcohol withdrawal where one agent, cross-tolerant with those substances in the brain, can be used to slowly wean a patient down and eventually off. And since there are no medications approved specifically for marijuana-related illnesses by the Food and Drug Administration (FDA), those agents are used off-label. This means there is a body of ancillary information suggesting possible efficacy.

Anxiety or irritability, another common complaint, can be helped with antihypertensive drugs such as propranolol. Some program physicians use antihistamine medications such as hydroxyzine (Vistaril): all these agents reduce excitation in the brain, thereby mitigating anxiety. Once again, benzodiazepines (Xanax, Ativan, Valium, Klonopin) are medications of last resort, as they have the capacity for abuse. Depending on the severity of the problem, medically supervised marijuana detoxification may or may not be a necessary precursor to treatment. Some patients may be at risk for complications and should be closely monitored.

Nabilone, a synthetic THC that it is hoped will ease the symptoms of cannabis withdrawal, is the latest drug to be investigated.[59] Although the sample was low—only 11 participants—this drug was found to decrease some of the most undesirable characteristics of cannabis abstinence syndrome, as well as diminished self-administrations of cannabis in response. Although similar to the older THC drug Dronabinol (Marinol), Nabilone has better bioavailability, as it is more easily absorbed and utilized by the body. Furthermore, Dronabinol has not been shown to decrease marijuana use, so Nabilone appears to be a promising synthetic THC alternative.[60]

Unfortunately, some studies demonstrate high rates of relapse at six-month follow-ups for marijuana dependent individuals.[61, 62] If medication-assisted treatment is to be a truly important adjunct, it must do more than just ease withdrawal, but also help individuals maintain significantly reduced use or abstinence long-term. In addition to the preliminary research from Nabilone trials, another study out of France suggested that the naturally occurring hormone pregnenolone might offer additional promise.[63] They found rats who were given high amounts of THC also exhibited elevations of this hormone, suggesting pregnenolone may be an inherent, signal-activated, protective mechanism against over-intoxication, attenuating the effects of THC at the C1 receptors. Pregnenolone, in a future preparation might mitigate the psychoactive effects of marijuana, possibly extinguishing the urge to use. This action is already used in the substance abuse pharmacology world with naltrexone for alcohol dependence and Chantix and bupropion to interfere with the reward of tobacco.

Medical management of cannabis use disorder symptoms is only one piece of the puzzle. Pharmacotherapy can be integral in providing support for individuals particularly in the early stages of recovery. Another major issue faced by individuals trying to cut down or abstain from cannabis is the social isolation that often comes with such a change. Fortunately, campuses have begun to address this barrier to treatment success by designing communities to enhance the well-being and function of students in recovery.

Recovery on Campus

One element almost everyone agrees with is the importance of a social environment supportive to sustained recovery. The culture of rampant substance use on the majority of college campuses makes this immensely challenging. In response to this reality, colleges have started to embrace the advantages of establishing recovery communities on their campuses, known as Collegiate Recovery Communities (CRC) or Collegiate Recovery Programs (CRP). These organizations provide supportive services such as social activities, case management, links to counseling, sober housing, and academic advising to those students who are in recovery from addictions. Although CRPs are not treatment modalities, they must work in partnership with area substance abuse and mental health providers. While many of the students have already been through some form of treatment prior to coming to CRPs, they often need assistance accessing follow-up counseling and medication management, especially when they have co-occurring depression or anxiety issues.

Twenty years ago, there were but a handful of universities pioneering this type of service, like Rutgers University, Texas Tech University, Brown University, and Augsburg College. As these programs proliferate, there is the emergence of national organizations devoted to the promotion of CRPs, such as the Association for Recovery in Higher Education (ARHE).[64] Prior to this, university administrators may have been reluctant to encourage the creation of such organizations on their campuses due to the stigma of addiction. Perhaps there was the fear: if we build it, *they* will come. The idea of luring prospective students who had already identified as battling an addiction was not an attractive one. But now we are seeing an almost 180-degree shift toward embracing this population: if we build it, they *will* come. One reason for this change in thinking is due to available data on recovering student performance and retention rates when given the assistance of CRPs. For example, at Georgia Southern University, the general student body averages a 2.7 GPA, but their CRP students average 3.69, and this reportedly has held steady for three years from 2011 to 2013.[65] Impressive student retention rates within CRPs are also being reported by these universities; to higher education administrators, this translates into increased graduation rates and an improved financial picture for these schools.

Among CRPs, one at Texas Tech University—the Center for Collegiate Recovery Communities (CCRC)—stands out for other universities to emulate. In 2011, this opinion was punctuated by the Office of National Drug Control Policy, when it honored CCRC as a model program. CCRC embraces a 12-step model, meaning that those student members are expected to attend meetings, have a sponsor, and engage in recovery fellowship and service. Sober housing is available to members—they have an entire dormitory floor dedicated to the program. In 2004, they were awarded a grant by the federal government to develop a curriculum that included how-to information and guidelines for other universities to utilize in developing their own collegiate recovery programs. The CCRC directly appeals to university administrators by contending on their website that ensuring continued enrollment of its 80 student members saves their school approximately $430,500 annually in tuition that could have been otherwise lost in attrition.[66]

Those students who become addicted to marijuana have been finding support in these groups. Sarah Nerad, former program manager of the Collegiate Recovery Community (CRC) and director of Recovery at Ohio State University, asserts those recovering primarily from marijuana have found acceptance within the group in spite of the majority of CRC participants being polysubstance users. "To the best of my knowledge, they have not encountered judgment or stigma [from] members of our community for 'only' being addicted to weed," she claims. There is an added advantage of having a Marijuana Anonymous meeting in the area. "I have met with our local Marijuana Anonymous group (started by an OSU alum), so we include information about it on our website and have referred students there. I know the members of MA felt [as though they were] not being taken seriously in AA or NA meetings because they 'just smoked pot.' " Other than this opinion, Sarah indicates that the other area 12-step meetings have been inclusive of students recovering from cannabis use disorders. As the field of collegiate recovery evolves, the potential assistance CRPs can provide marijuana-addicted students is inestimable.

Can we compare the type of dependent relationship people create with cannabis to that of other substances? In other words, is addiction to marijuana about being unable to quit, or rather a constant struggle with the question: "is quitting really necessary?" If we were to poll those persons dependent on tobacco, alcohol, heroin, and methamphetamine, the majority would undoubtedly agree that compulsive use injures in many ways. Nor would they advocate for others to use their drug of choice in-kind. The knowledge of damage done to their lives by use is clouded by the psychological mechanisms of denial, rationalization, and blame—not built on a rational, evidence-based platform. They recognize that these substances are bad for people—information they ignore when they decide to use. There are no advocacy groups for heroin or methamphetamine or crack cocaine use for its own sake; decriminalization, even legalization, yes—but there are no political action organizations extolling the virtues of using such substances. The alcohol industry and Big Tobacco, both incredibly large entities, promote use of their products with the singular goal of increased profits, not out of some higher purpose to society. With the sole exception of the antioxidants found in wine and beer (all of which can be found in other non-alcoholic beverages such as grape juice and green tea), there are no longer campaigns touting the health benefits of smoking, chewing, and drinking.

Many practitioners point to the complexities found in breaking down the meaning in the first step of the 12-step tradition; some even emphasizing the compound task of working through this seminal step: "We admitted we were *powerless* over (alcohol, drugs, gambling, etc.) and that our lives had become *unmanageable*."[67] Seasoned members of AA, NA, and other 12-step based groups often describe their struggles with both parts of this step. Earlier on in recovery, many are finally able to embrace their reality of being unable to use in a safe, controlled way—that they are "powerless" over their substance of choice. However, that their lives had become "unmanageable" can be influenced by many other factors including total losses directly attributable to their addiction and the reactions and behaviors of families and friends, whether they have incurred legal or financial consequences, as well as the stoutness of their defense mechanisms. More simply, while they may be able to admit they are addicted, another part whispers, "but it's not that bad."

In an interview with Jon Stewart, the late comedian George Carlin, who admitted having struggled with his use of alcohol, painkillers, and cocaine, framed getting sober as a shift from experiencing drugs as "good" to a place where negative consequences clearly outweigh any benefits of use.[68]

> Drugs and these things are wonderful, wonderful when you try them first—they're not around for all these millennia for no reason. First time mostly pleasure, very little pain . . . as you increase and keep using, the pleasure part decreases and the pain part, the price you pay increases, until the balance is completely the other way, it's almost all pain and very little pleasure.[69]

Due to the less swift and severe consequences directly associated with marijuana use, this personal shift may take longer for those dependent on it.

And, besides, it's just weed.

Notes

1 NBC News. (2014, April 7). *Storyline: America's heroin epidemic.* Retrieved from www.nbcnews.com/storyline/americas-heroin-epidemic/how-fix-rehab-expert-who-lost-son-addiction-has-plan-n67946

2 Trip. G. (2010, December 19). Mental health needs seen growing at colleges. *New York Times.* Retrieved from www.nytimes.com/2010/12/20/health/20campus.html

3 National Center for Education Statistics. (2012). *Digest of educational statistics.* Retrieved from https://nces.ed.gov/pubs2014/2014015.pdf

4 Iavorici, D. (2014, April 17). The antidepressant generation. *The New York Times.* Retrieved from https://well.blogs.nytimes.com/2014/04/17/the-antidepressant-generation/?_r=0

5 Buckner, J. D., Ecker, A. H., & Cohen, A. S. (2010, September). Mental health problems and interest in marijuana treatment among marijuana-using

college students [Abstract]. *Addictive Behavior, 35*(9), 826–33. doi:10.1016/j. addbeh.2010.04.001

6 Wu, L. T., Pilowsky, D. J., Schlenger, W. E., & Hasin, D. (2007). Alcohol use disorders and the use of treatment services among college-age young adults. *Psychiatric Services, 58*(2), 192–200. http://doi.org/10.1176/appi. ps.58.2.192

7 Caldeira, K. M., Kasperski, S. J., Sharma, E., Vincent, K. B., O'Grady, K. E., Wish, E. D., & Arria, A. M. (2009). College students rarely seek help despite serious substance use problems. *Journal of Substance Abuse Treatment, 37*(4), 368–378. http://doi.org/10.1016/j.jsat.2009.04.005

8 Alcoholics Anonymous. (1976). *Alcoholics Anonymous.* New York, NY: Alcoholics Anonymous Publishing Company.

9 Bill, W. (1960). *Proposal for twelve concepts for world service: 10th general service conference—1960.* Retrieved from http://aaohio-triarea.org/Articles/ Bill%20W%201960%20-%20Concepts.pdf

10 Alcoholics Anonymous (1976).

11 General Service Office (2016). *Estimated worldwide A.A. individual and group membership.* Retrieved from www.aa.org/assets/en_US/smf-132_en.pdf

12 Alcoholics Anonymous (1976).

13 Alcoholics Anonymous World Services. (1957). *AA comes of age. A brief history of Alcoholics Anonymous.* New York, NY: Author.

14 Timko, C. (2008). Outcomes of AA for special populations. In M. Galanter & L. A. Kaskutas (Eds.), *Research on Alcoholics Anonymous and spirituality in addiction recovery* (pp. 373–392). New York, NY: Springer Science. Retrieved from www.mentalhealth.va.gov/providers/sud/selfhelp/docs/5_Outcomes_of_ AA_for_Special_Populations.pdf

15 Donovan, D. M., Ingalsbe, M. H., Benbow, J., & Daley, D. C. (2013). 12-step interventions and mutual support programs for substance use disorders: An overview. *Social Work in Public Health, 28*(3–4), 313–332. http://doi.org/10. 1080/19371918.2013.774663

16 Tonigan, J. S., Miller, W. R., Juarez, P., & Villanueva, M. (2002). Utilization of AA by hispanic and non-hispanic white clients receiving outpatient alcohol treatment [Abstract]. *Journal of Studies on Alcohol, 63*(2), 215–218. https:// doi.org/10.15288/jsa.2002.63.215

17 LGBTQ in A.A. history. (n.d.). *Out & Sober Minnesota.* Retrieved from www.outandsoberminnesota.org/motivation/lgbtq-in-a-a-history/

18 Glasser, G. (2013, June 21). Why she drinks: Women and alcohol abuse. *Wall Street Journal.* Retrieved from www.wsj.com/articles/SB1000142412788732 3893504578555270434071876

19 Kelly, J. F. (2003). Self-help for substance-use disorders: History, effectiveness, knowledge gaps, and research opportunities [Abstract]. *Clinical Psychology Review, 23*(5), 639–663. https://doi.org/10.1016/S0272-7358(03)00053-9

20 Moos, R. H., Moos, B. S., & Timko, C. (2006). Gender, treatment and self-help in remission from alcohol use disorders. *Clinical Medicine and Research, 4*(3), 163–174. doi:10.3121/cmr.4.3.163

21 Timko, C., & Sempel, J. M. (2004). Intensity of acute services, self-help attendance and one-year outcomes among dual diagnosis patients. *Journal of Studies on Alcohol, 65*(2), 274–282. doi:10.15288/jsa.2004.65.274

22 Conway, K. P., Compton, W., Stinson, F. S., & Grant, B. F. (2006). Lifetime comorbidity of DSM-IV mood and anxiety disorders and specific drug use disorders: Results from the national epidemiologic survey on alcohol and related conditions [Abstract]. *Journal of Clinical Psychiatry, 67*(2), 247–257. doi:10.4088/JCP.v67n0211

23 Humphreys, K. (1997). Clinicians' referral and matching of substance abuse patients to self-help groups after treatment. *Psychiatric Services, 48*(11), 1445–1449. Retrieved from http://ps.psychiatryonline.org/doi/pdf/10.1176/ps.48.11.1445

24 De La Cretaz, B. (2016, February 26). Fundamentalist, atheist, gay . . . whatever you think of AA, know that every meeting is different. *The Influence.* Retrieved from http://theinfluence.org/fundamentalist-atheist-gay-whatever-you-think-of-aa-know-that-every-meeting-is-different

25 Harigan, F. (2000). *Bill W.: A biography of Alcoholics Anonymous co-founder Bill Wilson.* New York, NY: St. Martin's Press.

26 Nowinski, J., Baker, S., & Carroll, K. (1999). Twelve-step facilitation therapy manual. A clinical research guide for therapists treating individuals with alcohol abuse and dependence. *Project Match Monogram Series, National Institute on Alcohol Abuse and Alcoholism.* Retrieved from https://pubs.niaaa.nih.gov/publications/projectmatch/match01.pdfhttps://pubs.niaaa.nih.gov/publications/projectmatch/match01.pdf

27 Moos, R., & Timko, C. (2008). Outcome research on twelve-step and other self-help programs. In M. Galanter, & H. O. Kleber (Eds.), *Textbook of substance abuse treatment* (pp. 511–521). Washington, DC: American Psychiatric Press. https://doi.org/10.1176/appi.books.9781615370030.mg38

28 Connors G. J., Tonigan J. S., & Miller W. R. (2001). A longitudinal model of intake symptomatology, A.A. participation, and outcome: Retrospective study of the Project MATCH outpatient and aftercare samples. *Journal of Studies on Alcohol, 62*(6), 817–825. https://doi.org/10.15288/jsa.2001.62.817

29 Moos, R. H., & Moos, B. S. (2006). Participation in treatment and alcoholics anonymous: A 16-year follow-up of initially untreated individuals. *Journal of Clinical Psychology, 62*(6), 735–750. doi:10.1002/jclp.20259

30 Ferri, M., Amato L., & Davoli, M. (2006). Alcoholics Anonymous and other 12-step programs for alcohol dependence. *Cochrane Database of Systematic Reviews*, Issue 3, Art. No.: CD005032. doi:10.1002/14651858.CD005032.pub2

31 Laudet, A. B. (2008). The impact of alcoholics anonymous on other substance abuse related Twelve Step programs. *Recent Developments in Alcoholism, 18*, 71–89. Retrieved from http://pubmedcentralcanada.ca/pmcc/articles/PMC2613294/pdf/nihms62519.pdf

32 Meeting Search. (2017). *Marijuana Anonymous.* Retrieved from www.marijuana-anonymous.org/meetings#find

33 American Addiction Centers. (n.d.). *Alternatives to AA and other 12-step programs.* Retrieved from http://americanaddictioncenters.org/addiction-therapy-types/12-step-alternatives/

34 Bradshaw, N. (2017, June 27). *7 popular alternatives to alcoholics anonymous.* Retrieved from www.soberrecovery.com/addiction/5-popular-alternatives-to-alcoholics-anonymous-2/

35 Macgowan, M. J., & Engle, B. (2010). Evidence for optimism: Behavior therapies and motivational interviewing in adolescent substance abuse treatment. *Child and Adolescent Psychiatric Clinics of North America, 19*(3), 527–545. http://doi.org/10.1016/j.chc.2010.03.006

36 Miller, W. R. (1983). Motivational interviewing with problem drinkers. *Behavioural Psychotherapy, 11*, 147–172. Retrieved from www.vad.be/assets/1961

37 Miller, W. R., & Rollnick, S. (2002). *Motivational interviewing: Preparing people for change* (2nd ed.). New York, NY: Guilford Press.

38 Columbia University. (2009, October 22). *Motivational interviewing: Facilitating change across boundaries*. [Video film]. Retrieved from www.youtube.com/watch?v=6EeCirPyq2w

39 Miller 147–172.

40 Macgowan & Engle 527–545.

41 Miller 147–172.

42 Miller, W. R., Benefield, R. G., & Tonigan, J. S. (1993). Enhancing motivation for change in problem drinking: A controlled comparison of two therapist styles [Abstract]. *Journal of Consulting and Clinical Psychology*, 61(3), 455–461. http://dx.doi.org/10.1037/0022-006X.61.3.455

43 White, W. (2012). *The psychology of addiction recovery: An interview with William R. Miller*, PhD. Retrieved from www.williamwhitepapers.com

44 Macgowan & Engle 527–545.

45 Bradshaw (2017).

46 White, W. (2000). Addiction as a disease: Birth of a concept. *Counselor*, 1(1), 46–51, 73. Retrieved from www.williamwhitepapers.com/pr/2000HistoryoftheDiseaseConceptSeries.pdf

47 Miller, W. R., & Kurtz, E. (1994). Models of alcoholism used in treatment: Contrasting AA and other perspectives with which it is often confused. *Journal of Studies on Alcohol*, 55(2), 159–166. https://doi.org/10.15288/jsa.1994.55.159

48 Stea, J. N., Yakovenko, I., & Hodgins, D. C. (2015). Recovery from cannabis use disorders: Abstinence versus moderation and treatment-assisted recovery versus natural recovery. *Psychology of Addictive Behaviors*, 29(3), 522–31. doi:10.1037/adb0000097

49 Burnham, A., & Watkins, K. E. (2006). Substance abuse with mental disorders: Specialized public systems and integrated care. *Health Affairs*, 25(3), 648–658. doi:10.1377/hlthaff.25.3.648

50 Peters, G., & Woolley, J. T. (2017, June 17). Special message to the congress on drug abuse prevention and control. *The American Presidency Project*. Retrieved from www.presidency.ucsb.edu/ws/?pid=3048

51 Ross, H. E., Glazer, F. B., & Germanson, T. (1988). The prevalence of psychiatric disorders in patients with alcohol and other drug problems [Abstract]. *Archives of General Psychiatry*, 45(11),1023–1031. doi:10.1001/archpsyc.1988.01800350057008

52 Regier, D. A., Farmer, M. E., Rae, D. S., Locke, B. Z., Keith, S. J., Judd, L. L., & Goodwin, F. K. (1990). Comorbidity of mental disorders with alcohol and other drug abuse. Results from the Epidemiologic Catchment Area (ECA) Study [Abstract]. *Journal of the American Medical Association*, 264(19), 2511–2518. doi:10.1001/jama.1990.03450190043026Re

53 White 46–51.

54 Mangrum, L. F., Spence, R. T., & Lopez, M. (2006). Integrated versus parallel treatment of co-occurring psychiatric and substance use disorders. *Journal of Substance Abuse Treatment*, 30(1), 79–84. doi:10.1016/j.jsat.2005.10.004

55 Substance Abuse and Mental Health Services Administration. (2009). *Integrated treatment for co-occurring disorders: The evidence* (DHHS Pub. No. SMA-08-4366). Retrieved from https://store.samhsa.gov/shin/content/SMA08-4367/TheEvidence-ITC.pdf

56 Baker, A. L., Hides, L., & Lubman, D. (2010). Treatment of cannabis use among people with psychotic or depressive disorders: a systematic review. *Journal of Clinical Psychiatry*, 71(3), 247–254. doi:10.4088/JCP.09r05119gry

57 Dooley, S., Dawson, M., & Effron, L. (2016, September 9). ABC News anchor Elizabeth Vargas on her long battle with alcohol and her road to recovery. *ABC News*. Retrieved from http://abcnews.go.com/Health/abc-news-anchor-elizabeth-vargas-long-battle-alcoholism/story?id=41980399

58 Feinberg, I., Jones, R., Walker, J., Cavness, C., & Floyd, T. (1976). Effects of marijuana extract and tetrahydrocannabinol on electroencephalographic sleep patterns. *Clinical Pharmacological Therapy*, 19(6), 782–794. Retrieved from www.ncbi.nlm.nih.gov/pubmed/178475

59 Haney, M., Cooper, Z. D., Bedi, G., Vosburg, S. K., Comer, S. D., & Foltin, R. W. (2013). Nabilone decreases marijuana withdrawal and a laboratory measure of marijuana relapse [Abstract]. *Neuropsychopharmacology*, 38(8), 1557–1565. doi:10.1038/npp.2013.54

60 Haney, M., Hart, C. L., Vosburg, S. K., Comer, S. D., Reed, S. C., & Foltin, R. W. (2008). Effects of THC and Lofexidine in a human laboratory model of marijuana withdrawal and relapse [Abstract]. *Psychopharmacology*, 197(1), 157–168. http://doi.org/10.1007/s00213-007-1020-8

61 Babor, T. F., & The Marijuana Research Project Treatment Group. (2004). Brief treatments for cannabis dependence: Findings from a randomized multisite trial. *Journal of Consulting and Clinical Psychology*, 72(3), 455–466. doi:10.1037/0022–006X.72.3.455

62 Kadden, R. M., Litt, M. D., Kabela-Cormier, E., & Petry, N. M. (2007). Abstinence rates following behavioral treatments for marijuana dependence. *Addictive Behaviors*, 32(6), 1220–1236. http://doi.org/10.1016/j.addbeh.2006.08.009

63 Vallée, M., Vitiello, S., Bellocchio, L., Hébert-Chatelain, E., Monlezun, S., Martin-Garcia, E., . . . Piazza, P. V. (2014). Pregnenolone can protect the brain from cannabis intoxication. *Science*, 343(6166), 94–98. http://doi.org/10.1126/science.1243985

64 Association of Recovery in Higher Education. (2017). Retrieved from https://collegiaterecovery.org

65 Buchanan, S. (2014, September 4). *Recovery campus*. Retrieved from http://recoverycampus.com/smart-recovery/

66 Center for the Study of Addiction and Recovery, Texas Tech University. (2005). *Project one: Creating the vision*. Retrieved from www.depts.ttu.edu/hs/csa/docs/1.pdf

67 Alcoholics Anonymous (1976).

68 FreeAssange1. (2011, January 3). *Carlin on drugs*. [Video film]. Retrieved from www.youtube.com/watch?v=CdCklNNuEPw

69 Haney, Hart, Vosburg, Comer, Reed, & Foltin 157–168.

Chapter 11

Scottie

"I had been to Colorado a bunch of times before I made the decision to move here. When I came here the first time, it was before the passing of Amendment 64, and marijuana was legal only medicinally. I remember one time I was walking around the 16th Street Mall in Denver there was a guy with a cardboard sign that said, 'Need money for weed,' and I said to myself, 'really, whose going to do that?' I had grown up in the Midwest, where talking about it was really restricted, shut down, sort of in in hushed tones. Here in Colorado, even before it was legal recreationally, people were very open about it. It was part of the culture; people were a little more chilled out. It was always, as far I could tell, more out in the open. I'm sure people who have been here, have a longer history could say something different, but as far as I could tell, it's always sort of like integrated into the culture. So what happened, the law adapted to the culture. It wasn't like the law changed and then the culture shifted. The culture existed before the law was passed, so the law came to reflect the culture."

Originally, from the Midwest, Scottie moved several times before coming to Colorado. "The first time I ever used marijuana was between middle school and high school. My friend and I had been drinking, and he convinced me to smoke when I wouldn't have otherwise, because I thought it was a hardcore drug thing. I didn't touch it again until I was a sophomore in high school. I tried it again and came back to it. I kind of fell in love with it. I loved the way it smelled, the taste, the way it may it made me feel. It felt like starting a new relationship or something. Then from cannabis I started using other drugs. I can't say it was a gateway drug because I was smoking cigarettes and there was the people I was hanging out with." Scottie ended up shooting mephedrone (a synthetic stimulant), an episode that resulted in his entering a drug treatment program. He was seventeen.

"So, I went to treatment and got out and I was wrapped up in the system and couldn't smoke, and I wanted to smoke really bad. Cannabis has really changed in its nature [to me] as opposed to [what it was]. It was something akin to alcohol, or something to get high on, to get fucked up on—let me get fucked up, this is going to let me escape. After all the drug trouble went away, I resumed smoking, but my relationship with it has changed drastically. I don't know if it's the culture. I still smoke, but I don't think of it as 'I'm going to get fucked up.' I think it brings me in touch with my anxieties, and it lets me see myself in a different way, work with some of my flaws. It's like a self-work thing. I see it almost as a medicine, a psychological or spiritual medicine. I know if I were to say that to someone down in Texas (a state where he had lived previously), they would look at me sideways. But people here get that. People here used it in a variety of ways—some do use it as a party drug, or whatever. A lot of times for me it promotes deep thinking about myself that I wouldn't do otherwise. It's strange, because I was introduced to it as a drug, like heroin. They talked to us in school about cannabis at the same time they talked to us about the harder drugs." Scottie described some of his experiences in middle school with drug prevention, including going through the D.A.R.E program. "The things they told us were ridiculous, like one in four pills of ecstasy would kill you. If you do acid once, it will make you go crazy. They showed this thing with this kid taking a hit from a bong and dying, his mom finding him and becoming inconsolable. They were just lies. Reagan, Nixon—and now Trump, lies."

Scottie states that those people who come from states where it remains completely illegal are captivated by how different the cannabis culture is in places like Denver and Boulder. "I have friends who come here from Texas and South Dakota, and if you've never been here before, when you walk into a dispensary and you've heard your whole life that weed is the devil and weed is bad. Well, [they] can't believe it. But the people who live here, it's really so integrated, it has meshed really well. I think there were people who thought that there would be blood in the streets, a state full of 'pot zombies,' roaming around glossy-eyed, wrecking into each other. There's going to be chaos if you legalize pot! But what it really is that people are more respectful of each other, people are [calmer]." To illustrate his point, he tells of going out to bars in South Dakota (a former residence) with friends, and on several occasions some drunk patrons would try to pick fights with them. "But here in Colorado, like in Boulder, if I go to a bar and I walk outside, someone might hand me a joint. In other states where they talk in hushed tones about it, they might say, 'do you see that guy over there, that guy smokes weed.' But you don't see that with alcohol. Nobody says, 'do you see that guy over there, that guy likes whiskey.' It's just normalized [here], the way that it should be."

Scottie argues that, while used like alcohol by some, the more pervasive belief about marijuana in Colorado is that it is more a medicine.

He depicts people engaging in conscious cannabis circles, augmenting meditation with it. It has "given rise to a really beautiful attitude towards other people and ourselves." He adds that cannabis is not solely responsible for this transcendent spirit, but that there is a connection between the attitude toward the plant and an increased tolerance and respect. He also touts how the people who work in the dispensaries ("the budtenders") are very good at educating consumers—especially those from out-of-state—with products like edibles so that they do not overdose. He adds that, in a harm-reduction effort, there is even some talk about making edibles rather tasteless, explaining that sometimes people get the "munchies" before the full effect of the ingested THC, contributing to the rates of overdose. "They are really very good, tasty," he gushes of the scrumptious goodies, such as cannabis-infused baklava and cheesecake—regretting "biting off more than he could chew" himself once with the latter.

Scottie is working toward his degree in psychology, unsure yet what area of the field he wishes to focus his studies, although, not surprisingly, the attraction to the novel use of psychedelics in treatment is compelling. He also denies any conflicted feelings about modeling marijuana use for his children someday. "That's just pure social conditioning. Those people [who feel uncomfortable] wouldn't think that way about having a beer in front of their kid. And alcohol is a thousand times more dangerous. I think placing a bong in front of a child is better than having a beer. There is the idea of the authoritarian conscience, a voice of authority that works its way into your head so deep that you can't differentiate between it and yourself." He ventures even further, declaring that it would be his parental duty to instruct his children about the potential and the responsibility of cannabis use. "I would say 'this is what this is,' like what Bob Marley said, marijuana shows you to yourself. At least talk to them in a real way. Don't talk to them like 'it will drive you crazy kid, you're going to be a loser-stoner, living in a van and digging ditches!' First of all, it's safe; yeah, if you smoke too young, there can be problems. There's some research going on here about cannabis and the adolescent mind. It can exacerbate things like schizophrenia and psychosis and certain personality disorders. It's certainly not for everyone. For the people that it is for, it helps a lot."

Scottie is asked what he likes most and least about his relationship with cannabis. He returns to the element of introspection he feels cannabis brings to him: "It puts me in touch with the part of me that knows better. It acts as a teacher. It shows me where I need to grow, where I could have been better. It shows me where I could have brought more of myself forward. It can be intensely anxiety provoking. It's uncomfortable. But it's anxiety I can work with." That is what he likes *most* about it; what he dislikes is the severity of some of the lessons. "It's uncomfortable to see the places where I've fucked-up, been an asshole. It would be nice if I could just smoke and be better instantly, but it's not always nice, not always friendly. It can be harsh or punitive at times. I just have to sit with the feeling. Makes me squirm . . . opportunities that I've missed, let slip by."

Chapter 12

In the Wake of Legalization

*The amount of money and of legal energy being given to prosecute
hundreds of thousands of Americans who are caught with a few
ounces of marijuana in their jeans simply makes no sense—the kind-
est way to put it. A sterner way to put it is that it is an outrage, an
imposition on basic civil liberties and on the reasonable expenditure
of social energy.*

—William F. Buckley Jr.[1]

Many comparisons can be drawn between the past prohibition of alcohol and the current debate about marijuana legalization. Vocal advocates
of legalization and those who argue for the continued illegal status of
cannabis both refer to that "failed social experiment" called Prohibition—the Volstead Act enacted to enforce the Eighteenth Amendment.
Though repealed after 13 years, whether Prohibition was indeed a failure
has been debated, but its history provides a valuable lens through which
to view the current legal situation with regards to marijuana. Different
parallels can be made in relation to questions regarding changes in youth
consumption, impact on crime, and other public health consequences.
The story of a prime figure in Prohibition, Pauline Morton Sabin, puts
into high relief the debate about whether maintaining a drug's illegal status actually increases hazards for youth.

Sabin was born on April 23, 1887, into wealth and privilege, and later
served as the only female member of the Republican National Committee
(RNC). With the passing of the Volstead Act in 1920, Sabin was in favor
of alcohol prohibition as she thought it would protect her children from
the dangers of liquor. As the decade of the "Roaring Twenties" unfolded,
she found herself becoming increasingly disillusioned with what she considered to be the failed promise of prohibition as well as the hypocrisy
of many of the politicians with whom she socialized. They would preach
the virtues of an alcohol-free society, only to frequent private parties and
consume alcohol whenever they had the opportunity. She was disturbed

by the newspaper reports of the crime associated with illegal alcohol and the violence between rival bootlegging gangs. By 1926, she had had enough and began to mount a campaign for the repeal of the Volstead Act. After unsuccessful efforts to sway congress, Sabin resigned from the RNC and started the Women's Organization for National Prohibition Reform (WONPR). Demonstrating charisma and a keen sense of political strategy, she realized that she needed to extend her message to women of all socio-economic levels to garner enough political momentum. One of the arguments she used to sway opinion and support her movement was that Prohibition had made the world less safe for children in that they now had access to unsafe, unregulated alcohol:

> In pre-prohibition days, mothers had little fear in regard to the saloon as far as their children were concerned. A saloonkeeper's license was revoked if he were caught selling liquor to minors. Today in any speakeasy in the United States you can find boys and girls in their teens drinking liquor, and this situation has become so acute that the mothers of the country feel something must be done to protect their children.
>
> (p. 120)[2]

By the time Prohibition was repealed in 1932, she had mustered enough of the voting-age female population to outnumber the ranks of the prohibitionist Women's Christian Temperance Union (WCTU), a major force behind the passing of the Volstead Act.

Proponents and Opponents of Legalization

Just like Sabin's argument that prohibition gave youth greater access to alcohol, the pro-marijuana legalization movement asserts that cannabis is more easily accessible to youth because of its illegal status. According to former San Jose police chief, Joseph McNamara:

> Today, because it is illegal, teenagers have an easier time buying pot than beer. For any high school student, trying to purchase a six-pack without ID means being turned away by a liquor store owner who is concerned with losing his license. The same can't be said for drug dealers who exploit prohibition to profit off our kids.[3]

Have seventh and eighth graders confirmed this is true? Can they more easily score a bag of weed than a six-pack of beer? Middle and high school students were polled about substance use availability and attitudes.[4] Twenty-two percent of teens reported that marijuana was easiest to buy compared to beer (15%). Thirty-four percent obtained alcohol from friends, and 23% acquired it from home, while 24% reported marijuana was procured from friends and only 1% obtained the drug from their home or family.[5] A key point from these findings is that adolescents tend to get alcohol and marijuana from each other. In 2012, this survey was replicated changing the question to where youth could obtain which substances within an hour and within a day. Almost 27% stated that they could find alcohol within an hour, and just over 48% reported they could get alcohol in a day. Meanwhile, only 14% indicated they could score cannabis in an hour, and only 30% thought they could find some within a 24-hour period.[6] These statistics suggest that marijuana is more difficult to procure quickly than alcohol, contradicting assertions that underage access to marijuana is easier given its illegal status. Whether legalization would create an environment where teens could more readily acquire marijuana will continue to be debated.

Research offers some evidence suggesting legalization might not cause marijuana use rates to skyrocket among youth, but this could be attributed to how easy the drug already is to obtain.[7] Monitoring the Future's 2014 National Survey on adolescent drug use revealed that after a steady rise in marijuana use by eighth, tenth, and twelfth graders from 2007 to 2010, use leveled for two years.[8] In 2014, reported marijuana use modestly declined post-legalization in four states and the District of Columbia. The Healthy Kids Colorado Survey (2013) reported that high school student use remained unchanged following the legalization of marijuana the year before. In fact, rates of use had remained stable since 2005.[9] Additional reports have even found that after medical marijuana laws were passed, medical marijuana states claim decreased use,[10] that the jury is still out,[11] or no change at all.[12] These findings provide support for the contention that moving towards legalization of marijuana makes it less of a "forbidden fruit" to use and would direct access from the streets to inside dispensaries. Lastly, some research indicates elevated marijuana use among youth after medical marijuana laws were passed.[13] What confounds results in these cases may be the data showing marijuana use was already higher in states *before* they passed medical marijuana laws, suggesting other factors were at play.[14] As the picture remains unclear, it is of the utmost importance that monitoring trends continues.

One touted benefit of legalization has been that it would deal a crippling blow to the revenue stream of the violent Mexican drug cartels. There may be some truth to that assertion, as Mexican police departments have reported a decrease in drug-related murders from its peak of 23,000 in 2011 to 15,649 in 2014. Further, they have seized less marijuana being prepared for smuggling into the United States and elsewhere. Experts agree that the legalization in Colorado and Washington State along with associated increases in marijuana production in those states have impacted the trafficking flow of cannabis across the border. Despite these improvements, Mexican police departments are seeing an increase in the cartel's trafficking of other illicit drugs, as well as diversification into illegal activities.[15] Changing one drug's legal status may only serve to shift trends in illegal operations and which drugs are being trafficked.

Those who oppose legalization lack prominent voices, dynamic spokespersons, in mainstream media. While they provide information on the potential hazards of cannabis use, few attempt to directly counter the stated facts and opinions of pro-legalization forces. Some exceptions include prevention coalitions and even NIDA wades into the tussle on occasions—but rarely do they refute the other side's claims item by item or try to discredit their opponents. Debate is not usually the forte of researchers and scientists. The very passion needed to emotionally sway an audience has been subsumed beneath years of taut, objective discipline demanded by the rigors of the scientific method.

Notable exceptions are Joseph Califano (former Secretary of Health, Education and Welfare) and William Bennett (Drug Czar under President George H. W. Bush). Another is Kevin Sabet—assistant professor at the University of Florida, public speaker, Senior Advisor to the White House Office of National Drug Control Policy (ONDCP) under the Obama Administration, co-founder of SAM (Smart Approaches to Marijuana), and author of *Reefer Sanity: Seven Great Myths about Marijuana* along with other articles and monographs. Sabet goes on the offensive, arguing for continued prohibition while recommending modifications in our policies to soften further the lasting effects of criminalization on everyday marijuana users. If the amount of editorial pushback on the internet from the legalization advocates are a measurement, he has their attention. Among his many arguments is that Prohibition under the Volstead Act worked in a number of ways. He points out evidence that rates of cirrhosis and alcohol use decreased among the general population during this dry era,[16] though other data show the decrease in liver disease began before the start of Prohibition.[17] As Sabet summarizes: "If our experience with legal alcohol provides us with any lessons for drug policy, it is this: We have little reason to believe that the benefits of drug legalization would outweigh its costs."[18]

One of Sabet's direr prophecies of marijuana legalization is that of whom the producers of the product will be. Will Big Tobacco shift to Big Marijuana? "We're going to see the nightmare repeat," he states. "It's one thing to say you don't want see someone to go to prison for having a joint in their pocket. It's another thing to have Philip Morris-type tactics."[19] A 2014 investigation found that tobacco companies have indeed been actively exploring the potential of cannabis as an opportunity and a source of competition since the 1970s.[20] With their enormous financial resources and ability to navigate the government regulatory waters, companies like R. J. Reynolds and Phillip Morris would have a tremendous advantage of other growers, most of which are comparatively small, local operations. Much of the romanticized view of marijuana as a "plant of the people" would be lost. Instead of Joe Camel, we could have Joe Vape. Already tobacco companies are investing heavily in the e-cigarette business and producing vaporizers that would put them well ahead of the curve in the marketing of marijuana delivery devices. Presently, marijuana's Schedule I classification under federal law remains the primary roadblock to a full-scale Big Tobacco incursion into the cannabis marketplace.

What would the legalization of marijuana bring? Or maybe, what would this country look like if all drug use were decriminalized, even legalized, and regulated? Hypothetically, if this country were to move in that direction, the first step—and no small one—would be to resolve the herculean task of dismantling the edifice universally called the War on Drugs. It has metastasized greatly in the past 80 years of our country's history and every element connected to it—and opposed to it—has also swelled in kind: law enforcement, government bureaucracy, lobbyists, weaponry, business, correctional facilities, legal entities, internet marketing, banking, pharmaceuticals, laboratory testing, and, yes, scientific research, substance abuse treatment, and prevention organizations. It is an awesome, almost unfathomable, structure now. How does something that vast get pulled apart without also harming the thousands of well-meaning inhabitants within its body, people whose livelihoods are inextricably linked to and dependent on its continued survival? Answering that question thoroughly is another book entirely.

Those against prohibition point to the collateral damage it has caused, arguing that such harm far outweighs the benefits it affords us. At the top of this argument is how this policy has contributed to our country being the greatest imprisoner in the world. Furthermore, they assert prohibition of marijuana and the War on Drugs are racist policies, evidenced by the disproportionate number of minorities who are incarcerated. The pro-legalization argument states that marijuana is at the base of this outsized correctional population, since it is the drug for which Americans are most commonly arrested. To take this syllogism a step further, marijuana laws are the primary tool in the continued oppression of people of color.

That the United States incarcerates a great number of its citizens is indisputable. In her book *The New Jim Crow: Mass Incarceration in the Age of Color Blindness*, Michelle Alexander puts forth some unsettling statistics.[21] She states that even if we were to turn back the clocks to the 1970s, when critics and activists railed against what they saw as indefensibly high incarceration rates, to match those rates nowadays we would have to release 80% of the inmates presently behind bars. Although incarceration rates are beginning to dwindle, it remains a travesty. Having quadrupled since the end of the 1970s, our imprisoned population of 2.2 million is anywhere from five to ten times higher than any other western democracy. Almost a quarter of the world's incarcerated population is in our prisons and jails—nearly one out of every 100 adult Americans.[22]

However, here are some other statistics to consider: drug arrests account for between 20% and 25% of the prison population. Higher rates used by anti-prohibition groups of 50–60% are probably attributable to federal penitentiaries—therefore the result of a very serious drug crime—or that the numbers are mixed with other serious crimes on both federal and state levels. Only 8% of those incarcerated in prisons or penitentiaries for drug offenses are there for marijuana-related crimes.[23] Nevertheless, that 8%—around 50,000—represents a lot of individuals to have lost their freedom, and upon being released they face the disadvantaged future of a convicted felon.

One would think that the threat of incarceration on this scale would eventually have created deterrence and resulted in less drug use due to lack of availability, but this is plainly not the case. A comprehensive 2014 report sponsored by the London School of Economics and Political Science[24] suggests that prohibition multiplies the price of hard drugs like cocaine by as much as ten times. Since a significant number of those who are eventually jailed come from the lower socioeconomic stratum, the enticement of those kinds of profits can make selling an irresistible alternative to poverty.

Despite these impressive data, prohibition is not seen as an utterly failed policy. There are other indicators demonstrating that appropriate interdiction policies can prove to be cost-effective when compared to the potential damage incurred by unrestricted access to substances. The problem of prohibition versus legalization is far more complex when fully analyzed, and promoting legalization as a panacea may prove hazardously simplistic. The pros of legalization include: decreased social stigma; reduction in illegal trade and thus related crime; lower societal damage caused by incarceration; increased public revenue; less law enforcement expenditures leading to more fruitful reallocation of funds; regulated, safer cannabis products; and lower consumer costs due to an expanded, free market.

The potential downside is not to be ignored either. A prominent con laid out includes increased consumption by those already having drug dependency or are predisposed toward addiction—especially youth, impacting the families or dependents of those afflicted individuals. As noted, there might also be gains or losses from decreased or increased self-harming or socially harmful use of alcohol and other drugs. While there will certainly be states that take a "wait and see" stance on marijuana before committing to full legalization, other states will undoubtedly follow those that have already plunged in head-first.

What can be learned from those countries that have had de facto legalization for years, such as the Netherlands and Portugal? They have not legalized the drug and have only chosen a policy of non-enforcement for any laws pertaining to small amounts of cannabis sold in places like coffee shops or have decriminalized all drugs. How do they compare with the United States? The available data show that rates of cannabis use do not differ between the Netherlands and the United States, though Dutch females are less likely to report consuming cannabis in the past year.[25]

It is estimated that legalizing drugs within the United States would annually save roughly $41.3 billion, with $25.7 billion being saved among the states and over $15.6 billion accrued by the federal government.[26] This may be great for taxpayers and government officials, but, as more states legalize cannabis for recreational use, the more we will see the dynamic effects of an open market economy. As marijuana products increasingly saturate the market, competition and a greater supply will drive prices down, creating a buyer's market where there will be plenty of cheap weed. "If you make any attractive commodity available at lower cost, you will have more users," stated Thomas McLellan, former deputy director of the Office of National Drug Control Policy, when referring to Portugal's policies.[27] And yet, Portugal has seen a reduction in past-year drug use by 15- to 24-year-olds from over 8% in 2001 to 6% in 2012. Further, past-month drug use decreased even more, from just under 6% to 3%. Portugal has decriminalized marijuana to the status of an "administrative offense." Fines and classes still await those who are busted with small amounts of the drug, but penalty enforcement often never materializes. After a slight increase in use in 2007—a spike that was in line with other European countries—the rates of use diminished.[28] However, this reduction may not necessarily be a result of decriminalization, as other indicators muddy the picture.

Consequences for College Students

One peril for college students is that prohibition laws have created a threat to federal student aid. In 1998, Congress amended the Higher Education Act of 1965 to restrict eligibility for federal financial aid to students convicted of certain drug charges under federal or state laws. A single conviction under a drug offense could have resulted in immediate and permanent ineligibility for federal student aid such as Stafford and Plus loans, as well as federal work-study and Pell grants. However, as of 2009, modifications to the original rule were made allowing for paths to reinstatement for convicted students who had been ineligible for aid indefinitely.[29] Specifically, if a student is convicted of possession of illegal drugs, he or she loses eligibility for federal aid for one year for the first offense, two years for the second offense, and indefinitely for the third.

Students with one or two strikes may also be required to complete a drug treatment program as a stipulation for regaining eligibility.

Selling or conspiring to sell illegal drugs has a shorter leash. After conviction for a first offense, students lose aid eligibility for two years and then lose eligibility indefinitely after their second offense. The clock for the ineligible period starts from the date of conviction rather than the date of the offense, and it will only apply if the student was already receiving federal student aid at the time the crime was committed. Drug-related charges committed before or after the period a student was enrolled and receiving aid will not count except for trafficking arrests. Trafficking generally involves larger amounts of substances and often includes crossing state lines—allowing courts more leeway to impose funding penalties. These penalties cross state borders as well, so violations that occur in states other than where school is attended still count.

There is no need for a report to financial aid offices in states where marijuana possession of small amounts has been decriminalized to a fine or where accelerated rehabilitation-type programs lead to the charge being expunged. A federal study in 2005—conducted prior to the above changes—estimated that drug violations cause denial of 20,000 Pell grants and 40,000 student loans each year. Even with overlap between those two estimates, these figures represent almost an entire enrollment of a Big Ten university. This could be an underestimate since these numbers were only based on those who applied for aid and excluded the unknown number who may not have tried knowing the consequences.[30] With changes in the act, those numbers went down significantly between 2013 and 2014, as only 1,107 applicants lost eligibility for a full year of aid due to a drug conviction or failure to report one.[31] FAFSA applications ask about drug convictions directly. In earlier cases, students with drug records were counseled to lie as the Department of Education may not have had access to state and local crime records. The risk in doing so, however, was that fines for knowingly providing false information can be as high as $10,000.

A Glimpse at the Future: Colorado

The advent of medical marijuana and more recently legalization in several states, has ushered in a period where university policy on marijuana is both changed and yet not. In states with medical marijuana or even where it is legal for recreational use, universities risk raising federal ire and losing precious funding from the government if they allow cannabis on campus, regardless of the state statute. Most have found an easy enough compromise in that they prohibit marijuana to be physically on campus at any time for any reason. Devin Cramer, Associate Director of

Student Conduct at the University of Colorado, where recreational use of marijuana is legal by state law, commented that the legalization of weed did not significantly change that department's procedures. However, legalization necessitated education, especially for the influx of new out-of-state students, clarifying that marijuana was still a violation of the university code of conduct and disabusing them of the notion that they could come to the University of Colorado and light up a joint while walking to class.

As Colorado had a medical marijuana law for over a decade prior to the passing of Amendment 64, the culture of marijuana use was already imbued in everyday student life. Compared to other states with such a statute, medical marijuana in Colorado was fairly liberal, and students had relatively easy access to the dispensaries or at least had friends who did. Therefore, legalization did not result in a sudden tsunami of available marijuana on campus shocking the student culture and overwhelming the university student conduct, prevention, and police staff. Those students with state medical marijuana cards may live off-campus and use it there. The fact that the substance remains at least federally illegal appears to provide some ballast of clarity in this upheaval.

Immediately off campus, the rules change. The difficulties usually lie in police enforcement of these laws. Off-campus housing sites may be under town or state police jurisdiction and so cultivating a solid collaboration between the judicial system of that town and the one internal to the university can be paramount from a prevention standpoint. Colleges can handle this in a variety of ways, but there are some difficult knots to untangle. Cramer recounts that at the University of Colorado in Boulder, even prior to legalization, the mandate that freshmen live on campus their first year was challenged by one student who threatened to sue because he could not access his state-sanctioned medical stash if he were to comply with this rule. Now, students with medical marijuana cards can appeal for a waiver during freshman registration to live in off-campus apartments. Other schools in similar legal climates, such as Washington State University, have since followed suit allowing freshmen to live off-campus under such an appeal. Many other universities in medical marijuana states and with similar housing rules may have to accommodate this as well. The implications of this movement compound fiscal problems for universities that may be striving to retain students in residential housing on campus. Furthermore, the move of students off campus complicates efforts for schools to tackle alcohol and drug abuse issues in general. With off-campus living arrangements, students are less entrenched in the culture and mores of the school, where university safety officers can enforce policies surrounding drug use. The looser tether can impact the drug culture of a school and how effectively university professionals, hoping to promote wellness and retention among students, can stem the tide.

Schools in states bordering those that have legalized recreational marijuana will have to prepare for increased traffic of their students crossing state borders to score legal weed. In most of these states thus far, residents and visitors can have up to one ounce on their person by law. Returning to their universities is another matter. Police and federal authorities may regularly set up stops on the main throughways, intercepting any vehicle driven by or filled with twenty-something males—fish in a barrel. Immediately following legalization going online in one state, schools in neighboring states may have to cope with an uncomfortable number of students arrested for possession. As some of those students may get pinched with more than an ounce, these could be felony charges resulting in a rash of dismissals. It is even worse if DEA agents make the bust. Current federal law dictates that a first-time violation of marijuana possession laws can land you a minimum of a $1,000 fine and up to a year in prison. And that is if the feds do not think there was any intent to distribute. Over time, this should smooth out as students become savvier and police disinterested, but initially it could get ugly.

Many tourists of college age are disappointed when they travel to Denver or Boulder. Many expect to behold streets lined with clubs and cafes where they can walk in, belly up to the bar, and order a round of Mango Kush for themselves and their buddies. That is not the case. Unlike Amsterdam where tourists and locals can purchase marijuana inside a small café and consume it, in Colorado cannabis must be purchased at licensed stores and is usually eaten, smoked, or vaped in a private residence. There have arisen a small number of private clubs that people can easily join for a fee, then use their own weed on the location while socializing with others. These "budpubs" may offer smoking or vaping paraphernalia to patrons, but may not yet legally dispense pot. The reason these clubs are private is that *smoking* anything in public buildings is against the law. Marijuana advocates like Mason Tvert pushed for changes in city ordinances that would allow for restricted outside areas where marijuana could be used. Presently, under Amendment 64, Colorado's legalization law, marijuana may not be consumed in any outside public area. In November 2016, Denver passed Initiative 300 that approved a four-year study in which Denver establishments could apply for permits to allow marijuana smoking in restricted outside areas.

The movement toward legalization is unnerving for many, as it is a journey into uncharted territory. The future that lies before us is not clear, and unlike the repeal of Prohibition under the Volstead Act, where Americans knew what a "wet" world would look like once again, there is no a familiar historical relationship with legal marijuana. It was banned before the average citizen knew anything about it. If there is any reassurance to be found, it is that it will happen state by state, piecemeal over time. This will allow other states to study those that have taken the plunge, weigh the pros and cons, and learn from mistakes before moving forward themselves, or not.

Notes

1 Koch, C. G. (2015, November 19). Freedom's framework. *National Review*, 67(21). Retrieved from www.nationalreview.com/nrd/articles/426272/freedoms-framework

2 Kyvig, D. E., & Jeffers, H. F. (2000). *Repealing national prohibition*. Kent, OH: The Kent State University Press.

3 McNamara, J. (2010, October 25). Let's be honest: The war against marijuana has failed. The Blog, *Huffington Post*. Retrieved from www.huffington-post.com/joseph-mcnamara/lets-be-honest-the-war-ag_b_773627.html

4 The National Center of Addiction and Substance Abuse. (2009, August). *National survey of American attitudes on substance abuse XIV: Teens and parents*. Retrieved from www.centeronaddiction.org/addiction-research/reports/national-survey-american-attitudes-substance-abuse-teens-parents-2009

5 Ibid.

6 The National Center of Addiction and Substance. (2012, August). *National survey of American attitudes on substance abuse XVII: Teens*. Retrieved from www.centeronaddiction.org/addiction-research/reports/national-survey-american-attitudes-substance-abuse-teens-2012

7 Caulkins, J. P., Hawken, A., Kilmer, B., & Kleiman, M. A. R. (2012). *Marijuana legalization: What everyone needs to know*. New York, NY: Oxford University Press.

8 Johnston, L. D., O'Malley, P. M., Miech, R. A., Bachman, J. G., & Schulenberg, J. E. (2015). *Monitoring the Future national survey results on drug use: 1975–2014: Overview, key findings on adolescent drug use*. Ann Arbor, MI: Institute for Social Research, The University of Michigan. Retrieved from www.monitoringthefuture.org/pubs/monographs/mtf-overview2014.pdf

9 Nelson, S. (2014, August 7). Pot use among Colorado teens appears to drop after legalization. *U.S. News & World Report*. Retrieved from www.usnews.com/news/articles/2014/08/07/pot-use-among-colorado-teens-appears-to-drop-after-legalization

10 Lynne-Landsman, S. D., Livingston, M. D., & Wagenaar, A. C. (2013). Effects of state medical marijuana laws on adolescent marijuana use. *American Journal of Public Health*, 103(8), 1500–1506. http://doi.org/10.2105/AJPH.2012.301117

11 Wall, M. M., Poh, E., Cerdá, M., Keyes, K. M., Galea, S., & Hasin, D. S. (2011). Adolescent marijuana use from 2002 to 2008: Higher in states with medical marijuana laws, cause still unclear. *Annals of Epidemiology*, 21(9), 714–716. doi:10.1016/j.annepidem.2011.06.001

12 Harper, S., Strumpf, E. C., & Kaufman J. S. (2012). Do medical marijuana laws increase marijuana use? Replication study and extension [Abstract]. *Annals of Epidemiology*, 22(3), 207–212. doi:10.1016/j.annepidem.2011.12.002

13 Stolzenberg, L., D'Alessio, S. J., & Dariano, D. (2016). The effect of medical cannabis laws on cannabis use [Abstract]. *The International Journal on Drug Policy*, 27, 82–88. doi:10.1016/j.drugpo.2015.05.018

14 Hasin, D. S., Wall, M., Keyes, K. M., Cerdá, M., Schulenberg, J., O'Malley, P. M., . . . Feng, T. (2015). State medical marijuana laws and adolescent marijuana use in the United States: 1991–2014. *The Lancet Psychiatry, 2*(7), 601–608. http://doi.org/10.1016/S2215-0366(15)00217-5

15 Grillo, I. (2015, April 8). U.S. legalization of marijuana has hit Mexican cartels' cross-border trade. *Time Magazine*. Retrieved from http://time.com/3801889/us-legalization-marijuana-trade/

16 Sabet, K. (2013). *Reefer sanity: Seven great myths about marijuana*. New York, NY: Beaufort Books.

17 Thorton, M. (1991, July 17). Prohibition was a failure. *Auburn University Cato Policy Analysis 157*. Retrieved from www.cato.org/publications/policy-analysis/alcohol-prohibition-was-failure

18 Sabet, K. (2011, October 5). Prohibition's real lessons for drug policy. *Los Angeles Times*. Retrieved from http://articles.latimes.com/2011/oct/05/opinion/la-oe-sabet-prohibition-20111005

19 Hughs, T. (2015, April 11). Will big tobacco become big marijuana? *USA Today*. Retrieved from www.usatoday.com/story/money/business/2015/04/11/cigarettes-and-marijuana/70746772/

20 Barry, R. A., Hiilamo, H., & Glantz, S. A. (2014, June). Waiting for the opportune moment: The tobacco industry and marijuana legalization. *The Millbank Quarterly, 92*(2), 207–242. doi:10.1111/1468–0009.12055

21 Alexander, M. (2010). *The new Jim Crow: Mass incarceration in the age of color blindness*. New York, NY: The New Press.

22 Travis, J., Western, B., & Redburn, S. (2014). *The growth of incarceration in the United States: Exploring causes and consequences*. Washington, DC: The National Academies Press. https://doi.org/10.17226/18613

23 Caulkins, Hawken, Kilmer, & Kleiman, (2012).

24 The London School of Economics and Political Science. (2014, May 14). *Ending the drug wars: Report from the LSE expert group on the economics of drug policy*. Retrieved from www.lse.ac.uk/IDEAS/publications/reports/pdf/LSE-IDEAS-DRUGS-REPORT-FINAL-WEB01.pdf

25 Simons-Morton, B., Pickett, W., Boyce, W., ter Bogt, T. F. M., & Vollebergh, W. (2010). Cross-national comparison of adolescent drinking and cannabis use in the United States, Canada, and the Netherlands [Abstract]. *The International Journal on Drug Policy, 21*(1), 64–69. http://doi.org/10.1016/j.drugpo.2009.02.003

26 Miron, J., & Waldock, K. (2010, September 27). The budgetary impact of ending prohibition. *Cato Institute*. Retrieved from www.cato.org/publications/white-paper/budgetary-impact-ending-drug-prohibition

27 Ingraham, C. (2015, June 5). Why hardly anyone dies from a drug overdose in Portugal. *Washington Post*. Retrieved from www.washingtonpost.com/news/wonk/wp/2015/06/05/why-hardly-anyone-dies-from-a-drug-overdose-in-portugal/?utm_term=.eaef7a8dcaf7

28 Stevens, A., & Hughes, C. E. (2012). A resounding success or a disastrous failure: Re-examining the interpretation of evidence on the Portuguese decriminalisation of illicit drugs. *Drug and Alcohol Review, 31*(1), 101–113. http://doi.org/10.1111/j.1465-3362.2011.00383.x

29 Mayotte, B. (2015, April 15). Drug convictions can send financial aid up in smoke. *U.S. News and World Report*. Retrieved from www.usnews.com/education/blogs/student-loan-ranger/2015/04/15/drug-convictions-can-send-financial-aid-up-in-smoke

30 Lederman, D. (2005, September 28). Drug law denies aid to thousands. *Inside Higher Ed*. Retrieved from www.insidehighered.com/news/2005/09/28/drug

31 Liebelson, D. (2016, February 11). College kids caught with drugs may not get kicked off financial aid anymore. *Huffington Post*. Retrieved from www.huffingtonpost.com/entry/drug-policy-financial-aid-college_us_56bcbe7fe4b08ffac1242cf9

Chapter 13

Changing the Dialogue

If you talk to a man in a language he understands, that goes to his head. If you talk to him in his language, that goes to his heart.
—Nelson Mandela[1]

Despite the challenge of reaching college students in an honest, productive discourse on cannabis, there is remarkable work being done in research, prevention and counseling, and other areas across the higher-education landscape. Sincere, dedicated people are striving to protect young brains, futures, and careers. Regardless of funding or underlying agenda, there exists a massive body of knowledge demonstrating the potential health impact of regular marijuana use. Yet, for many students who regularly consume cannabis products, the information they glean from their friends and the pro-marijuana internet sites simply carries more weight. This is true even for students who are struggling most with dependency on marijuana; there is a refusal to acknowledge that their beloved plant is harming them.

Then there are those for whom the struggle over cannabis is much larger than the drug itself; it is political, about social subjects important to them like justice and individual freedom. We have plenty of data that give some insight into what college students think about marijuana overall, but there is little research on student attitudes toward drug policies. One such study found students' perceptions about marijuana policy vary by major, but overall the pool is meager.[2] To a smaller card-carrying cohort of politically inclined students within the cannabis culture, college prevention and counseling professionals come from an alien, weedless planet whose inhabitants view marijuana use only as a developing disorder, a health hazard, illegal behavior tainted with immorality . . . and there is some truth to this. Meanwhile, students perceive it as an exhilarating, adventurous, mind-expanding, curative, comforting, social, and misunderstood recreational activity. From the outset, these incongruent platforms create a disconnection that makes meaningful communication difficult.

Driving the wedge deeper is the underlying stigma associated with drug use. Drug addiction is the most stigmatized illness in the world, even more so than the runner up: alcoholism.[3] Students finding themselves caught up in the drug enforcement system experience a sense of shame that is discordant with their beliefs about marijuana use. They feel judged, even oppressed, by a misguided system that refuses to look at itself. College campuses are populated by groups that identify with prejudice and marginalization, such as the LGBTQ community, students of color, or those of different religious and cultural backgrounds. And while it may seem a stretch equating a bong hit with having a same-sex partner or wearing a *hijab*, it is the students' perception of their experience that matters. We can interpret the righteous defiance of many cannabis consumers as defending against their experience of being stigmatized. To reject this entrenched edifice of social stigma serves as a blow against the empire. If this seems an exaggeration, one only needs to Google pictures of the throngs at 4/20 rallies. Universities are fertile soil for disenfranchised groups to find a sense of community and speak out. Yet cannabis consumers see themselves as an ignored class, and school policy reinforces this perception.

All of this boils down to finding a way to bridge the gap and fully connect with cannabis using students in a meaningful way. After close to three years exploring this issue, we, the authors, have found no singular method that brilliantly outshines the rest of the field. Despite this (not unexpected) disappointment, there are some principles worth recommending as a starting point.

Moving Toward a Harm-Reduction Model

As more states begin to move toward legalization in some form, neighboring states will have to confront the reality that unless they follow suit, they will inherit the consequences legalized cannabis may bring, while reaping none of the tax revenue it promises. It is both a difficult and easy choice to make: difficult, because it will chafe at beliefs and raise fear in many policy makers; easy, because the huge state budget shortfalls will force those politicians to resign to a bitter pragmatism. Meanwhile, the zero-tolerance foundation in college cannabis prevention will become increasingly hard to defend in the face of a pervasive environmental normalcy.

What can help our students is information about marijuana detached from an overarching goal of making them stop weed completely. This approach echoes extant prevention strategies to reduce risks associated with drinking in college. We need to retool our efforts toward curricula that make students better-informed consumers, because that is and will be the reality. This also means exploring ways to minimize possible harmful effects of marijuana use. Several areas of college students' experience with marijuana can be targeted:

1 Know all the cannabis products they will be exposed to, especially the difference between smoking a joint at a party and doing "dabs" or consuming an entire edible. Discuss the pharmacology of THC; the relative levels in all the products should become a basic part of any prevention program. Some schools are already beginning to do this. For example, Emerson College in Boston has a prevention pamphlet titled "Let's Be Blunt," with a section "Use Smart" with tips on reducing harm for those who choose to use cannabis. For those at-risk students, dabs and other potent extracts will be a bigger problem in the future than marijuana the plant. As students use more cannabis products, the tolerance levels these high-THC products create will be the next tier of dysfunction.

2 For regular consumers, encourage more "tolerance breaks" to allow THC to leave their systems. This will also minimize the withdrawal they might experience in future periods of abstinence. Reduction in use and breaks have an added benefit of allowing consumers to re-experience what they enjoyed about the high at first, while needing less marijuana as they are not developing tolerance as quickly. These conversations may involve acknowledging positive attributes of marijuana for consumers. Acknowledging that the high from marijuana is enjoyable is disagreeable to many in the prevention arena. This may be attributed to the predominance of drug prevention targeted toward children and may send an unwanted message. College students are no longer kids, and most have already experienced the euphoria of some substance. We need to meet them where they are, not where we think they should be.

Another benefit from tolerance breaks is the often-reported improvement in cognitive abilities and memory. Lastly, tolerance breaks have another benefit: those who cannot achieve even shorter periods of abstinence may become more open to the idea of needing abstinence-based treatment. The unpalatable truth that they are addicted does not always hit home until they make a sincere effort to stop, and fail. This painful insight leads to contemplating a more dramatic change. Self-evident truths are the most powerful ones.

3 Along a similar vein, convince students to take a break from using cannabis before studying or writing a paper. At some point, there will be students who claim it enhances their academic abilities; they need to know that this is a very small minority. Furthermore, improved performance after use can indicate tolerance, and those individuals

may be basing these claims on the times they stopped before an exam and experienced acute withdrawal that could be relieved only by use. This comes down to helping students find a better balance between their academic lives and partying behaviors.

4   Explain the pitfalls of driving while under the influence of cannabis. Many believe that they are driving carefully when high—they think safer because they may be driving slower than normal. Still, their reaction times slowed, they will not be able to respond swiftly to a sudden hazard or someone running out into the street. As marijuana laws change, so will the DUI regulations, along with the technology to accurately measure if someone is under the influence. Those students who have high tolerance may think they are driving better while buzzed, but it will be a moot point if pulled over for a broken taillight and their car smells like a Dave Matthews concert.

5   Review potential drug interactions with cannabis. While marijuana does not cause severe drug interactions, marijuana has been shown to inhibit the liver enzyme cytochrome 450, which is known to be responsible in the metabolism of many medications, including psychotropics and THC itself.[4] Therefore, heavy marijuana use can affect how medications work. Students should be encouraged to be candid with their prescribing doctors to allow for dosage adjustments.

6   Educate on individual characteristics associated with addiction: tolerance, withdrawal, etc. Emphasizing personal risk factors such as ADHD, co-occurring anxiety and depression, family history, and trauma can also help circumvent the argument over marijuana itself since it will be less of a confrontation about the drug itself and more of a discussion about characteristics of the consumer.

7   Consider potential health hazards, such as chronic bronchitis resulting from regular use. There can be more risk if the marijuana is mixed with tobacco in *spliffs*, though there has not yet been a robust amount of research about this combination. Students are also doing bong and pipe hits of a tobacco-weed mix, sometimes referred to as "moles." We do not know the effects of this at present, but, given what we do know about tobacco, it probably is not therapeutic. Additionally, certain infectious diseases that are spread through contact with saliva can be spread by sharing joints, pipes, and bongs. Recommend that students avoid direct contact with the cigarettes, try to clean the rim of the bong first, or completely avoid sharing delivery systems of any type involving oral contact.[5] Guiding students to avoid sharing cannabis using the same delivery system will be a hard sell, but some may be more inclined to take certain precautions.

The list of possible subjects for a marijuana harm reduction campaign is vast and is a relatively unmined area. Prevention has already made great strides developing strategies for safer alcohol use among college students. Schools routinely preach guidelines (e.g., "safer" drinking versus binge-drinking, B.A.C. cards, educating students to recognize the signs of alcohol poisoning). Higher education has accepted the inevitability of student alcohol use and has adjusted to this reality by teaching students how to drink safely. To do so with marijuana would not be a quantum leap.

Marijuana prevention self-assessments like Marijuana eCHECKUP TO GO head in this direction by taking the participating student's use profile and comparing it to a large database of college students. The next step would be more direct media campaigns and other strategies recommending healthier marijuana use guidelines, a clear departure from zero-tolerance.

Prevention Strategies to Include Longer-Term Follow-Ups

Many researchers and prevention specialists concede that following students over an extended period after intervention would be ideal and improve outcomes. However, universities, as a whole, have not yet provided the funding and resources to incorporate such programs into regular practice. College prevention and counseling programs are often combined and understaffed, running on meager budgets. In many cases, it is a staff of one, especially in small schools. To do periodic follow-ups with students would stretch resources to a breaking point. Nevertheless, it is unrealistic to expect a two-session intervention or an online program to be resistant to effect decay, especially in the adverse environment of drug use found on college campuses. Furthermore, even the most effective prevention and intervention will not yield immediate results; it requires an institutional commitment for the long haul. There is not yet a robust body of research demonstrating improved rates of change in the college prevention realm, but studies of treatment interventions of longer duration (more than 12 months) appear to have a greater effect than more time-limited ones.[6]

Our students who want to cut back or stop using marijuana entirely must endure constant temptations, as reminders to smoke or vape are presented to them in their dorms and apartments; on Snapchat, Instagram, and other social media; and in regular gatherings with friends. The bong is right there on the coffee table—the aroma wafts through the apartment, and their friends cajole them to join in. Meanwhile, inside their heads, a conflict is waging between information encouraging reduction or abstinence, and the more practiced and still captivating devotion to weed. In order to remain resolute with any commitment to change, they will need ongoing encouragement and support. Regular follow-ups throughout the year at reasonable intervals could be just enough investment to help students maintain change. This is an area where well-designed research studies on frequency and duration between follow-ups would be an invaluable addition to the field.

Having services available to provide such support will be key, including access to counseling or collegiate recovery programs. Contrary to what administrators might believe, these services are more than just another expense for schools in an already tight fiscal situation. Research-based prevention programs have shown to be cost-effective, at least in other educational arenas.[7] Like earlier findings, recent studies demonstrate that if school-based prevention were implemented nationwide, $18 would be saved for every $1 dollar invested. The problem is that these savings do not easily show up on a spreadsheet and are difficult to attribute directly to programming. More analysis is needed to examine the inter-related variables involved. Spending money short-term to save more in the future is not as clear-cut as simply restricting expenditure.

Increased Use of Technology

The present generation of college students has grown up with computers and mobile devices. In a 2015 study by the Pew Research Center, 92% of teens, ages 13 to 17, report going online daily: 24% reported doing so "constantly." A mere 6% answered that they only go on weekly.[8] The development of online programming, available through mobile devices like smartphones, will undoubtedly prove to be a key feature in college prevention. Online programs have two attractive features. First, they afford more privacy, minimizing contact with other people. Students can complete the online intervention confidentially and have the results or confirmation of completion sent to the Office of Student Conduct, if required. No one else is involved, and those who are get minimal information about that student. Second, it costs less than in-person interventions. This is an attractive feature for schools that cannot afford to staff prevention departments adequately, such as small institutions and community colleges. Hiring and training staff to meet the challenges of collegiate alcohol and drug prevention is expensive, and it is easily predicted that online products will become more prevalent.

Focus Research on College-Specific Consumption

Given the rapaciousness of collegiate substance use, one would think pertinent research could be measured in sheer tonnage, but that is not the case. Consider Harvard University. A thorough search within the seemingly endless maze of the 400-year-old archives would yield hundreds of studies, papers, and dissertations on the entire scientific-social-political atlas of cannabis chronicled by generations of Harvard professors and students—with one glaring omission: there is hardly anything about marijuana use at Harvard itself.[9] It is highly unlikely that Harvard students through the years have refrained from cannabis use, making one wonder about the censorship of research that could potentially put the university in an unfavorable light.

Overall, our own research revealed collegiate cannabis use remains an area ripe for further investigation since marijuana studies have predominantly focused on primary and secondary prevention among adolescents. Research tailored specifically to the college population would help prevention and treatment efforts with these students. Although we can generalize from present literature, nothing replaces population-specific research demonstrating what works and what does not. Although colleges have the useful practice of routinely collecting data on cannabis use and attitudes through instruments like the Core survey,[10] it is only a first step.

Understanding Them Versus Them Understanding Us

In welcome, or in dread, we are not only entering an era of legalized, but *legitimized* marijuana use. It will one day become, just like alcohol and tobacco before it, woven into the fabric of everyday life: completely integrated, and yet still tinged with hazard. The efforts of primary and secondary prevention in middle and high school will accomplish what it can, altering the trajectory of experimentation for some, but not for others. The focus in college needs to be connecting with students who show signs of greater risk and intervening quickly and effectively. Given the inevitable cultural integration of marijuana, we need to collectively rethink and retool how we communicate with students. Since we are the ones who educate, counsel, direct, and model, we must make the adjustments.

Some experts predict that stripping away the barrier of illegality will cause the rates of cannabis use disorders to spike. It is possible this would be a temporary trend where the majority will eventually tire of the previously forbidden fruit, followed by a gradual decline back to pre-legalization norms. Since 2001, the rates of addiction to alcohol and drugs appear to stay the same, at least as measured by admissions to chemical dependency treatment programs.[11] What fluctuates over time are the demographics of the consumers and the substances consumed. However, these statistics may be affected by the limited treatment slots available nationwide or by the low treatment-seeking behavior among those with substance use disorders. SAMHSA estimates that close to 95% of all persons needing treatment do not receive it.[12] This problem may worsen, particularly for those with cannabis use disorders given the normalization of marijuana and denial of any related addiction potential. These data suggest at the very least that cannabis use disorders will not be declining any time soon, so the problem of prevention and treatment remains relevant post-legalization.

If given the opportunity, young people will share their thoughts and attitudes about marijuana, and they are much more insightful than they have been given credit for by older adults. This area has not had the attention it deserves; however, there have been some efforts to study and document how high-school age adolescents perceive marijuana-related topics.[13]

Research has also demonstrated what collaboration with young adults and adolescents on prevention can achieve. They are willing to not only talk but to help problem-solve around harm reduction messaging if given the opportunity,[14] recommending more focus on marijuana in earlier prevention initiatives, harm-reduction vs. abstinence-based messaging, and avoidance of scare tactics.[15] Another theme that came out of listening to youth was that consumers are a diverse group—if you have met one weed smoker, you have met one weed smoker. This has important implications for the need to target a wide range of different groups for prevention efforts.

The next step would be to incorporate input from these participants into overall prevention strategies and look closely at future outcomes. At the college level, schools could start by holding similar focus groups on marijuana use including consumers at all levels and non-consumers alike. Feedback from such groups along with evidenced-based strategies can inform the development of prevention programming, particularly for incoming freshman.

The key to fruitful dialogue lies in listening, more so than talking. The good news is that there are templates available to help with this shift. In many current prevention programs in schools across the nation, Motivational Interviewing (MI) provides a framework from which to begin communication. Since their first publications on MI, Miller and Rollnick have focused more on what they describe as *the spirit of motivational interviewing*.[16] The primary goal remains helping clients examine and resolve their ambivalence, but with a greater emphasis on the spirit vs. the techniques of the method, reinforcing the supportive collaboration between counselor and student identified by inclusive language and a clear description of teamwork. The relationship is not directly persuasive, manipulative, or underpinned by any ulterior motive to move the student toward abstinence or even improved health; students must see change as their choice.

This may sound simple enough, but it is very hard for some counselors to sequester their own biases or fears and set aside organizational mandates concerning cannabis use that could muddy the partnership.

Something remarkable happens to many professionals when it comes to working with substance use, especially when they are older and parents. Parents want to shield, direct, and at times—out of their own anxiety—lecture, scold, and even punish to protect youth. Seasoned therapists, skilled in discussing a wide range of sensitive and provocative topics, suddenly become flummoxed when heavy substance use becomes the subject of discussion. The need to intervene can feel reflexive, almost irresistible. Institutions such as universities reinforce this parental stance in many ways as they are legally bound to exercise authority over their student body. To truly embody the spirit of MI, those working with students must allow them that basic freedom of choice—difficult when the mission of one's department is to promote a drug-free lifestyle. This also demands affirming client-students' positive attributes and strengths, without disingenuously trying to prop up their self-esteem or indirectly endorse their cannabis use. MI acknowledges skills the students already possess to create change in their lives. Engaging these strengths in a partnership is key.

Students should be the ones doing the talking. This can be difficult because marijuana prevention is heavily weighted with research and messaging for dissemination to at-risk groups. But, if students are to be responsible for the transformation, eliciting language of change is paramount. Research still plays a critical role in providing education that increases ambivalence necessary for change, provided it pads *both* sides of the argument. The key to using information effectively is determining what to provide and when to do so. It must be introduced judiciously to facilitate the work and not be force-fed to students. Choice information is tantamount to just the right ingredient in a recipe that enhances a dish. A generous pinch of saffron transforms the paella. Eating an entire plate of saffron would be a very unpleasant gastronomic experience. A student who desires change will want, will seek, the information research studies have availed us. We just need to be informed and ready when that opportunity presents itself.

Perhaps no principle is misapplied more than *empathy*. Empathy, the ability to understand and experience the feelings of another person, is a key interpersonal process in psychotherapy. Miller and Rollnick describe it as the ability to accurately reflect what a client has said.[17] But this accuracy requires more than just repeating the words correctly. Crucial in the art of counseling, over time it has devolved into a mere technique—a parroting device used as a means to an end, as the necessity to train counselors quickly grew to meet the burgeoning demand. Many college prevention counselors are graduate students, set to depart at the end of the year, requiring annual retraining for the following cohorts. As colleges incorporated MI into their prevention and intervention programming, the need to be able to package MI into pre-made, user-friendly, and easily marketed toolkits became increasingly important. Personally facilitated or online MI trainings have become ubiquitous in the prevention marketplace as a way of packaging such skills. While these trainings are helpful, it is much more complicated to operationalize something as basically human as empathy. We can teach the behaviors associated with it, but true empathy must come from within—otherwise it is analogous to knowing the lyrics to a song, but being unable to hum the tune.

We must appreciate the internal conflict of the students themselves and why marijuana is important to them. Having this compassion by itself is insufficient to move forward with the process of change, but it must be present. For practitioners without any personal experience with drug or alcohol use, being able to identify with a student's struggle can be hard, like trying to understand the cultural customs of a foreign people. Those who have never used marijuana, or perhaps found it unpleasant or unrewarding, may not have an internalized experience for identification. They do not get what it is all about—why the reluctance to quit in the face of mounting consequences. Worse, some practitioners may have grown up in homes where the entire family process rotated on the axis of addiction—subjected to constant fear, threats, losses, disappointments, and, in some cases, abuse and trauma. In these situations, there can be an irresistible drive to intercede with students independent of what they want, but in doing so it becomes the practitioner who wants understanding. In the lore of addiction psychotherapy, there is an axiom that warns of an unconscious struggle between the therapist and the client. Even if never stated or overt, clients who believe their therapist is trying to take away their beloved substance without their consent will, in turn take away something precious to the therapists: their experience of efficacy.

Having experience with marijuana is not a prerequisite for being able to offer help and guidance to those who use or struggle with it. Although personal experience is not essential to be effective, having a base of knowledge about cannabis can be helpful to engender confidence in students. Personal experience is not a requirement to work with other types of mental health problems—does one need to have experienced psychosis to help people with schizophrenia? Over-identification with presenting problems and sharing our own histories can be counterproductive and interfere with the intervention. However, everyone, regardless of background, can access a shared experience with attachment to something like a place, time of life, person, or drug. Most of us know the feeling of being absolutely enthralled with something or someone. Some of us have even had the experience of being in love to a detriment, yet persisted in that relationship long after we reached that conclusion. Cannabis, as with other substances and addictive behaviors, activates many of those chemicals in our brains that allow us to fall in love, make a home, become committed to a cause, and parent a child. It just does so in a way that ceases to be healthy for some people. Knowing this can engender the compassion necessary to serve as catalysts for change.

What we view as a harmful drug may initially have been a transformative agent for some college students. It may have allowed the socially phobic to suddenly, even "miraculously," connect with others. Like shared food it incorporates others into a family or culture. Drugs like marijuana become valuable currency in the previously exclusive market of relationships. Students congregate around it in fellowship. Nothing we can promise students will affect them as swiftly, as dramatically, and as predictably as their favorite drug does—or at least did at one time. We need to understand not marijuana itself but the primacy and intensity of the relationship students have with it. Otherwise, we may end up in a tug-of-war we can never win.

We Need to Talk Openly About Marijuana

This may seem obvious, even simplistic, but it may also be the biggest obstacle. How often do those who work in higher education sit around at lunch or on break, discussing the possibility of getting together later and smoking a bowl? Beers or margaritas, yes, but (almost) never weed. It is illegal and therefore a subject forbidden to discuss at work even by those who consume it. Because it is a prohibited topic, perhaps some students wonder if those talking to them about cannabis have ever even tried it. Others who grew up seeing their parents smoke—even joining them on occasion—do not. Others could care less. Nevertheless, questioning older adults about their own use often leaves these adults tongue-tied. The razor's edge between openness and fear of poor role-modeling can feel perilous, especially when it comes to thorny subjects consigned to the deviations of one's own youth, such as criminal mischief, alcohol, drugs, or sex. Those conversations are couched as safety instructions. Cautionary tales. Prevention talks. For their own good. Adults in authority roles struggle to find a sweet spot in discussing uncomfortable topics like sex and drug use. The unavoidable paradox in the fantasy of hitting the bull's-eye is educating with commanding authority, while simultaneously disavowing any personal experience.

More specific to the collegiate world and education as a whole, there can be no discussion about normal, healthy substance use behavior. We can talk about safety, but not about those behaviors in a positive, enjoyable way. Marijuana use is officially, at baseline, deemed pathological because it is illegal or in violation of policy. We talk about norms, but only in a statistical way as a comparison with a database of other students. *Healthy* marijuana use is not a subject for discussion, creating a roadblock in communication.

The present focus on collegiate marijuana, without incorporating healthy norms data, may actually have the effect of escalating use. Berkowitz and Perkins were the first to suggest the important role social norms play in college drinking.[18] Berkowitz explains:

> When drug prevention emphasizes problem behavior without acknowledging the actual healthy norm, it may foster the erroneous belief that drinking problems are worse than is actually the case and inadvertently contribute to the problem it is trying to solve. In contrast, interventions based on social norms theory focus on the healthy attitudes and behavior of the majority and try to increase it, while also using information about healthy norms to guide interventions with abusers.[19]

Many working in the fields of prevention and treatment are trained to simply dismiss such inquiries about personal drug use in a direct, commanding manner with scripted responses such as, "This isn't about me. We're here to talk about your use." Those questions—especially within the context of conduct violations—pose a potential trap; admission of past use courts the label of hypocrite; denial nullifies credibility. To dismiss the question entirely is equivalent to a legal plea of *nolo contendere*; it presents no defense, nor does it admit guilt. Yet both parties know the question was answered.

And we wonder why students seek other sources for information?

Those on the pro-legalization side of the debate are less burdened by the same internal conflicts over marijuana. They have no qualms admitting to using the drug and serve as models with whom students can identify. If they are not regular consumers, then this is seen as a choice and perfectly understandable. Openness about their use aims to diminish stigma around marijuana and has the objective of normalizing the idea of legal cannabis. The more commonplace it feels with a sense of ease and comfort, devoid of internal dissonance, the less resistant the public will be. The passing of Amendment 64 in Colorado arguably was paved years beforehand by the state's medical marijuana law, desensitizing the public. Those who advocate for marijuana have advantages. At least they get it. They are the "cool" parent, the understanding one who allows for reasonable exceptions and may even ignore the rule if it is inapplicable or nonsensical. In the struggle for the hearts and minds of students, they do not fear being perceived as hypocritical. They have swallowed whole the immeasurable possibilities of marijuana as medicine and relatively safe intoxicant, while only giving a nod to its potential damaging effects on developing brains.

It is always harder to be the tough parent.

––––––

The short and long-term effects of legalization will undoubtedly change the college campus culture in a myriad of ways: some good, some bad, some expected, others completely unforeseen and disturbing. The far-reaching impact of legalized marijuana on the collegiate landscape will likely be as complex as the plant itself. No matter what side of the marijuana debate one falls on, the core value appears to be centered on the search for freedom: what is going to support personal freedom, freedom from suffering and the achievement of authentic well-being. The ways one meets this goal are varied, and philosophical questions are raised regarding how much institutional structure should assist the pursuit of freedom and health. Certainly not everyone is addicted to marijuana, but there are those for whom marijuana use has become unmanageable. What then? What resources and policies do we have in place to help those who need it the most? This is especially important to consider for adolescents and young adults whose maturing brains are bombarded by increasingly popular messages that "nothing is wrong with marijuana use—it is normal, benign, a rite of passage" and so forth. Freedom does not mean buying into a black or white ideology, but planning and preparing for life in the gray. With all the confusion surrounding marijuana, it makes sense that there should be a beacon to cut through the fog. The guiding light for students, practitioners, and prevention specialists are policies and procedures that support clarity of mind and body and the ability to make choices.

Notes

1 Opomo, K. (2012, November 18). *NUHA foundation*. Retrieved from www. nuhafoundation.org/home/blog/bloggingentries/2012/adult/if_you_talk_ to_a_man_in_his_language_k_okpomo#.WYCBZ2eWwdV

2 Garland, T. S., Bumphus, V. W., Sara, A., & Knox, S. A. (2012). Exploring general and specific attitudes toward drug policies among college students. *Criminal Justice Policy Review*, 23(1), 3–17. doi:https://doi.org/10.1177/ 0887403410389807

3 Crisp, A. H., Gelder, M. G., Goddard, E., & Meltzer, H. (2005). Stigmatization of people with mental illnesses: A follow-up study within the changing minds campaign of the royal college of psychiatrists. *World Psychiatry*, 4(2), 106–113. Retrieved from www.ncbi.nlm.nih.gov/pmc/articles/PMC1414750 /?report=reader#!po=1.19048

4 Yamaori, S., Ebisawa, J., Okushima, Y., Yamamoto, I., & Watanabe, K. (2011). Potent inhibition of human cytochrome P450 3A isoforms by cannabidiol: Role of phenolic hydroxyl groups in the resorcinol moiety. *Life Science*, 88(15–16), 730–736. doi:10.1016/j.lfs.2011.02.017

5 Tatarsky, A. (2010). Harm reduction psychotherapy. In J. Holland (Ed.), *The Pot book: A complete guide to cannabis—its role in medicine, politics, science, and culture* (pp. 223–241). Rochester, VT: Park Street Press.
6 McKay, J. R., & Hiller-Sturmhöfel, S. (2011). Treating alcoholism as a chronic disease: Approaches to long-term continuing care. *Alcohol Research & Health, 33*(4), 356–370. Retrieved from www.ncbi.nlm.nih.gov/pmc/articles/PMC3625994/pdf/arh-33-4-356.pdf
7 Miller, T. R., & Hendrie, D. H. (2008). *Substance abuse prevention dollars and cents: A cost-benefit analysis* (DHHS Pub. No. (SMA) 07–4298). Rockville, MD: Center for Substance Abuse Prevention, Substance Abuse and Mental Health Services Administration. Retrieved from www.samhsa.gov/sites/default/files/cost-benefits-prevention.pdf
8 Lenhart, A. (2015, April 9). Teens, social media &technology. *Pew Research Center: Internet and Technology*. Retrieved from www.pewinternet.org/2015/04/09/teens-social-media-technology-2015/
9 Senser, B. D., & Wang, L. (2017, March 8). It's high time: Weed at Harvard. *Harvard Crimson*. Retrieved from www.thecrimson.com/article/2017/3/8/weed-at-harvard/
10 Southern Illinois University. (2017). *Core Institute*. Retrieved from http://core.siu.edu/
11 Substance Abuse and Mental Health Services Administration. (2010). *National survey on drug use and health*. Retrieved from www.samhsa.gov/data/sites/default/files/NSDUHNationalFindingsResults2010-web/2k10ResultsRev/NSDUHresultsRev2010.pdf
12 Ibid.
13 Moffat, B., Haines-Saah, R. J., & Johnson, J. L. (2016). From didactic to dialogue: Assessing the use of an innovative classroom resource to support decision-making about cannabis use. *Drugs: Education, Prevention and Policy, 24*(1), 85–95. http://dx.doi.org/10.1080/09687637.2016.1206846
14 Moffat, B. M., Jenkins, E. K., & Johnson, J. L. (2013). Weeding out the information: An ethnographic approach to exploring how young people make sense of the evidence on cannabis. *Harm Reduction Journal, 10*, 34. doi:10.1186/1477-7517-10-34
15 Porath-Waller, A. J., Brown, J. E., Frigon, A. P., & Clark, H. (2013). *What Canadian youth think about cannabis*. Ottawa, ON: Canadian Centre on Substance Abuse. Retrieved from www.ccsa.ca/Resource%20Library/CCSA-What-Canadian-Youth-Think-about-Cannabis-2013-en.pdf
16 Hall McMaster & Associates Limited. (2016). *The spirit of motivational interviewing*. Retrieved from www.hma.co.nz/wp-content/uploads/2016/01/The-spirit-of-motivational-interviewing.pdf
17 Miller, W. R., & Rollnick, S. (1991). *Motivational interviewing: Preparing people to change addictive behavior*. New York, NY: Guilford Press.
18 Perkins, H. W., & Berkowitz, A. D. (1986). Perceiving the community norms of alcohol use among students: Some research implications for campus alcohol education programming. *International Journal of the Addictions, 21*(9–10), 961–976. Retrieved from www.alanberkowitz.com/articles/social_norms.pdf
19 Berkowitz, A. D. (2004, August). *The social norms approach: Theory, research and annotated bibliograph*, 6. Retrieved from www.alanberkowitz.com/articles/social_norms.pdf

Index